日本文学
現実と虚構

水田宗子

REALITY AND FICTION IN MODERN JAPANESE LITERATURE

NORIKO MIZUTA LIPPIT

日本文学
現実と虚構

水田宗子

M.E. SHARPE INC., WHITE PLAINS, NEW YORK

Copyright ©1980 by M. E. Sharpe, Inc.
901 North Broadway, White Plains, New York 10603

Library of Congress Catalog Card Number: 79-67859
International Standard Book Number: 0-87332-137-5

Printed in the United States of America

*In memory of my Father,
Mikio Mizuta*

CONTENTS

PREFACE

This study emerged during the years when, my sojourn in the United States having become longer than I had initially anticipated, my consciousness turned increasingly toward questioning and evaluating my own relation to Japan's literary heritage. For Japanese who have witnessed (at least intellectually) the violent attraction to and rejection of foreign cultures of many of their predecessors in the Meiji, Taisho and Showa eras, and their final, often sentimental and abstract, glorification of the Japanese cultural heritage, nihon kaiki (return to Japan) still presents enormously complex intellectual as well as emotional problems.

To view the long-held ambivalence of Japanese artists and writers — the desire to be a member of the cosmopolitan artists' society and the desire to maintain a unique and closed world of their own — only as the Japanese struggle over cultural identity, as many critics have done, will miss the most crucial element in shaping modern Japanese literature. For since the Meiji period, writers have been seriously concerned with the function of art and literature in the historical process of the formation of a society on the one hand and with the ethical function of art in the writers' personal lives on the other. Only in the Taisho period, when Tanizaki, for example, deliberately identified himself as an artisan of the pre-modern era, did writers and artists try vigorously to separate art from politics and morality, and themselves from intellectuals. Yet in both the Meiji and early Showa periods, writers struggled passionately

with questions of politics and ethics, trying to relate themselves
vitally to the complex reality of modern Japan.

Just as the I-novel, the most distinctive fictional genre in Japanese literature, must be understood in terms of the writers'
attempt to deal with their isolation from social reality in the
overly utilitarian Meiji era, the return to the Japanese heritage
of such writers as Tanizaki, Kawabata and Mishima must be understood as a reaction against the preoccupation of their contemporaries with the relation between art and political and historical reality, and with the relation between art and morality,
as well as in the context of the severe national control of art and
literature. The works written by members of the ultra-nation-
alistic group Nihon Romanha (Japanese Romantic Group), many
of whose members converted from Marxism, only clarifies the
escapist elements of nihon kaiki. Although the present study is
not an attempt at literary history, I have tried to maintain a perspective which regards the development of modern Japanese literature in relation to the Meiji goal of modernization and its
consequences.

I am most indebted to Professor Shoichi Saeki, a literary
critic and professor of comparative literature at the University
of Tokyo, for illuminating my "return" passage to Japanese literature. Since the time I was his student in English and American literature at the graduate school of Tokyo Metropolitan University, he has been my unfailing mentor and a model for the
most sensitive critical intelligence. I am also deeply indebted
to Dominic Cheung, a poet and my colleague at the University of
Southern California, for deepening my understanding of the importance of cultural tradition in writers' creative consciousness.
I also learned much from co-teaching with him courses on the
Asian aesthetic tradition, and this is reflected especially in the
chapter on Akutagawa. Professor Roy E. Teele read the entire
manuscript and made invaluable criticisms and suggestions.
Professors Earl Miner, Jun Eto, Yoshio Iwamoto and Dominic
Cheung read some of the chapters when they were to appear initially in several journals, and their criticisms proved indispens-
able in the final revisions of the manuscript. I would also like

to express my gratitude to Tsukao Kawahigashi of Tokyo Metropolitan University for his assistance in preparing the manuscript for publication.

Above all, my warmest gratitude goes to Victor D. Lippit,
whose devotion to our family made this study possible. Most of
the chapters were written during the time when I watched in
agony from six thousand miles away my father falling fatally ill
and passing away. The book is dedicated to him.

Riverside, California
June 1979

INTRODUCTION

In twentieth century Japanese literature, the opposition and interaction of realism and romanticism on the level of literary concepts, and of Marxism and aestheticism (including, in part, modernism) on the level of literary ideology, supplies a most vital basis for writers searching for new methods of literary expression, fostering debates among the writers and creating the setting for active experimentation with style, form and language. Cosmopolitanism and traditionalism were also vital cultural concerns for Japanese writers, whose exposure to Western culture and literature supplied a significant source of imagination and energy for their creative activities. Many Japanese writers who went through a period of active learning from the West, however, later turned to the cultural and literary heritage of Japan as their source of inspiration. Although their "return" was certainly influenced by Japan's nationalistic war effort and their feeling that the cultural tradition was threatened, at a much more basic level, it was the outcome of their vital concern with the relation of art to the self, reality, and the cultural tradition of Japan. This concern, underlying the aesthetic and ideological debates of the modern period, was shared by practically all writers and, as expressed in the major literary movements of the twentieth century, may indeed be regarded as the defining characteristic of modern Japanese literature.

The studies in this volume approach an understanding of modern Japanese literature by focusing on three of the most basic

1

concerns of modern Japanese writers: the relation between
their art (literature) and themselves, the relation between their
art and social and historical reality, and the relation of their
art (and themselves) to Japan's cultural tradition and the archetypal creative imagination underlying it. These concerns do not
exist independently of one another but are deeply intertwined.
Thus, for example, Miyamoto Yuriko believed that literature
must reflect social reality, but only as mediated by the experience of the self in history, while Tanizaki's fastidious exclusion
of social and political issues from his literary works in his attempt to create a private aesthetic world of his own was justified in terms of the relation of his art to Japan's cultural tradition. The wide variety in form, expression, style and use of language that characterizes modern Japanese literature reflects
the interaction of these basic concerns with the aesthetic and
ideological questions of the modern period.

The I-novel (watakushi shōsetsu) stands out in this context as
the single most significant form of novel that modern Japanese
literature has produced. The I-novel emerged from Japan's naturalist literary movement with its focus on the author's self as
the object of naturalistic study. Although its narrow focus on
the self as subject and point of view helped make it possible for
writers, isolated from social reality, to write novels of realism,
the I-novel also quickly developed into a novel of lyrical confession, both as a novel of bald exposé of the secret side of the self
and one of philosophic contemplation of the author's own state of
mind. Whether as lyrical confession or self-oriented realism,
the dominance of the I-novel as a literary form in the early part
of the twentieth century imposed a heavy burden on younger
writers whose historical and social concerns or aesthetic attitudes required a different form of novel. The writers of the
Taisho (1912-1926) and early Showa (1926-present) periods had
to take the I-novel as their point of departure and frame of reference. Underlying their criticism of the I-novel is their criticism of the Meiji writers' narrow, egocentric concern with the
self and their overly ethical concern with the modern ego. The
writers of the Taisho period sought universal values and prin-

ciples which would relate them to the historical, social and cultural reality, enabling them to transcend the excessive involvement in their egos which characterized the I-novelists. Whether the writers pursued Marxism, cosmopolitanism or traditionalism, they all sought values larger than that of the individual self. The first chapter of this book addresses itself to some of the generic problems of the I-novel and to critics' attitudes toward it. The I-novel is a unique product of Japanese writers' efforts for "modernization," efforts pursued in the context of their vital exposure to Western ideas and basic isolation from Japanese society.

Although modern Japanese literature emerged during Japan's overall modernization effort and is rooted in the history of the era of modernization, literature occupied a peripheral position in the mostly utilitarian activities of the era. As Futabatei Shimei's ambivalence when confronted by the choice of becoming a diplomat or a writer indicates, literature was not the field which a bright and aspiring young man would choose for his career in the Meiji era (1868-1912). Writers and artists were considered social failures — good-for-nothings — and they willingly considered themselves social outsiders and outlaws. As Nakamura Mitsuo points out, writers converted their initial exclusion from the society's mainstream activities of modernization into a privilege of the artist and proudly endured poverty and the neglect of society.[1] Because they were excluded from society, they took the role of social critics quite naturally, even while demanding purity in their artistic quest. Their demand for purity and sense of mission was often geared to their own lives, making their art an ethical attempt to elevate themselves.

At the same time, because writers were neglected and excluded, they kept together in a small, closed circle referred to as the bundan (literary circle), which enabled them to explore and develop the most avant-garde ideas and methods of the West as they were introduced to Japan. Their basic isolation also contributed to bringing certain questions to the fore, and they were all forced to confront the question of the relation between art and social life on the one hand, and that of the relation between art and the artist's life on the other.

The novel emerged as a genre in the West when writers' eyes
were turned to social life — during the eighteenth and nineteenth
centuries — and especially when their interest became directed
to grasping and expressing the life of the bourgeois class. By
the end of the nineteenth century, however, as rapid industrial-
ization continued, many European writers became increasingly
isolated from the bourgeois class and the values it maintained.
Modern Japanese writers, never having occupied the secure position of respectable citizens, shared the fate of these turn-of-
the-century European writers. Without experiencing the novel's
initial stage of development, that of realism, Japanese writers
were placed in the same predicament as that encountered by
Flaubert, Thomas Mann, Virginia Woolf and Oscar Wilde, among
others, a predicament which resulted from the writers having
dropped out of the mainstream of their society's social, economic and cultural life. Excluded from their society, the Japanese writers could treat only their own lives, and not the life
of society, in dealing with the human experience. The I-novel
emerged from this situation.

The fundamental isolation from society which the writers experienced certainly justified their seemingly exclusive, egotistical concern with and interest in themselves as the subjects of
search and materials for literature, and the question of the modern ego was one of the major themes of Meiji literature. Yet as
Saeki Shoichi points out, the I-novel is not necessarily a novel
in which writers insist on, praise, investigate or express themselves openly; nor is it one in which self-search is the sole purpose.[2] Rather, the writers of I-novels sought to write through
or in terms of the "I," and therefore watakushi in the I-novel is
partly a novelistic convention, a medium which enables the
writers to construct the novel, as well as the purpose of their
pursuit.

The use of the "I" as a convention determining the novelistic
perspective of the work as well as a concrete subject of literature, however, complicates the relation between literature and
the self on the one hand and that between literature and society
on the other, for both uses of the "I" compensate for the absence

of a direct relation between the author and social reality and
therefore for the lack of a direct means of describing that reality. Although the I-novels cannot exist without the "I," they often
lack thorough and profound exploration of the self simply because
that was often not their main purpose.

In the West, the isolation of writers from the industrial order
and mechanical civilization was basically comparable and had a
similar effect, turning such writers as Gide and Woolf to their
inner worlds, where they confronted the question of the self and
literature. Yet in the West, which had experienced historically
the Christian confrontation between man's ego and God, and later
an era of positivistic science, delving into their inner worlds
meant for writers, at least in part, experimenting with insistence
on their human egos in a studio-like enclosure (their works), as
Kobayashi Hideo correctly points out.[3] The inner world of ego,
at least for the Western writers of the early twentieth century,
still existed firmly and autonomously, and was the terra incog-
nito which they ventured to explore further.

Japanese writers, with the possible exception of Natsume
Sōseki and Shiga Naoya, were not so egocentrically obsessed
with the question of the ego as Nakamura Mitsuo and Kobayashi
Hideo tended to think in their criticism of the I-novel.[4] It is
true that for such writers as Shimazaki Toson and Shiga Naoya,
art was the means to explore oneself and life, and thus that the
dimensions of art and life were overlapping for them, if not
identical. However, even for Tayama Katai, the writer who is
usually considered to be the creator of the I-novel, the "I" in
his novels was only a reflection of the ironic perspective with
which he regarded the Meiji writers, including himself. Katai's
Futon (The Quilt, 1907) is a confessional novel, but if the protagonist is the author himself, then he is presented from an
ironic perspective — one that is detached as well as attached —
making the novel something more than "a confession" in which
the author tries to reveal his secret self. Futon can only be
considered a work of fiction in this respect.

Thus the I-novel provided not only a means to place the self
in the center of literary pursuit, but also a means, when writers

were isolated from society, to relate the author's self to larger
questions of human life. Indeed, the I-novelists believed that to
explore the self was to explore humanity. Thus the I-novel is
more than an extreme expression of the writers' concern with
the self and literature; it is also an expression of their effort to
relate their literature to social reality. The I-novelists often
justified the self-scrutiny which they conducted with pseudo-
scientific realism not in terms of their self-interest, but as
part of their naturalistic study of human nature.

The confusion surrounding the I-novel is in large measure due
to critical failures to clarify the theoretical issues presented by
the genre. Its early critics assumed that it expressed only the
author's personal experiences and feelings, and that it resulted
from self-search and metaphysical pursuit of the modern ego
only. These early critics failed to grasp the many significant
theoretical questions posed by the I-novel form, including the
question of the "I" in the novel (as protagonist and narrator, and
their relation to the author), the use of confession (the relation between the lyrical and dramatic confession), and the
relation between realism and the lyrical expression of the
author's emotions.

The questions which were central to the I-novelists, the questions of the self and literature and of literature and reality,
were also central to Kawabata Yasunari and Mishima Yukio, but
Kawabata and Mishima dealt with them in a quite different manner. Kawabata's Yukiguni (Snow Country, 1937), for example, is
a lyrical novel which is close to the I-novel in its lack of novelistic devices, yet its successful dramatization of the protagonist's psyche in terms of women characters enables it to escape from being a narrow, egocentric expression of the protagonist-author's inner world. Kawabata's aspiration for self-
transcendence, his romantic quest for unity with nature and the
Japanese aesthetic tradition, also prevents his work from being
a concentrated expression of the self.

The aspiration of the ego to exist in relation to something
that transcends or overwhelms it is also the central theme of
Mishima's novels. Mishima's protagonists constantly seek a

tragic fate that will define their lives and create their raison
d'être, a fate against which they can carry out a tragic struggle.
Mishima dramatizes his aspiration for a tragic life in different
personae, with his characters serving as the masks through
which he confesses his ego's desire. Declaring deliberately that
art and life are separate from one another and that, even in the
writer himself, the self that writes and the self that lives belong
to different dimensions, Mishima justifies the absence of any
reflection of immediate social reality in his works. As a person
living firmly in the mundane world of physical existence as well
as a writer, Mishima even makes the dichotomy between art and
life, soul and body, one of the central themes of his literature.
Yet he does try to place his characters in Japanese history, to
make them symbolic heirs of samurai warriors and kamikaze
pilots, whose existence was indeed determined by their tragic
fate. Mishima's anachronistic romanticism results from his
realization that any such tragic fate is completely absent from
modern, postwar life. He responds to this by placing his heroes
in ever-returning human history — in the cycle of metempsy-
chosis in his later works — thereby enabling his ego to attain
an archetypal relevance.

Although Mishima was egotistically interested in himself, he
did not write typical I-novels.* Mishima's famous dislike of
Dazai Osamu is due mainly to his irritation over a writer who
unselfconsciously writes about himself, who openly places himself at the center of his literary pursuit and reveals all his
weaknesses. Mishima was more embarrassed than appalled by
Dazai, for he certainly shared Dazai's egotistic desire for self-
expression. As a highly self-conscious writer, loving paradox,
Mishima reacted violently to the intellectual artists of Japan
brooding over their alienation and to their sterile coiling into
their inner worlds. Mishima's works are characterized by ver-
satile characters, well-developed plots, complicated stories,

*Confessions of a Mask is very close to an autobiographical novel, yet it is
clearly a work of fiction. For a discussion of the work, see Chapter 10.
Mishima has also written extensively about himself in nonfiction form, including
two lengthy autobiographical essays.

ironies and dramatic tension, yet every work contributes to the
formation of Mishima's prototypal tragic hero with whom it
seems as if Mishima tried to identify himself with fastidious
care and effort.

Akutagawa and Tanizaki — representative writers of aestheticism, which formed a mainstream of modern Japanese literature — bury their egos in a world of story with its own autonomous structure, yet they too are connected with tradition and
consciousness of culture through the archetypal patterns maintained in their stories. Both authors appear to be content with
the role of storyteller, yet as their debate over plot and story
in fiction reveals, Akutagawa could not bypass the question of
the self in literature. For Akutagawa, who was basically a poet,
storytelling and the creation of a well-made world of fiction,
in which the lyrical expression of his "poetic spirit" had no direct means of expression, would eventually prove inadequate as
a form of expression.

The Akutagawa-Tanizaki controversy represents one effort of
the Japanese writers to overcome the problems and limitations
of the I-novel in their attempt to establish the modern novel as
a new genre. While Akutagawa sought to justify his new efforts
to write lyrical inner novels integrating the lyrical tradition
into the novel, Tanizaki tried to articulate his attempt to create
a novelistic space between storytelling and the author's inner,
aesthetic search. Tanizaki's argument is among the first of a
series of theoretical explorations which pointed toward the concept of the chūkan shōsetsu, the middle novel. Yokomitsu Riichi's idea of the junsui shōsetsu (pure novel) provides the most
articulate clarification of this concept. Yokomitsu regards the
ground of the modern novel as lying between junbungaku (pure
literature), the intellectual literature of self-search, and tsūzoku bungaku (popular literature), which deals sentimentally
with everyday life in society. Yokomitsu argues that the space
for the modern novel is that which lies between the diary and
storytelling, between describing human beings internally and
externally, and between realism and romanticism. While Yokomitsu was more inclined to grasp individuals in terms of human

relations in social life and to locate his literary efforts in relation to literary trends abroad, Tanizaki, who together with Kawabata and Mishima was baptized in Western dark romanticism,
found the perspective for dramatizing himself in Japan's cultural tradition and the even broader cultural consciousness beyond tradition.

This does not mean that Kawabata, Tanizaki and Mishima can
be regarded solely as offshoots of Western romanticism, particularly dark romanticism. Their involvement in Japan's classical literary tradition and clear vision of their archetypal
consciousness in terms of the cultural tradition make them
Japanese romantics first and foremost. Placing them within the
larger framework of Western romanticism is meaningful, however, not only because they were "influenced" by dark romanticism and Western fin-de-siècle literature — which clarifies
such aesthetic ideas as the grotesque and the ugly in their
works, for example — but also because to evaluate modern Japanese literature in relation to Western literature and aesthetic
ideas provides one of the essential perspectives in the study of
modern Japanese literary development.

The shock of encounter with Western literature was one of the
important sources of energy in Japan's literary development,
with writers struggling to convert Western literary and artistic
ideas into legitimate tools for writing in the Japanese environment. Such writers as Kawabata, Tanizaki and Yokomitsu Riichi, all of whom earnestly learned from the West, turned in
their later years in precisely the opposite direction, to their
own literary and cultural tradition, and tried to place their own
works within it. The relation between their literature and Japan's cultural tradition, and that between imagination and archetypal consciousness, should not be understood, however, merely
in terms of these writers turning their backs on Western literature and returning to their own national tradition. Rather,
their turning to the Japanese tradition is an extension of their
effort to place their literature — and the author's ego — in a
larger framework, in an organic, archetypal body of creative
consciousness and imagination. At the same time, it must be

pointed out that their effort to link their works and imagination with the cultural tradition is one means of bypassing social and historical reality.

Proletarian and modernist writers, to the contrary, were more intensely concerned with the question of the relation between the self and reality — social as well as individual reality — and the relation between literature and reality. For this reason, their approach to literature was quite different from that of those whose eyes were turned to the archetypal origins of Japan's cultural tradition. Connecting their opposing concerns and perspectives was the writers' concern with the relation between literature and the self. Miyamoto Yuriko, for example, elevated her personal ego (and its growth and liberation) to a position representing the intellectual spirit of the age by placing her personal growth in history (in the context of the writers' struggle against the war and the oppressive forces of history). Her novels, which trace her growth as a person and as a woman, thus become Bildungsroman, integrating the Japanese I-novel with the historical, social novel. If the concern with the relation between literature and the self represented by Tanizaki, Kawabata and Mishima remains within the ideological and artistic tradition of romanticism, the way Tayama Katai and Miyamoto Yuriko dealt with the same question remains within the tradition of realism.

It is frequently said that Showa (1926-present) literature started with the death of Akutagawa. In "Aru kyūyū e okuru shuki" (A Note to an Old Friend, 1927) Akutagawa had written a literary will in which he indicated that he had had a vague fear of death for the past two years. His death gave a tremendous shock to writers and was taken as symbolic of the death of the intellectualism and aestheticism of those writers who had stayed away from the waves of history and from a vital interaction with their social environment. Itō Sei wrote, "The feeling that the ideas and practice of such writers as Shiga Naoya, Satō Haruo, Ryūnosuke (Akutagawa) and Junichiro (Tanizaki), writers who composed the core of the aesthetics of the Taisho era (1912-1926), formed the forefront of the literary activities

of the bundan (literary circle) vanished with the death of Akutagawa."5 Itō stated, "The necessity for a revolution in thinking
which Marxism forced the bundan to face" around the end of the
Taisho period, and "the necessity for a revolution in literary
style" which the New Perceptionists (including Yokomitsu and
Kawabata, among others) advocated, were the two "new factors"
governing the literary tides to come.6

Although modernist literature and proletarian literature are
diametrically opposed ideologically, both are first and foremost
a response to the new human predicament, which was characterized by the alienation produced by the aggressive machine-
culture of the capitalist system. The New Perceptionist movement, led by Yokomitsu Riichi, emerged at the end of the Taisho period as the most fruitful outcome of Japan's modernist,
avant-garde art movement. After the brilliant initial stylistic
experiments which culminated in his short-story collection
Shanghai (1928), however, Yokomitsu turned to psychological
realism, the results of which can be seen in "Kikai" (Machine, 1930). While the proletarian literature movement was
aborted by a combination of ruthless police suppression and the
confusion its adherents showed in their theoretical understanding of the relation between literature and politics, the modernist writers also lost direction during the oppressive war, and
Yokomitsu and Kawabata increasingly turned to Japan's cultural heritage as the source of imagination.

Tomioka Taeko, one of the most talented novelists to emerge
in the 1970s, is a legitimate successor to those writers who ad-
dressed themselves to the questions of self and literature and
of reality, tradition and literature. Standing at an historical
juncture which enables her to reevaluate the development of
modern literature in its totality, Tomioka has embarked on the
ambitious task of creating a literary perspective, that of the
self in literature, which dramatizes the reality of human beings
in relation to both their social environment and cultural heritage. Deeply immersed in Western and Japanese avant-garde
art movements (she is one of the poets who represents Japan's
postwar modern poetry), Tomioka integrates in her novels the

ontological quest of the modern individual and a form of narration which has its origin in the traditional bunraku. Central to her works is the question of the relation between self and literature, the question of why write. Critical of the alienation of intellectuals and artists from the life of common people, which is particularly pronounced in modern Japan, Tomioka has consistently explored the life of common people as her own personal heritage and the source of indigenous Japanese culture. Her exploration of classical Japanese literature and culture has never been that of the high culture of courtiers and scholars but of the culture of the Edo merchants and other socially peripheral people. Her search for the meaning of life and origin of culture through the exploration of the daily life of common people has resulted in novels of existential realism without intellectual abstraction. Tomioka's conscious turning away from intellectualism represents one phase of the transformation of the consciousness of the artist and the idea of art in contemporary Japan, a transformation characterized by the artists' reaction against the predominant intellectual elitism of art and their conscious effort to make art compatible with the life of common people in the age of mass culture.

My purpose in this volume is not to survey the history of modern Japanese literature or to treat all major writers, but to present a perspective which will help to illuminate some of the central concerns of modern Japanese writers, and especially their concern about the relation of their art to the self, reality and Japan's cultural tradition. Because these concerns were pursued and developed in the midst of Japan's vital exposure to Western literature and the literary and aesthetic movements of the modern period, the comparative perspective which I have applied in some of the analysis in this volume will, I believe, prove to be a useful one.

IRONIC PERSPECTIVE AND SELF-DRAMATIZATION IN THE CONFESSIONAL I-NOVEL OF JAPAN

The most peculiarly characteristic form of the modern Japanese novel is the I-novel, in which the author appears as the protagonist and describes his private affairs and experiences. Avoiding the use of fictional devices, the author presents his state of mind, ideas and realization almost directly. Not only is the subject matter narrowly confined to the author's personal life and experience, but the perspective is almost entirely limited to that of the author-protagonist, and the novel typically lacks such structural and fictional mediation as plot, story-development, dramatic tension and characterization. The author's inward-turning eye observes his inner self in minute detail, leading to a profound insight, a distilled and crystallized sensibility, and a heightened awareness of life which make this type of novel close to poetry, while the lack of fictional devices brings it close to the impressionistic essay and diary.

At the same time, writing about oneself is an act of exposing the hidden self and desire, and often constitutes a challenge to the norms of social morality. It involves a confrontation between the individual and society, resulting in the sacrifice of the individual's (author's) social respectability. The author engages in this confrontation for the sake of art and the pursuit of truth. The self-exposure that characterizes the confessional I-novel is thus at once exhibitionistic and self-destructive.

Two distinct types of I-novel can be discerned in modern Japanese literature.[1] The poetry-like, essay-like I-novel,

usually called the "state-of-mind novel" (<u>shinkyo shōsetsu</u>),
reached its peak in the works of Shiga Naoya. It expresses the
writer's understanding of life — his realization. It is not necessarily confessional and in most cases is not rebellious toward
society, however unconventional and individualistic the author
may be. It most characteristically expresses the author's sincere and stoic determination to search for the self, for a higher
knowledge of life. Rather than being destructive both to society
and to the self, the <u>shinkyo shōsetsu</u> is a purified form of autobiographical novel in which the author meditates upon himself
or herself with a profound, if egocentric, inward-turning eye
and with the accurate eye of a realistic painter. It becomes a
presentation of the heightened moments of the author's life and
thus a philosophic novel as well as a realistic one. In the author's endeavor, the "I" is purified and even approaches self-
lessness. The optimistic, idealistically humanistic belief that
the expansion of one's ego means the expansion of all human
consciousness supports this process.

The other form of I-novel, the confessional novel, was established at the same time, in the late Meiji (1868-1912) and Taisho (1912-1926) periods, by the works of Tayama Katai, Shimazaki Tōson, Iwano Hōmei and Chikamatsu Shūko, and was further developed in the Showa period (1926-present) by the works
of Dazai Osamu.[2] All of these writers depict their sinfulness,
perversity, shamefulness and irrational contradictions without
presenting any explicit aspiration for a solution or salvation.
The act of exposure becomes the purpose in itself, yet with
their persistent, unsentimental presentation of themselves,
their novels gain an existential dimension and become expressions of the sinfulness of human nature itself. Underlying this
destructive type of I-novel is a view of human beings and of literary expression that is essentially naturalistic. Thus it is not
surprising that the first confessional I-novels were produced
by such naturalist writers as Katai, Tōson and Iwano Hōmei.

The confessional novel is usually considered to have been
initiated by Tayama Katai's <u>Futon</u> (The Quilt, 1907), a work
strongly influenced by naturalism. Although the unveiling of

the self is not an essential element of the original French naturalism and the confessional I-novel is not a simple extension of
European naturalism, the basic concepts of the Japanese confessional novel were fundamentally influenced by the tenets of
naturalism, and the form or genre of the I-novel emerged from
the short-lived movement of naturalism in Japan. Indeed we can
even say that the mature era of naturalism in Japan started when
the writers became engaged in writing about themselves.

According to the naturalistic view, people are controlled basically by their instinctive drives and conditioned by their social and biological environment. People either struggle unsuc-
cessfully to control their drives through reason and moral will
or achieve success only superficially. To understand people's
lives as they are, the writer unveils the false social masks they
wear and describes the naked human self in all its contradictions as baldly and as truthfully as possible. The reality of human life and nature is understood as determined by objective
forces, and thus it can be described precisely through "flat description" (heimen byōsha) and "one-dimensional description"
(ichigenteki byōsha).[3] Not only is the unfictionalized exposure
of one's ugly and secret side thus justified, but also the self and
the author's life become the most suitable materials for his art,
serving as the basis for both intellectual scrutiny and the detailed, realistic description which exists as the core of the nat-
uralists' theory of description.[4]

Both types of I-novel (the shinkyo shōsetsu and the confessional novel) are also based on the author's sense of crisis, a
sense which is not abstract, metaphysical anxiety or despair but
the result of a specific crisis in life (such as his wife's love affair or his infatuation with a young girl). While the shinkyo
shōsetsu is an expression of the writer's victory over the sense
of crisis or of his effort to overcome it, however, the confessional novel is an expression of the sense of crisis as it is. The
sense of crisis in the destructive I-novel stems from the sinfulness and shamefulness inherent in human existence which, unless overcome, leads people to self-destruction. The shinkyo
shōsetsu, on the other hand, is based on a belief in struggle to

transcend the sense of crisis and attain enlightenment. The shinkyo shōsetsu reflects a belief in life according to which art is used as a means for arriving at a higher consciousness of life, while the destructive I-novel reflects an effort to find salvation in art, that is, in the act of writing the novel itself.

In both cases, the question of the relation between art and life is central. For the writers of the I-novel, art was a path of mental and spiritual training, and their ethical passion to live honestly made the artists expose their thoughts and desires openly and frankly, thus converting life to art and making art serve life.

Both types of I-novel dominated the development of the modern Japanese novel. Although there were such writers as Natsume Sōseki and Tanizaki Junichiro who strongly opposed both the I-novel and naturalism, it continued to be the dominant form of Japanese novel until the emergence of proletarian literature in the Showa period. For new writers, the I-novel was a heavy burden of tradition to struggle with and to surpass, and in the period following World War II, a major critical effort was devoted to criticism of the I-novel.

The limitations of both types of I-novel are quite obvious. The I-novel excludes almost completely the elements of the outer world, of others and of social problems. It tends to be narcissistic, self-satisfying dialogue with oneself or an exhibitionistic exposure of oneself. The most fundamental problem of the I-novel, a problem which has been pointed out by such critics as Kobayashi Hideo, Nakamura Mitsuo and Hirano Ken, is the writers' lack of a concept of the modern self.[5] The reader can readily discern the easy assumption of the I-novelists that the self could be grasped by themselves and that to know the self was to know human beings in general. While the I-novelists justified their egocentric interest in writing about themselves accordingly, their works in fact present merely impressionistic and often sentimental and self-righteous, if realistically accurate, observations of themselves.

The I-novelists also assumed too easily that to expose oneself was to rebel against society. Their effort, although understood by themselves as an essential part of their struggle to establish the modern ego, became too often merely a personal reaction to their narrow and immediate circumstances, reflecting a fundamental lack of insight into the relationship between the individual and society in the modern age.

The I-novel was originally the product of writers who were influenced by such French writers as Rousseau, Flaubert, Maupassant and Gide, all of whom were concerned with the question of the "I" in society and in the novel. In criticizing the Japanese novelists' superficial understanding of the French writers, Kobayashi Hideo points out that when Rousseau declared in his famous Confessions that he would undertake the unprecedented act of exposing himself to society, he was not really concerned with knowing himself or with how he would describe himself, but was concerned with the question of the individual in society.[6] Above all, the Japanese writers never experienced the desperation of Flaubert, Maupassant or Gide over their lack of faith in the possibility of understanding the self and reality with the methods of positivistic science — the French writers were concerned with the question of how to restore the "I" which is killed by positivistic science. For Gide, to believe in the "I" meant to believe in the "I" in his experimental studio. Although the French writers esteemed daily life in art, they did not seek salvation in life itself, unlike the basically ethical Japanese I-novelists, whose primary concern was salvation in life. Kobayashi states that the I-novelists were sentimental and romantic, and that they were fundamentally feudalists with a naturalistic outlook.[7]

The other principal criticism directed toward the I-novel concerned its form and method of expression. The I-novel rejects fictionalization and the mediation of materials through fictional devices. Although the author's limited perspective and firm grasp of the materials convince the reader of the truthfulness and accuracy of the description, the essay-like novel, with its crude, bare facts, hardly entertains the reader; nor does it evoke understanding of people's complex relation to society. It tends, rather, to be boring and irrelevant. Thus it leads to such violent reactions as that of Tanizaki Junichiro, who stated that he loses interest in the work immediately if he senses that the author is going to talk about himself, and who declared that he loves made-up stories with complicated, shocking plots.[8]

In fact, the question of form and the necessity of structural and fictional mediation in the novel became one of the central points of the critical controversy among the young writers of the Taisho period who, dissatisfied with the I-novel and naturalistic writing, began writing neo-romantic literature. The debate carried out between Akutagawa and Tanizaki — which is usually referred to as "the plot controversy" — is typical of the critical disputes which arose during this period.[9]

Dissatisfaction with the I-novel spurred as well the arguments for the honkaku shōsetsu (the orthodox novel), whose model was the works of European, English and Russian realism.[10] Such dissatisfaction also aroused a critical dispute concerning the difference between the I-novel and the German Ich Roman, in which the process of the protagonist's mental growth is traced. Since the critics who favored the honkaku shōsetsu were usually enthusiastic about the German Ich Roman, they could base their arguments against the I-novel only on the grounds that it lacks social scope and fictional devices, both of which the I-novelists deliberately excluded as irrelevant to their endeavor.

The pursuit of the question of the self is a major concern of most modern novelists and a characteristic of the modern novel which distinguishes it from the early nineteenth century and Victorian novels. Although the Meiji I-novel narrowed novelwriting to the pursuit of the self, excluding the possibility of social novels, its modernity exists exactly in this fact, that is, in the writers' search for the self in art and indeed in the very act of writing novels during the overly utilitarian Meiji period, when writers were excluded systematically from the mainstream of society's efforts to modernize itself. Although the protected, hothouse situation of the writers' in-group literary circle, the bundan, isolated them from the reality of social life and forced them to coil into themselves, it did create a fertile environment for radical and abstract literary and philosophic

experimentation. The modernity as well as the fundamental
weakness of the I-novel stems, therefore, from the basic isolation of the writer from the reality of society in the process of
industrial development, the very situation which characterizes
modern Western writers as well.

Underlying the emergence of the genre of the novel, there existed the diaries, confessions and letters in which the private
experiences and feelings of individuals are expressed with vary-
ing degrees of fictitiousness. The novel as a form and as a literary perspective absorbed these underlying forms of expression.[11] The novel is often a concealed form of autobiography and
in particular in modern literature, the modern literary technique of stream of consciousness facilitates this concealment,
enabling the author to expose the inner self of the protagonist
without necessarily making the work overtly autobiographical,
and often resulting in the fusion of dramatic confession with
autobiographical confession.[12] Writing about oneself using the
device of confession, thus, is an inherent part of the novel as a
form. In modern confessional novels, the confession was deliberately isolated by the author and made into the sole basis of
the novel. Restoring the self in the novel through confession
was a new, if desperate, literary venture for the modern author
at a time when writers had become isolated from social reality,
and thus the spontaneous relation between the individual and society, life and art, a relation which the novel had taken for
granted, had ceased to exist. The I-novel must be viewed then
not only in the context of the unique development of the Japanese novel, but also in the context of this overall history of the
development of the modern novel in which the self became a
major theme — indeed the sole theme — and the artist and art
turned increasingly and exclusively to themselves.

In Japanese literature in particular, the I-novel emerged
from the naturalistic investigation of the self, but it was modi-
fied by and integrated into the romantic tradition of the pursuit
of the self, a tradition which was first introduced to Japan
through Emersonian romanticism and to which many of the naturalist writers subscribed even before turning to novel-writing.

In particular, the confessional I-novel integrates the naturalistic unveiling of the self with the destructive exposé of the inner
self inherent in the tradition of Western dark romanticism.
Iwano Hōmei, for example, defined his confessional works as
neo-naturalistic and was a proponent of the naturalistic theory
of expression which he called "one-dimensional description,"
yet he was also deeply indebted to the romantic literature both
of the West and of Japan in the mid-Meiji period. An ardent
admirer of Poe and Baudelaire, he was a proponent of the "diabolism" in the literature of dark romanticism.[13] Thus he embodies the link between the naturalistic unmasking of the self
and the diabolical self-exposure inherent in the literature of
dark romanticism, a link which is of particular significance in
the development of modern Japanese literature. This link between naturalism and dark romanticism in the confessional
novel's investigation of the self is responsible for rendering the
Japanese confessional novel uniquely modern and is one of the
major factors which enabled the I-novel to continue as a dominant form even after naturalism died as a literary movement
and when anti-naturalistic — in fact anti-I-novel — aesthetic
literature, strongly influenced by the Western decadent literature of Poe, Baudelaire and Oscar Wilde especially, came to
be a major literary force in the Taisho period.

Indeed, many of the overly hasty denunciations of the I-novel
are due to critics' uncritical identification of the novel with the
author's life and their inability to assess the works as part of
the emerging modern genre of the confessional novel. Japanese
literary criticism ironically has been dominated by a view and
method which form a counterpart to the I-novel; it is characterized by the critics' heavy emphasis on the study of the authors' lives rather than their works. Instead of appreciating
the works as autonomous works of art, critics have used them
as documents which illustrate the writers' minds and lives, re-
ducing too readily every element in the works to the authors'
ideas, attitudes toward life and actual experiences. Most of the
severest critics of the I-novels failed to analyze the works as
separate from the authors' actual life experiences and attacked

the authors rather than the works, basing their attacks on their
uncritical identification of the authors with the protagonists.

Even if the concern with the author's life is recognized as legitimate in some cases — since the subject matter of the I-novel
is usually the author himself or is derived from his life —
evaluation and reading of the works solely in the light of the author's life becomes absurd in most cases. Hirano Ken, for example, argues in his essay on Shimazaki Tōson's Shinsei (New
Life, 1920), a confessional I-novel in which the protagonist confesses his illicit love affair with his niece, that the author had
no literary or artistic purpose in confessing the love affair in
the book but did so in order to end the relationship with her
when it became a burden to him. He argues that Shinsei thus
cannot be understood fully without understanding Tōson's real
motivation for writing the novel, that is, to rid himself of his
niece. Hirano believes that it was only Tōson's consistent egotism which caused him to sacrifice others' social life by exposing them in his novels, pretending that he did so for the sake
of his art while in fact using art to solve his personal problems.[14]

It is striking that Hirano's criticism lacks completely any
analysis of the work itself. Shinsei in particular uses the confession of the protagonist as the basic plot, and the confession
provides the climactic point toward which the novel develops.
Although the story is based on the author's life, the novel as-
sumes the form of an art novel in which the protagonist struggles to bring himself to write a confessional novel (Shinsei is
the product), and the theme of the novel becomes the process
of a man being born anew as an artist. Although Hirano's essay reveals unintentionally the basic structure of the Japanese
I-novel (true in particular of the works of Tōson) — the interweaving of actual life and art in the works, with actual life frequently receiving priority over art and art serving life — his
complete failure to analyze the work itself renders the relations between his essay and literary criticism tenuous at best.

One of the central questions of the I-novel is indeed the extent to which it can be appreciated meaningfully without re-
ducing it to the author's actual experiences, and it is to this

question that I now turn with an analysis of Tayama Katai's
Futon (The Quilt), which is considered to be the starting point
of the I-novel. I try to show that Katai uses an ironic perspective in portraying the protagonist, creating a critical distance
between the author and the protagonist, and that consequently
the protagonist emerges as an ironic dramatization of the author, not as a faithful portrayal or subjective self-dramatization. Thus, the protagonist can be viewed as a fictional representation of the Meiji high-collar intellectual or as an ironic
representation of the author's self, comical as well as tragic,
who is made to typify the Meiji intellectual. According to this
reading, the demarcation which is usually made between Futon
and Shimazaki Tōson's Hakai (The Broken Commandment,
1906)[15] — treating Hakai as a genuine modern novel of realism
and Futon as a distorted, pseudo-modern I-novel[16] — is not ac-
ceptable. Instead, Futon is a work close to Ukigumo (Floating
Cloud, 1888, the "first" modern Japanese novel and a work
which Katai himself admired),[17] a work in which the Meiji intellectual, infatuated with the new Western ideas, is portrayed as
a quixotic hero with a touch of self-parody on the part of the
author. This point will be illustrated in the following analysis
of the ironic dual perspective which Katai carefuly implants in
Futon but which is also inherent in the confessional novel in
general.

To grasp the dual perspective, it will be necessary to clarify
some of the confusions which led critics to read Futon exclusively as a document of the author's life. These confusions
stem from the very basic fact that the I-novel exists in the
"slender margin"[18] between art and life (or fiction and reality)
and exploits this fact artistically and intellectually, although
sometimes without clear self-consciousness on the part of the
author. The fascination of the confessional I-novel, of the
masochistic self-exposé of Iwano Hōmei and Chikamatsu Shūko
or of Henry Miller, for example, exists precisely in this artistic exploitation of the "slender margin" between reality and
fiction as the sole basis of the genre. Although it is one type
of autobiographical novel, the confessional I-novel forms a dis-

tinct genre of its own on the basis of its manipulation of the confession and of its ironic perspective in particular, which facilitates both self-search and self-exposé, and both self-glorification and self-parody.

The "evils" of the I-novel are usually traced back to Futon.
The publication of Futon in the fortieth year of Meiji (1907) was
received as a shocking event by Katai's contemporaries. Futon
and Tōson's Hakai, which appeared a year earlier, mark the beginning of the late naturalism period, a period in which major
naturalistic works integrating crude, imported theories into
Japanese milieus and themes were produced. Futon alone, it
has been argued, also determined the direction of the mainstream of Japanese literature in the post-Russo-Japanese-War
period by establishing the genre of the confessional I-novel.
Thus, Nakamura Mitsuo argues that the I-novel warped and distorted the Japanese literature of realism and that Futon played
a decisive role in making the autobiographical I-novel the mainstream of modern Japanese literature.19

He argues, moreover, that the success of Katai's Futon over-
shadowed Hakai, relegating Hakai to a state of complete neglect
and thus foreclosing the possibility of developing Japanese realism along the lines of the social novel Hakai. Even Tōson
himself followed the path of Katai and after Hakai began to write
autobiographical I-novels (Haru [Spring, 1909], Ie [The Family,
1912], and Shinsei [New Life, 1920]), until in the end he left the
form to write Yoake mae (Before the Dawn, 1935), an historical
novel describing his father's life and the struggle of the intellectual caught up in the process of cultural dissolution. Thus,
according to Nakamura, although Hakai and Futon are usually
recognized as the first modern Japanese novels, the two are almost diametrically opposed in nature; while Hakai is a genuine
modern novel of realism, Futon is representative of the typically Japanese brand of pseudo-modern novel, the I-novel, a
confessional, exhibitionistic, egocentric, narcissistic, autobiographical novel.

Tōson's Hakai is the story of a young man who, belonging to
the Eta caste, receives a command from his father not to reveal

his Eta identity. Obeying this command faithfully, the protagonist, Ushimatsu, successfully progresses through the educational hierarchy and becomes a teacher in a local town in Nagano prefecture. His colleagues and pupils never suspect his Eta identity. Ushimatsu's self-contempt at his own life's deception increases, however, as he witnesses the merciless ostracism of other members of the Eta caste. His admiration for the Eta intellectual Inoko Rentaro, a humanistic ideologue who openly admitted his Eta identity, increases his desire to lead a life of self-respect and moral and intellectual integrity, and he finally overcomes his fear of social ostracism. At the climax of the novel, Ushimatsu confesses his Eta identity and leaves the school and, in fact, Japanese society altogether.

The central question of Hakai is the dilemma of the new Meiji intellectuals who were torn between the desire for an ideal life with moral and intellectual integrity and the feudalistic social values and system which hindered the development of the modern individual ego. The essential tension of the novel, Ushimatsu's fear of social ostracism and his contempt for his own moral and intellectual deception, is that of the modern intellectual of the Meiji period.

Tayama Katai's Futon also deals with the inner conflict or dilemma of the new intellectual writer. Takenaka Tokio, a middle-aged writer, feels weary frustration over his lack of success as a writer and his drab marital life. The novel is a bald exposure of his inner struggle over his sexual attraction to his young female pupil, Yoshiko, an attraction which turns into an obsession when he comes to conceive of their relationship as the sole and absolute solution for his life of frustration. Yoshiko is a "high-collar" girl, the new breed of modern Meiji girl. Infatuated with the new Western ideas, she had come to Tokio to be his apprentice, to have him teach her to be a writer.

Takenaka Tokio finds consolation in teaching Yoshiko foreign literature and what the modern woman should be. When he discovers that she is in love with a young man who has given up his religious studies and followed her to Tokyo to become a writer himself, he is tormented by jealousy. Yet he also sup-

ports their love, for love is what a new individual must celebrate,
and he even defends the young couple before Yoshiko's parents.

His infatuation with Yoshiko is not solely sexual; in fact, his
infatuation is with ideas — the new ideas of man, of life and of
literature. Katai writes: "Into Japanese literature, which had
only Chikamatsu and Saikaku, the great European thought came
with the full violence of a typhoon.... Every young man aspired
to it."[20] Feminine liberation, that is, the creation of the new
woman, was one of the imported ideas which inspired Meiji
writers. Reading Ibsen to Yoshiko, Tokio urges her to grow out
of feudal submissiveness and to develop her modern personality. Free love was central in this female liberation, the establishment of the modern self. Tokio argues the importance of
love, yet love of the flesh, sexual love, he rejects as morally
wrong.

Tokio's inner conflict is thus dual in nature. On the one hand,
he aspires to be a liberated modern individual, and finding life
with his old-fashioned, unintellectual wife deplorable, dreams
of having an intellectually vital life with the modern Yoshiko.
He cannot force himself, however, to act according to his desire and dream, for his moral sense as a teacher, husband and
father prevents him from doing so. His romantic ideals meet
defeat before his moralistic concern for social integrity, and
he emerges as a compromising realist to his own great sorrow.

On the other hand, the novel presents the protagonist as a
middle-aged man who, though driven by the dark force of sexual
desire, is basically a conventional, feudal moralist. Although
he desires Yoshiko himself, he finds her sexual relations with
her lover morally unacceptable. He can approve only of spiritual love as necessary for the attainment of the modern self.
Thus the inner conflict he experiences is not only between his
romantic ideal vision of life and the drab reality of his daily
life, and between his uncontrollable sexual longing for a young
pupil and his moral social integrity, but also between his Western, radically modern ideals and the old feudal values to which
he himself still subscribes. His moral outrage (and subsequent
rejection of Yoshiko), which is based on the young lovers' phys-

ical relations, exposes his inner feudal self. The most devastating revelation is indeed the fact that the Western ideology of the modern man and the romantic, humanistic idealism to which he enthusiastically subscribed proves to be superficial attire for him. He emerges as a conventional moralist as well as a sentimental dreamer who is unable to accept the burdens and responsibilities of man's daily life.

The novel was accepted as a shocking yet brilliant achievement by Katai's contemporary writers. The main reason for the shock is the bold exposure and description of the protagonist's inner secret, his sexual longing for a young girl. A year before the publication of Futon, Katai had written an essay entitled "Rokotsunaru byosha" (Bald Description) in which, rejecting what he called "gilded literature," he advocated the presentation of reality as it is by the one-dimensional, bald description of facts.[21] Futon is the implementation of this naturalistic theory of description. Following its appearance, heated debates took place with regard to the legitimacy of sexual description as literary and artistic expression. Erotic realism as a part of the naturalistic theory of literary creation came into focus.

At the same time, the work was considered to be a bold confession of the writer, who was regarded as willing to sacrifice his social respectability, family life and even his relation with his model for the sake of artistic creation. It was considered a confrontation with and even a revolt against the social values confining individuals within the framework of feudal morality. In this way, the novel was accepted as a radically modern novel, a confessional novel through which the writer challenged society fundamentally at the risk of his own social destruction. Katai himself later wrote, using Maupassant's expression in a somewhat different way, that he experienced the pain of peeling off his skin, of exposing himself.[22] It is exactly on these grounds that Nakamura Mitsuo defines Futon as the prototype of the confessional I-novel.

It is not incorrect to call Futon a naturalistic novel, for we can discern the strong influence of the naturalistic concept of

man in Katai's portrayal of the protagonist. Katai presents man
as basically controlled by his instinctive drives and conditioned
by his social environment. He struggles to control his desire
by reason and moral will. In order to understand man as he is,
the author unveils the false social mask he wears and describes
him as baldly and as truthfully as possible. Before this task of
unveiling the truth of human nature, fictionalization or rhetori-
cal devices seem superficial and unnecessary. Indeed, with the
publication of Futon, the mature era of Japanese naturalism
began. The naturalistic concept of man found a congenial genre,
the I-novel, the subject of investigation being the author himself. The I-novel supplied a form in which Japanese writers
could dramatize their investigation of man in a milieu where a
tradition of literary realism was lacking.

What is problematic, therefore, is not the question of the naturalistic elements in Futon, but the question of the confession
in this I-novel, that is, the relation between the author and the
protagonist, and the author's treatment of the protagonist. Nakamura Mitsuo argues that Katai, moved by the protagonist
Johannes in G. Hauptmann's Lonely People, tried to recreate
his own image accordingly without understanding Hauptmann's
treatment of his hero. He criticizes Katai for what Tokio is:
a sentimental intellectual, fundamentally alienated from the reality of his life, who is infatuated with Western ideas of humanism and the modern self — a romantic dreamer who laments
over the drab reality of mundane life yet is himself a conventional, feudal man.[23]

Hirano Ken, on the other hand, disagrees with Nakamura's
contention that the protagonist's drama is the direct portrayal
of the author's.[24] He states that the author himself behaved
perfectly as a teacher and a family man, and that the publication caused no problem to those who were directly related to
him or to the events in the novel, for it was evident to them
that the story was indeed fiction. He says that Katai's intention
was ethical, that the central theme of the novel is the author's
struggle for moral growth, for self-reform even at the risk of
social respectability. Hirano says that Katai, unlike Toson in

Shinsei, had no need to reveal or confess his secret infatuation
with his pupil. The deliberate confession of his secret desire
served only his literary and ethical ambition, his desire to
break through the deadlock he felt both as an artist and as a
modern man. While Nakamura argues that the hero-author gen-
uinely suffers from the loneliness of modern man in the mold of
Hauptmann's Johannes and thus is a self-dramatization as a
tragic figure, Hirano argues that the protagonist is the old self
which the author outgrew by writing the novel.

While on the surface the point of divergence between Nakamura and Hirano appears to exist in their assessment of the
critical and aesthetic distance between the hero and the author,
an essential and crucial point in the assessment of the I-novel,
in actuality both accept the protagonist as a direct and faithful
portrayal of the author, or assume that it was the author's intention to make him so, whether the protagonist is the author
in the present or the past. The novel, according to them, is a
direct autobiographical confession, and their critical efforts
are directed at evaluating the author, present or past, as a person and his motivation for writing the novel.

Here again a simplistic identification of the protagonist
with the author exists behind their critical assessment. It
is a truism that Katai had both the ethical intention of reform-
ing himself — enabling himself to be reborn as a writer and to
break the artistic deadlock from which he felt he suffered —
and an urge for self-dramatization, an emotional urge to reveal
his inner feelings through his protagonist as a projection of the
self.[25] To argue these points can only reveal the motivations of
all writers in creating works of art. The central issue is to
evaluate the author's artistic treatment of the self, his relation
to his art, in terms of the literary or even philosophic perspective of the novel. This is particularly to the point in the confessional novel, in which the treatment of the inner self and the
artistic exposé of the self provide the sole structural and thematic basis of the novel.

It is exactly in the ambiguity and complexity of the author's
treatment of the protagonist that the main point of Futon lies.

Indeed, Tokio is portrayed as a hopelessly sentimental intellectual who can see himself only by comparing himself to characters in Western literary works. Western novels are always
open on his desk, and when he lectures on them to Yoshiko he
is in a heightened or drunken state of consciousness, having
identified himself with the heroes of the novels. In his mind he
is Johannes, and he believes that his sorrow is that of a high-
minded intellectual who has confronted pre-modern social
norms and human relations and met defeat. Tokio believes that
he is a tragic hero and is not aware of the fact that his pathetic
despair may appear comical to others. He is not himself aware
that he has exposed the superficiality of his belief in Western
ideas and that his tragic posture reveals only the puerile sentimentality of the intellectual who cannot see himself in the light
of reality.

This is exactly how Nakamura sees Katai himself. Basing his
opposition on this book, he defines not Tokio but Katai as a
product of bummei kaika ("the flowering of civilization," a
phrase in vogue in the Meiji period), a man who believed joining
international society as a modern military power meant the
modernization of the Japanese mind. Nakamura states that the
comical nature of Tokio's drama, the drama of one who is drunk
with ideas, escapes from the author's eye and that to appreciate
this novel, it is necessary for the reader to be as drunk with
the same ideas as is the author. Thus, according to Nakamura,
for the sober reader the book cannot bear critical evaluation.

Actually, however, Tokio cannot simply be Katai, for the author presents a dual perspective for observing his protagonist:
Tokio's subjective view of himself and the perspective of ordinary people absorbed in everyday life. Although Tokio himself
does not understand fully the complexity of his inner conflicts
and above all is not aware of the comical nature of his tragic
posture, Katai is aware of it and presents Tokio both from
Tokio's own point of view and from this antithetical point of
view. Tokio's lack of self-knowledge as well as his genuine
suffering becomes the main point of the novel, and according
to the dual perspective which Katai presents, Tokio is a comi-

cal hero as well as a tragic one.

Tokio's change of mood and obvious high spirits caused by Yoshiko's presence in his house is viewed from the perspective of daily life simply as a nuisance, as an obvious brightening of the spirit any ordinary middle-aged man would experience. Nakamura states that Tokio's infatuation with the young girl is too ordinary for a man of the world to take seriously, and that his inner suffering is not at all intellectual or tragic as Tokio believes it to be. He points out the comical nature of the self-dramatization of an ordinary, mediocre man who thinks his drama is unique and tragic. Yet this is exactly what Katai wishes the reader to think about his protagonist. This is exactly how he is viewed by his wife and his sister in the novel, although they, being old-fashioned women, never articulate their views. His wife and sister, both of whom he ignores or constantly compares to the modern Yoshiko as old-fashioned, ignorant women, consistently present the "healthy," although conventional, realistic viewpoint of daily life and regard him as a big child.

Moreover, Yoshiko is portrayed as she turns out to be — a superficial modern girl who was only attracted to Western ideas as if to fashionable clothes; she was actually interested in men, and her intellectual pretension was an unconscious device to attract them. Katai reveals this true nature of the Meiji "high-collar" girl mercilessly.[26] In fact, Tokio's wife and sister see this from the beginning, and the reader too is led to see Yoshiko from their perspective. Only Tokio is blind to it and continues to defend her free behavior with men (until he finds out that her object of interest is not him but a young man), telling his wife that she does not understand the new woman or the ideas in which she believes.

Yoshiko's lover also turns out to be a vulgar, superficial fellow, and this time even Tokio recognizes it. Although he is critical of the lover, however, he never blames Yoshiko for choosing him. It is his wife who takes the lover's superficiality almost for granted since Yoshiko is herself superficial. Tokio's wife, as if watching the play of children, observes a

drama whose ordinariness is hidden from its participants by
high language, and it is she who comes to fetch and mother Tokio when, overwhelmed by his misery and frustration, he drinks
himself into a stupor. Katai views this drunken, middle-aged
man, lying on the floor of the bathroom, through the eyes of his
wife, a woman rooted in the business of her daily life and do-
mestic cares. His self-pity and pathetic drunkenness lack dignity and are viewed as such by people in daily life. A stranger
passing by Tokio, who is lying drunk in the park and brooding
over his loneliness, regards him simply as an ordinary drunk-
ard, a good-for-nothing, while Tokio compares himself to an
intellectual hero in Russian literature who is insulted by a
crude common citizen.

Tokio's lack of understanding and self-knowledge are also
clearly portrayed. Even when he finds out about Yoshiko's
sexual involvement with her lover, he does not realize the fundamental shallowness of this "high-collar" girl. On the contrary, he tries to believe that her love is still platonic, while
her own father simply laughs at such an idea, taking their sexual relation for granted. When Tokio learns the truth, he believes that they have betrayed the high ideals of love which he
advocated, and acting like a severe, moralistic guardian with
uncompromising standards, he decides to send her back home.
Yet after Yoshiko leaves, he breaks into tears, still dreaming
that someday she may become his wife.

Even Yoshiko and her lover Tanaka are somewhat at a loss
over Tokio's high language and persistence in advocating ideal,
spiritual love. Yoshiko knows too that what Tokio sees in her
is not herself as a person but the idea of love, the egotistical
projection of his aspiration. Yoshiko knows well, however, that
in order to stay in Tokyo, she must please Tokio by pretending
to go along with his high ideals. Even when her sexual involvement is revealed, she tries to justify herself to Tokio in terms
of the high ideals of the modern woman, while Tokio, torn between his desire to accept her high language and his moralistic
indignation over her corrupt love, merely indulges himself in
his own misery and loneliness. At this point it is clearly Tokio

alone who believes he is the Johannes of <u>Lonely People</u>.

The scene in which Tokio sees Yoshiko off describes Tokio's blindness and lack of self-knowledge mercilessly. Tokio, wrapped up in his feeling of sadness, speculates that Yoshiko's mistake, the fact that she is no longer a virgin, might enable her to marry him who is much older and has many children. He then compares his fate to that of the protagonists in Turgenev's novels. He firmly believes that Yoshiko is in the same state of sorrow over their imminent separation; Katai informs his readers that only Tokio did not see that another man was at the station secretly bidding farewell to Yoshiko.

The last scene of the novel depicts Tokio after Yoshiko's departure, indulging himself in inhaling the body odor retained in the <u>futon</u> (quilt) which Yoshiko had left in her upstairs room in his house. It is this last scene of the novel which was considered the most shocking.

When he opened one shutter of the eastern window as he did on the day of separation, the sun's rays streamed into the room. The desk, bookcase, bottles and cosmetic dish were left there as they had been before, and he was caught by the illusion that his beloved was at school, as it had been in the past. Tokio opened the drawer of the desk. An oil-stained ribbon had been left there. Tokio took it in his hand and inhaled the odor. After awhile, he stood up and opened the closet door. Three large chests were packed there, ready to be sent off, and behind these chests was the bedding which Yoshiko used to use — the bottom quilt in pale yellow with an arabesque plant design and a top night-cover with the same design and thickly stuffed with cotton were folded on top of each other. Tokio took them out. The nostalgic odor of oil and the perspiration of the woman made his heart swell. Putting his face to the velvet collar of the night-cover where it was particularly soiled by use, he inhaled to his heart's content the odor of his beloved woman.

Sexual desire, sadness and despair struck his heart immediately. Tokio spread the quilt, covered himself with the night-cover and burying his face in its soiled velvet collar, he cried.

Outside the dark room, the wind blew fiercely.[27]

Nakamura Mitsuo expresses his disgust over Katai and over his sentimental treatment of this folly of a middle-aged intellectual who, after everything is over, still remains without self-knowledge and indulges himself in this pathetic outburst. On the other hand, Hirano Ken argues that the scene is obviously a fiction, that this is not what Katai himself actually did. He says that Katai could not have done this because of what would have happened if his wife had come upstairs and seen him. He also argues that it is highly improbable that a young girl whose father came from far away to take her home would leave her personal belongings behind.

As I have shown, however, Futon is not meant to be the author's truthful exposé of his inner self; nor is it simply a moralistic novel in which the author criticizes away his past self by deliberately exposing his inner secret. As Yoshida Seiichi points out, Katai had previously dealt with basically the same theme as that of Lonely People in Onna Kyōshi (Woman Teacher, 1901), a novel which is not based on his real experience.[28] He had also written a novel called Shōjyobyō (Young Girl Fanatic) in which a middle-aged, frustrated and sentimental writer who has a "bad habit" of falling in love with young girls is mercilessly parodied. The protagonist, Kojyō, is a sentimental dreamer who, completely lacking self-knowledge, comically becomes isolated from the reality of his life. He is almost the same as Takenaka Tokio, yet is presented clearly as a comical anti-hero. Thus it is not possible to regard Futon as a direct dramatization of the author's inner self.

What we see in Futon is a dramatization of the sentimentality as well as of the despair and loneliness of the Meiji intellectual who was infatuated with Western ideas and thus was alienated from society; it is a dramatization of the artist's alienation in its tragicomical duality. Viewed from the perspective of daily life, Tokio appears to be a comical, quixotic hero, yet the reader also feels the frustration of a middle-aged writer living in an environment hostile to art and modern ideas, and the despair of a man who fails to find a sense of life. The man who cries in the quilt of the young girl whose very superficiality is the cause of his misery is indeed comical as well as pathetic, and Katai portrays this well. The point of the novel lies in the fact that it is neither a clear self-parody nor an empathetic self-portrayal, but a representation of the Meiji writer in his tragicomical duality. The ironic perspective and use of confession facilitate the presentation of this duality: the novel is indeed an ironic self-dramatization.

The basic structure of such novels as Futon is the exposé of the protagonist's inner self — an exposé which destroys his social respectability before the reader. Whether the confession is autobiographical or dramatic is not important, for the reader, forced to hear the confession, is taken into an alliance with the protagonist. The confessor masochistically abandons himself before the reader, who is fully exposed to his embarrassing contradictions or disgusting criminality. The reader's complex reaction to the confession, his disgust and empathy, is caused by the complex psychological relation between the confessor and his audience. Confession, whether it is that of the extrovert or that of the introvert, to use Northrop Frye's terminology, is a masochistic exhibition of the self and thus an aggressive challenge to the consciousness of the other. By deliberately exposing himself, the protagonist becomes a clown, challenging the reader's consciousness but also glorifying his own subjectivity, a subjectivity which is established by the reader's disgust over or moral rejection of his clowning self-dramatization. In most cases it is the reader more than the protagonist himself who is embarrassed by the self-exposé.

The confession of the secret self of the protagonist has been used by various authors, including Edgar Allan Poe, who was influential in Japan, to establish a complex relationship between the protagonist and the reader. Poe's "mad" heroes confess their gratuitous crimes, exposing the perversity of their criminal selves which desire to do wrong for its own sake. Not only do they challenge the reader's moral and social sensibility by fascinating the reader, they also establish their singularity by evoking the reader's sense of disgust at being forced to see something which he does not desire to see. Thus the reader is caught between feelings of disgust over the hero's persistent self-dramatization without self-knowledge and the fascination of glimpsing some forbidden truth about human nature. Poe skillfully draws the reader into the inner world of the protago-

nist, but at the same time does not forget to remind us that the
heroes are mad. Through the use of the confessional technique,
therefore, the author introduces dual perspectives for regarding
the hero, one involved and the other detached.

Iwano Hōmei, a writer of confessional I-novels who was
greatly influenced by the "diabolism" of Poe and Baudelaire,
exploits this existential-psychological challenge of the confession to its extremity in his novels. His persistent exposure of
the protagonists' shamefulness, lack of integrity, and self-
destructive indulgence in sex is as masochistic and intimi-
datingly obnoxious as that of Henry Miller's protagonist in
Tropic of Cancer or Erica Jong's in Fear of Flying, yet because
of his persistence and extremity, the self-exposure becomes
almost an act of conscious self-parody. In the confession,
therefore, self-glorification and self-parody, the expression of
the singularity of the self and of the universality of human nature, are presented simultaneously. Iwano Hōmei's novels
clarify the integration in Japanese confessional novels of naturalistic self-investigation with the self-destructive self-search
inherent in the tradition of dark romanticism. Tanizaki's early
works also demonstrate this unique mixture clearly. Dazai
Osamu, whose deliberate use of the confession as a fictional
device comes very close to that of Poe, also integrates these
elements skillfully.

The tragicomedy of the Meiji intellectual, whose radical
ideas and Western influence isolated him or her from the reality of contemporary life, is indeed the main theme of Futon.
This has been one of the major themes of modern Japanese literature. Such major writers as Futabatei Shimei, Mori Ogai,
Natsume Sōseki, Shimazaki Tōson, Akutagawa Ryūnosuke and
Yokomitsu Riichi pursued it with obsessive concern, revealing
both the superficiality and the tragic despair of the Japanese
intellectuals in their struggle to modernize themselves. The
confessional novel proved to be an effective vehicle for the expression of the theme, enabling the author to present his ironic
understanding of the self both as a clown and as a tragic hero.
Above all, the dual perspective which the confession itself con-

tains enables the author to present an ironic self-dramatization, a uniquely modern treatment of the self.

Despite its egocentric narrowness and narcissistic obsession with the self, and despite its lack of articulate artistic devices, the confessional I-novel emerged as an extension of the Meiji writers' awareness of realism, as advocated by Tsubouchi Shōyō, and it realizes one extreme possibility of the modern novel. For Meiji writers, isolated from society in the closed world of the bundan, the question of one's self and one's relation to art was the sole matter of import. There is no doubt that Meiji writers did not and could not fully understand the struggle of French writers against bourgeois society and against science. Yet the Japanese writers, living in an overly utilitarian yet feudal society that was hostile to art and the artist, shared with them the same isolation and the same concern with the question of the restoration of the self in art. It was only natural that Tsubouchi Shōyō's hito no nasake (human feelings)[29] made sense to these isolated artists only as his own nasake.

The conflict between art and life is central in their confessional novels. Tōson's Shinsei, although seriously colored by Tōson's desire for purification and self-punishment (bringing the novel closer to shinkyo shōsetsu), exploits fully the psychological, social and above all literary challenge the confession itself contains. The reader's disgust over the protagonist's egotism stems from the deliberate self-exposure, contrary to Hirano Ken's contention, and the self-righteous insistence that the protagonist's rebirth as an artist will be achieved by it.

Almost all modern confessional novels are in fact art novels, with the protagonist trying to write or to be reborn as an artist. Whether an artist will be reborn, as in the case of Stephen Daedalus, or whether the protagonist continues to be unable to create is irrelevant with regard to the fact that in confessional novels, art and life are curiously interwoven. The confessional novel becomes a form of art novel in which the artist's self-search, the process of making an artist, is the structural basis and major theme. Although the life of the artist is the subject, it is a life justified in terms of art. The art or the seriousness

of the protagonist in his attempt to become an artist supplies the
fundamental justification for writing about oneself. Thus confessional novels are curiously philosophic and intellectual despite their narcissistic, egocentric perspective.

Yoshida Seiichi dismisses the confession in Futon as a point-
less display of inner experience, for the protagonist does not
suffer from any sense of guilt and his secret infatuation with his
young pupil does not merit being called a crime.[30] He argues
that in the absence of an absolute God or established religious
and social orthodoxy in Meiji Japan, there could not be any serious, uncontrollable urge for confession, except the vague fear of
social criticism. Yet in modern confessional novels, art re-
places religion, and the confession becomes not that of a moral
sinner seeking religious salvation or spiritual resurrection, but
that of an artistic failure trying to be born or reborn as an artist. The loss of imagination or creative sterility is the crime
(sin) for which the protagonist seeks salvation. Artistic sterility rather than religious sinfulness drives the artist-hero to
confess, and the artistic sincerity or commitment to art justifies the exposure of the inner self as material suitable for art.
The Japanese confessional novelists, because they were exempt
from religious struggle, were able to attain radical modernity
in this sense, presenting the wasteland of art in modern society
and the struggle of modern man, for whom art has replaced God
as the sole means of salvation.

The interweaving of art and life, one typical characteristic of
the Japanese I-novel, is thus a characteristic of the modern
confessional novel in general. The protagonist of confessional
novels, who is neither an aloof artist nor a realistic social existence, appears tragicomical. He appears to be a comical,
quixotic hero without self-knowledge when regarded from the
perspective of everyday life, but a tragic hero who suffers
enormously in a hostile society and from the artistic sterility
caused by it when regarded from the perspective of art. This
tragicomical quality itself expresses the isolation of the artist
in a utilitarian, industrial society in which art and life are incompatible with each other. Unlike Tanizaki Junichiro, who

abandoned life without reluctance for the sake of art, or Shiga
Naoya, who assumed responsibility for life by placing it above
art, the authors of the confessional I-novels based their artistic
creation on this very duality. The confessional novel is a form
which enables the author to convert life into art and art into a
means of serving the artist. Its raison d'être is its exploitation
of the "slender margin" between the real and the unreal, between truth and fiction, and between the author's self-glorification and self-parodization, integrating the artist's egotistical
insistence on his artistic self and his awareness of life's retal-
iation against it.

Following in the path of Mori Ogai and Natsume Sōseki, writers whom he especially admired, Akutagawa Ryūnosuke (1892-1927) started his writing by rejecting the confessional self-revelation and open self-search which characterized Japan's I-novelists, including the naturalistic writers like Katai and the idealistic Shirakaba writers. Akutagawa, who was also strongly influenced by Western fin-de-siècle literature, chose the short story as his form from the start, and studied Poe, Anatole France, de Maupassant, Gautier, and Merimée, among others.

Although the short story has been the dominant form in modern Japanese literature, it was often — particularly in realistic works — meant only to be a short form of the novel. In fact, the Japanese term shōsetsu is used to refer to both the novel and the short story. Such writers of the I-novel as Shiga Naoya (who wrote major novels) and Kajii Motojiro (who wrote short fiction exclusively) excelled in using the short-story form to present situations which led to the height of the author's or protagonist's perception and to a moment of profound realization in his daily-life experiences. Precisely for this reason, however, precisely because they used the short-story form to explore openly the self and life, centering on the protagonist-author's self-search and self-expression, the form of their short stories was no different from that of the novel, except in

---

*A version of this chapter appeared in Asian Culture Quarterly VI:4 (Winter 1978), pp. 25-34, under the title "Akutagawa's 'Toshishun' and the Chinese 'Tu Tzu-ch'un.'"

length. For writers pursuing self-growth, the novel is definitely a
more suitable form, and even Kajii, who was devoted to the genre of
the short story, turned to the novel just before his untimely death.

Akutagawa, on the other hand, approached the short story in
a manner completely different from the I-novelists. First of all,
the short story for him was a modern form of storytelling and
had to center around the story element (the lack of which characterizes the work of the I-novelists). Second, the stories had
to present a self-sufficient world of their own. The art of the
short-story writer, therefore, had to concentrate on creating in
the works a perfectly autonomous "architectural structure," to
borrow Tanizaki's phrase (which, ironically, he used in his debate with Akutagawa1).

The most characteristic feature of Akutagawa's short stories
is the fact that they are based almost exclusively on other stories: classical tales, foreign tales, the works of other writers,
and so forth. In other words, Akutagawa's short stories do not
usually deal with human reality directly, but with materials
which have already been fictionalized in tales or stories. On the
rare occasions when he dealt with situations in his own experience, they were almost invariably limited to those in his childhood. He did deal with historical situations, learning much from
Mori Ogai, but even there his interest was not in dealing with
the actual human experience, but in the use of stories which had
already been told in history.

The borrowing of old stories or the use of someone else's
stories, immediately and on a superficial level, frees the writer
from having to confront the epistemological question of how to
know, grasp and present reality, a question which has been vital
to modern fiction. The reality in Akutagawa's works is one or
two steps removed from the reality of the author and the reader,
and the reality in his twice-told tales is replaced by the "story,"
temporarily solving the problem of the relation between reality
and art. Moreover, the story element, which he made central,
helps to create the structure of the works and to make them
self-contained. Their perfection can be evaluated in terms of
the narrative structure, that is, by the art of storytelling and

the extent to which the story presents a world complete in itself.

The borrowing of old stories also exempts the author from confronting directly the question of self-expression in his works. He is a storyteller, one whose business is to mediate between the readers and the story. Not only does the story give shape and boundaries to the world of his works, but it also defines the author's identity in relation to his works as a storyteller, both inside and outside the works. Akutagawa was amazingly unconcerned with the question of the relationship between the author and the work. He often appears openly as a narrator in his works (as in "Rashomon"), and the author as narrator is surprisingly free from self-consciousness in his intrusion into the world of the story.[2]

Thus, the use of existing stories, particularly old stories, whose credibility the author did not have to defend, enabled Akutagawa to circumvent dealing directly in his works with the two vital problems of modern fiction, reality and self, and to avoid the deadlock which the I-novelists reached in dealing with these problems. In Akutagawa's short stories, the question of reality and fiction and that of their relation to the search for the self in literature are temporarily suspended because of the dominance of the story itself. In that world of story, the questions of reality and the self are converted into technical or aesthetic problems of narration.

This does not mean that Akutagawa lacked concern with the problems of reality and self or that he tried to avoid dealing with them. By borrowing stories and taking the reader away from the immediate reality, Akutagawa sought to present symbolic situations relevant to all human reality. A self-avowed literary cosmopolitan, Akutagawa was confident of the universal validity of his works, confident that his works transcended the particular time and place in which they were set. Most of Akutagawa's works deal with complex psychological situations that exist in human relations, and they often reveal his fundamental skepticism about human life and belief in the relativity of human relations. In other words, Akutagawa's borrowing of the stories was a device for dealing with the modern human situation and

psychology. The borrowed story provided the distance of time
and space which helped give universality to the situation with
which he was dealing. In this sense, the story provided only a
convenient framework.

Moreover, Akutagawa's consistent use of old stories, stories
twice or thrice told, reveals his belief in or reliance on archetypal literary themes and patterns of human life. Often in his
stories, the narrator evades the responsibility even for being the
witness or providing firsthand information on the story. By
relying on the archetypal patterns of his stories, Akutagawa was
able to expand his imagination to present his own story. In fact,
his short stories are characterized by the exceptional integration of storytelling with the presentation of modern phychologi-
cal reality.

In depending on earlier literary works, Akutagawa was certainly not alone among Japanese authors; such dependence has
been one of the major techniques of Japanese (and Chinese) literature. Japanese fiction in particular, including the monogatari, setsuwa and short fiction of Saikaku and Ueda Akinari, has
relied extensively on the use of earlier works as source materials. In utilizing earlier works, therefore, Akutagawa was only
revitalizing a deep-rooted tradition of Japanese fiction, and in
doing so, he countered the dominant trend of his time which
treated the short story as a form of direct self-search and self-
expression or as the presentation of a slice of life, a form without a story. In the Western short story too, the development of
the modern genre involved liberal borrowing from earlier stories as, for example, in the case of Edgar Allan Poe, often regarded as the father of the modern short-story genre.

Furthermore, Akutagawa was far from indifferent to the question of self-expression or the author's ego. Indeed, he admired
and envied Shiga Naoya and Goethe, both of whom openly exposed
their internal lives as the materials for their literature and the
subject of their literary pursuit. Considering himself a poet,
Akutagawa was strongly inclined toward the pursuit of self-
exultation and self-transcendence. His persistent concern with
egotism, particularly the egotism of the artist, was reflected in

various ways in his works, but most often in the recurring theme
of conflict between the decadent pursuit of art and beauty and the
humanistic acceptance of the self as part of humanity. "Jigoku-
hen" (The Hell Screen, 1918) is the most brilliant dramatization
of the conflict. By assuming the role of a storyteller, therefore,
Akutagawa was only wearing a mask which would hide the author's ego in the archetypal drama contained in the stories. In
fact, it can be said that the development of modern fiction is the
history of the authors' search for the appropriate masks in
which to confess.

Mishima Yukio, who is the proper successor to Akutagawa in
this respect, reveals plainly the mechanism of the confession of
a mask. Unlike Mishima, however, Akutagawa was never successful in dramatizing the self in different personae; not only
was the short-story form decidedly unsuitable for it, but also
the narrative structure in which the narrator assumed the role
of storyteller imposed inherent limitations on such dramatization.

The plot controversy between Akutagawa and Tanizaki, which
took place in the last year of Akutagawa's life, sheds considerable light on these issues. In this dispute, Akutagawa, almost
negating his entire literary achievement, advocated the writing
of stories without a story and the expression of the author's
"poetic spirit" as the purpose of literary expression rather than
the creation of an autonomous world of fiction with architectural
beauty. The dispute took place at a point when Akutagawa's confidence as a storyteller was deeply shaken and he had come to
doubt whether storytelling was an adequate form to provide the
mask for the search for the self and the meaning of life. (A full
discussion of this controversy appears in the next chapter.) Although it would be too simple to take his last work, "Aru ahō no
isshō" (A Fool's Life, 1927), as a straight confessional, autobiographical work, the change of his literary stance and form
of expression, the open and direct dealing with himself at the
time of his mental crisis, only impresses us the more with his
earlier effort to hide his vulnerable self under the mask of a
storyteller.[3]

Such critics as Saeki Shōichi have pointed out that Akutaga-

wa's failure as a storyteller in his later years was due mainly
to his failure to clarify the relation between the narrator and the
author himself.[4]   Such modern writers as Henry James, Mauriac
and Jean-Paul Sartre have long cast doubt on the ontological legitimacy of the author assuming the role of narrator, and in contemporary fiction, the narrator has become nothing but a fictional character. Akutagawa's turning to the story without a story, therefore,
was only the result of his doubt about having the author assume
the role of narrator and of his recognition of the problems which
became acutely felt in the modernist era. Akutagawa was thus
anticipating, in his later years, the direction which modern fiction itself would take.

In this sense, Akutagawa's early works present a happy union
of storytelling and the presentation of the psychological or inner
reality of human beings, a union between the architectural beauty
of a self-sufficient, artificial world of art and the human condition. In other words, Akutagawa found in his stories, his twice-
told tales which borrowed from earlier works, a means of overcoming the dichotomy between art and life, a dichotomy which
was the major literary and aesthetic concern of the fin-de-siècle
writers.

Akutagawa was an indefatigable experimenter in his expression and in his effort to develop the poetics of the short story.
Each story, therefore, reveals not only his unending search for
new materials, but also his awareness of the problems of narration. One of the genres he successfully developed was stories
for young adults, the most representative of which is the famous
"Kumonoito" (The Thread of the Spider's Web, 1915). He wrote
about eleven such stories, all during the middle period of his
writing career (1918-1924), a period in which he was especially
concerned with the relations between art and life.

The Taisho period (1912-1926) was a time when stories for
children were seriously pursued as a new genre. Such writers
as Ogawa Mimei and Suzuki Miekichi turned completely to children's literature and led the movement to raise the genre to the
level of art. Other writers, including Uno Koji, Kubota Mantaro
and Sato Haruo, were also devoted to the genre. Akutagawa

wrote the stories for young adults under the influence of Suzuki
Miekichi, who was one of the pupils of Sōseki. Akutagawa's
dowa (tales for children), like most of his other works, were
based on a wide range of old and legendary stories, including
Buddhist, classical Chinese and Japanese tales, and Western
fairy tales. Since they were ostensibly written for young adults,
however, they enabled Akutagawa to express more openly his
own ethical views and attitude toward life, and his lyrical ap-
praisal of innocence and purity.

"Toshishun," which was published in 1920 in Akai Tori (The
Red Bird), a journal of children's literature edited by Suzuki
Miekichi, is not only one of the masterpieces of children's literature but also occupies a significant place in Akutagawa's
literature.[5] The work is an adaptation of a tale, or ch'uan-ch'i,
of T'ang China entitled "Tu Tzu-chun," which falls into a major
category of supernatural tales in the ch'uan-ch'i genre.[6] Although Akutagawa followed the basic plot and story of "Tu Tzu-
chun," essentially retelling the story to young adults, by changing
several key elements in the story he converted the Chinese tale
into a quest-story of his own.

The original Chinese story is about a young man, Tu Tzu-
chun, who dissipated his inheritance. A good-for-nothing wast-
rel who neglected all his duties, he is deserted by his relatives
and friends when he loses his money. At this point he meets at
the city gate an old man who gives him money to restore his
former life of dissipation. When he again wastes his money
within a few years, the same old man appears and gives him a
still larger amount of money. He intends to do something good
with the money, but the minute he receives it he resumes his
decadent life. When he receives money for the third time, Tu
Tzu-chun is determined to use it to promote public welfare, and
after attending to his worldly affairs in this way, to place himself at the old man's disposal. After spending a year helping
orphans and widows and contributing to the social good in other
ways, he goes on the appointed day to see the old man at the appointed place. The old man takes him to his mansion on a
mountain which penetrates deeply into the clouds. In the man-

sion there is a cauldron for making holy medicine. The old man,
returning in his Taoist's clothing, tells Tu Tzu-chun not to utter
a single word at the trials he is about to experience, for whatever he experiences will not be real.

Subsequently, Tu Tzu-chun is tortured by soldiers, attacked by
ferocious animals, and tortured by monsters and ogres who boil
him and cut up his limbs. Through all this, Tu Tzu-chun utters
not a single word. Next his wife is brought before him and cut
up inch by inch. Tzu-chun survives this too without saying anything. After this, Tzu-chun is killed and sent to hell. Having
gone through the torture of hell, he is sent back to this world as
a daughter of a family in Sung-chun. She is a mute woman who
suffers pain and illness silently. A man marries her, and they
have a son. Angered by his wife's remaining silent even when
she sees their son, the husband bangs the son's head against a
stone, cracking it. When she sees this, she feels love in her
heart and utters, "A!" in spite of herself.

Tu Tzu-chun finds himself once more at the cauldron beside
the old man. The old man is grieving and tells him that he failed
to become immortal. He tells Tzu-chun that he was successful
in repressing such human feelings as joy, anger, sorrow, fear
and desire, but not love. He then sends Tzu-chun back to the
world. Tzu-chun is ashamed of his failure to assist his benefac-
tor and once more tries to seek him out to offer his services,
but he can never find him again.

In the original Chinese tale, the life of man, searching vainly
for unattainable immortality, is portrayed as absurd. The tale
is filled with obvious Taoist ethical teachings. Tu Tzu-chun is
not selected by the old man for the test because he is a Taoist
interested in becoming an immortal, nor is he selected because he
requested it. He goes through the test simply because he is "told"
to do so. In the story, he is asked to find the old man deep in the
mountains, and when he arrives, he is asked by the old man to
sit down and neither to move nor to utter a single word. In other
words, when he was put to the test, he knew nothing about the
nature of the test and was therefore following the Taoist prin-

ciple of purposelessness, or the Buddhist principle of mindless-
ness. The test was a direct experiment on human nature, and
only human will, not intention, would help one succeed in it. In
addition, Tzu-chun was selected because he had been a spend-
thrift, a parallel of the prodigal son whose return was especially
blessed because he had sinned.

The nature of the old man's test, therefore, can be understood
as an ironic statement on the vulnerability of the human will,
which is so closely connected to human relations with others.
Success in the test — or rather, the attainment of immortality —
lies in the elimination of all the human attachments which detain
man so powerfully on the mortal level. The achievement of immortality, therefore, requires the filtration of all human sedi-
ments, enabling the protagonist to reach the realm of "non-man"
and the ultimate "silence."

Tu Tzu-chun's being mute in the test is a second mask laid
over the first, which is created by his conversion into a woman.
Being a mother, he experiences the maternal human nature of
love for his/her child. Being mute, however, he/she experiences an initial non-attachment to worldly matters. She grows up

With incomparable beauty, but mute. Her family treated her as a born mute.
There were indecent relatives who intimidated her in many ways, but she made
no response.[7]

In other words, being mute is a mask which protects her from responding to human experiences. Unfortunately, the mask is ripped
asunder at the moment when she sees her child dashed to his death.

Although Akutagawa's "Toshishun" appears to follow "Tu Tzu-
chun" quite faithfully, it differs from its source story in two
fundamental respects. The first difference is in Toshishun's
motive for leaving the human world; the second is in the attitude
of the sennin (old man) toward Toshishun's attempt to become
an immortal sennin himself.

In the original story, Tu Tzu-chun becomes ashamed of his
wasteful life, and when he is made rich for the third time, he
spends money for public welfare. Toshishun, to the contrary,

never becomes ashamed of his life of luxury; nor does he spend any of the money he receives for the social benefit. Moreover, Akutagawa describes in detail the gorgeousness of Toshishun's life and the decadent beauty in which he indulges himself. This does not exist in the original. When the pensive Toshishun is asked by the old man whether it is the luxurious life itself that he has become tired of, he answers positively no and refuses to live a life of poverty.[8] It is not a distaste for luxury that made him dissatisfied with life, but the fact that he had "given up on man." He then asks the sennin to make him his pupil and to train him to be a sennin of high virtue, to enable him to transcend human life. Tu Tzu-chun, on the other hand, wishes to place himself at the Taoist's disposal, to assist him in making an elixir, in order to return the favor the Taoist did for him. Moreover, this takes place after Tzu-chun has established himself as a virtuous and respectable social existence, restoring his respect as a human being. Although both Tzu-chun and Toshishun were disillusioned by people who were nice to them when they were rich and deserted them when they were poor, Tzu-chun's return of the favor is fundamentally different from Toshishun's despair over humanity as far as the motive for leaving the human world is concerned.

From the start, Akutagawa's "Toshishun" presents the languid, melancholy air of a decadent life, and Toshishun is portrayed as a man who, disillusioned with the pursuit of beauty and luxury, searches for the meaning of life. Akutagawa's opening narration conveys this sense immediately:

It was a spring day; nightfall was approaching. At the west gate of Lo Yang, the capital of T'ang, a young man was gazing vacantly up at the sky.[9]

Then he describes a busy street of this gorgeous, prosperous city, contrasting it with the lonely, pensive Toshishun who stands leaning against the gate, looking vacantly at the sky. When the old man appears before Toshishun, he asks him what he is thinking. Toshishun just answers him, "Me? I was thinking about what I should do, since I do not even have a place to sleep tonight." In the original, the old man hears Tzu-chun's complaint about his cold-hearted friends and relatives, and offers him money.

Akutagawa's Toshishun is, indeed, a decadent hero, who, turning his back on morality, has stoically pursued a life of beauty and luxury and become disillusioned by his pursuit. He is presented as a quester-hero, who, having seen and been disgusted with everything about men and life, desires to transcend human life, to be above human beings. He is not a naive Tzu-chun who is simply weak at the temptation of luxury and a lazy life and has just learned a lesson about the selfishness of people. Through his experiences, Tzu-chun turns into a morally and socially respectable man, even an honorable man who does not forget to show his gratitude by returning the favor done him. What Toshishun learns is disillusionment with human life.

Akutagawa wrote two other works which contain the story of a man who was made rich instantly by meeting a wizard. The first of these, "The Sennin" (1914), also takes place in China. One of his earliest works, it is a story about a street magician who endures poverty and rigorous training for the moment of glory when his skill in his art will reach its height and the audience will throw him money in excitement. At the end of the story, the protagonist, his performance over, is walking on the deserted street, his magic tools on his shoulder, wet in the evening drizzle. He meets an old man to whom he tells his life's sufferings and hardships, and the old man, who is a wizard, makes him rich instantly. In another story of the same title written in 1922, an honest idiot who wishes to become an immortal works without pay for a greedy doctor who promises to make him one at the end of a long period of service. Although the doctor has no power to make him an immortal, the doctor's wife suggests at the end of the promised years of service that he try flying, and the idiot flies away as an immortal. It is evident, therefore, that the theme of "Toshishun" was one with which Akutagawa was consistently concerned.

Akutagawa was obsessed with the theme of the "condensed life," a life comprised of moments of intense feeling. His often-quoted saying that life is not worth a line of Baudelaire's poetry [10]

indicates not only his ideal of art for art's sake, but also his desire for a short but brilliant life. "Fireworks in a dark sky"[11]
was how he envisioned his own life. Indeed, many of Akutagawa's
protagonists risk the destruction of their social and moral integrity for the sake of brilliant, intense moments of experience.
One of Akutagawa's masterpieces for young adults, "Torokko"
(The Truck, 1922), describes a boy who pursued the excitement
of coasting downhill in a truck (a coal-car on rails). He offers
to help miners push the truck up the hill for the thrill of coming
down. After the pursuit of excitement, he finds out that he has
come too far away from home to return in the daylight. The
story ends with a brilliant description of the boy running back
home in fear, barefooted in the twilight, and of his outburst of
crying when he finally reaches home.

Akutagawa's Toshishun pursues a life of luxury and beauty at
the risk of his social and moral destruction, and his gorgeous,
decadent life is not the result of his weakness as in the case of
Tu Tzu-chun. He has no intention of living the long and dull life
of a morally upright, socially respectable philanthropist. When
he becomes disillusioned with the life he envisioned, he desires
to leave human life, to go beyond human experience. His request
to the sennin to make him a sennin too, therefore, is a quest for
an above-human existence, not an effort to return the wizard's
favor. The ordeal he goes through — the same maintenance of
silence in the face of physical and mental agony — is clearly a
trial through which a quester-hero must pass to attain his ideal.
The tortures which Toshishun has to bear are much more simple
than those to which Tu Tzu-chun is subjected. The wife does not
appear at all, and he is not reincarnated as a woman. Although
both heroes break their oaths because of concern for loved ones,
in Toshishun's case it is the torturing of his parents in hell that
he finally cannot bear and that causes him to break his silence.

The ending of "Toshishun" is also fundamentally different
from that of the original. Both stories are about the failure to
attain immortality, the transcendence of human life, because of
human love. Although both Tzu-chun and Toshishun fail in the

face of human love, however, Toshishun's happiness with his
failure contrasts sharply with Tzu-chun's shame. Above all, the
sennin in Akutagawa's "Toshishun" tells Toshishun that if he had
not said anything when his parents were in agony, he would have
killed Toshishun instantly. The Taoist monk in "Tu Tzu-chun,"
on the other hand, laments over Tzu-chun's failure and sends
him back to the world. Tzu-chun tries again to transcend human
existence, while Toshishun is reborn as a new human being with
a new vision of life. He decides to live truthfully as a human being, and the sennin assists him in doing so by giving him a house
with a plot of land for farming.

"If you had remained silent, I was determined to take your life instantly. I imagine you no longer wish to be a sennin. You have already become disgusted with
the life of a rich man. Then what do you think you would like to be from now on?"

"Whatever I become, I intend to live an honest life, a humane life." In Toshishun's voice there was a tone of cheerfulness which hitherto was absent.

"Do not forget your word. Then I will not see you again from today." Tekkanshi
[the sennin] began walking away while saying this, but he suddenly stopped and
turned to Toshishun, adding cheerfully,

"Oh, fortunately I just remembered that I have a house at the southern foot of
Taizan [Taishan]. I will give you the house together with the plot of land next
to it for farming. Go and live there. Just now peach flowers must be in bloom
all around the house."[12]

Toshishun attains his desire to be human, and his quest for a
meaningful life ends with his regaining trust in humanity. Here
immortality is the negation of humanity, and Toshishun learns
the value of being human through his effort to become immortal.
The sennin, representing the point of view of the story, maintains that it is not worthwhile to attain immortality by negating
humanity.

The dichotomy between immortality and humanity is the central theme of both the Chinese and Japanese stories. The Taoist monk in "Tu Tzu-chun" tells Tzu-chun that he successfully
conquered all human feelings except love. Tzu-chun's failure
is that of a common Chinese pursuing immortality. His trial is

not a heroic quest because the tale lacks the grandeur to portray
him as a hero. Indeed, it emphasizes Tzu-chun's awareness of
a sense of shame when he is thrice financed by the old man, but
only to add to his personality the element of human dignity, a
virtue perhaps, but one of common mortals. His failure shows
the existence of an unbridgeable gap between the realm of mortals and the realm of immortals. The harder human beings try
to attain the unattached immortal realm, the more they realize
their unbreakable ties to their human surroundings. This is why
the Taoist monk finally sighs:

"Alas, how hard it is to find the talent with the potential to become immortal!
I can make my medicine once again, but you will have to go back to the human
world. I wish you well."[13]

Both the Taoist monk and Tu Tzu-chun consider the pursuit of
immortality to be positive, and there is no moral statement in
"Tu Tzu-chun" with regard to humanity. But Akutagawa, by
contrast, tells us that it is not human to conquer love, and that
we should be human.

Akutagawa's "Toshishun" thus is a story of a quest for the
meaning of life, a quest which leads to humanity itself. Humanity is weighed against immortality and art, or the decadent life
which pursues art for art's sake. Toshishun's attempt to attain
immortality was doomed from the start, for the sennin would
not have granted it in any event, even if he had remained silent
until the end. Therefore he did not fail the trial, but passed it.
His quest was actually for humanity, and his attempt at immortality was a necessary part of his quest.

It is worth noting here that in a Ming version of "Tu Tzu-chun"
which appears in Hsing shih heng yen (Lasting Words to Awaken
the World), collected by Feng Meng-lung in 1627, Tzu-chun does
finally attain immortality with his wife in the most glamorous
manner, even after failing the test.[14] The change may be attrib-
utable to the storytelling tradition in which the storyteller always attempts to satisfy his audience, mainly unsophisticated
merchants and commoners, with a happy ending. Indeed Tzu-
chun's attainment of immortaility in the Ming version appears

more ludicrous than instructive. The Taoist monk, instead of
retaining his identity as a symbol of higher transcendence, becomes Lao Tzu, the Taoist god commonly known to lay followers
of the Taoist religion. Consequently, the story is degraded to a
mere instance of Taoist didacticism, advising people to give
away their belongings to achieve immortality. Compared to the
T'ang tale, the Ming version lacks tragic intensity.

In contrast to the original "Tu Tzu-chun," Akutagawa's "Toshishun" has a clear message for the reader: To learn the value
of being human is the meaning of life; to be human means to be
true to one's feelings and to accept the life of emotions. The
humble recognition of joy and sorrow, and submission to love as
the substance of human life is what saved Toshishun from the
life of decadence and inhuman immortality. The sennin in the
story is a moral teacher. Among art, immortality and life (humanity), humanity receives the highest value. When he wrote
"Toshishun," Akutagawa had just finished writing "The Hell
Screen," whose central theme is the conflict between art and
life. The painter in the story sacrifices love and human life for
the sake of art. The work of art which was produced through
this negation of humanity, however, stands as a brilliantly true
work of art. Akutagawa condemns the artist as a human being,
but never dismisses the value of his art, which demands perfection and purity in the sacrifice of human emotion. In "The Hell
Screen," therefore, the dichotomy between art and life is left un-
solved.[15] In "Toshishun," the conflicts presented are among the
selfish pursuit of beauty (art), the transcendence of life
(immortality), and humanity (life). Akutagawa clearly states
that the aspiration for humanity is more valuable than the
other two.

Akutagawa was torn between art and life throughout his life.
Unlike Tanizaki, who chose to live in a way that would serve his
art, and Shiga Naoya, who used art to attain a higher realization
of life, Akutagawa despaired of life in human society from his
early years and wished to live the condensed life of a line of
poetry, while remaining aware of and torn by the sacrifice of
humanity such a life would demand.

In one of his later works, "Shūzan zu" (The Autumn Mountain,
1921), Akutagawa even considers art to be an illusion; a masterpiece of art is certainly the product of man's imagination
dreaming of the ideal, perfect beauty, but the actual work may
not exist at all. The conflict between art and life presented in
the case of "The Hell Screen" no longer exists here. Art is
meaningful not because of itself but because man aspires for it.
The question of realism Akutagawa raised in "The Hell Screen,"
the question of the artist's need to see reality in order to paint
it, is also dismissed here. The significance of art is reduced
to the point of denying art, for art without visible work is no
longer art. "Toshishun" reflects Akutagawa's turning toward
life, moving away from his belief in art for art's sake.

The central theme of "Toshishun" is indeed a theme in Akutagawa's own life as an artist. In the place of realism and confession, Akutagawa used an old tale to dramatize his own search.
He thus converted the classical Chinese tale into a short story
which contained his own quest and his own clear message. By
confining the work clearly within the framework of the ancient
tale and directing it to young adults, Akutagawa was able to
avoid being didactic despite the existence of a moral. In "Toshishun," Akutagawa successfully combined brilliant storytelling with the presentation of a symbolic situation in which the
quest of modern man can be dramatized. In his search for a
method to dramatize his quest for reality and self, Akutagawa
revived the tradition of storytelling in fiction, a tradition which
had been lost in the era of modern realism and naturalism.

The famous Akutagawa-Tanizaki plot controversy (shōsetsu no suji ronso) began in February 1927 (the second year of Showa) and continued until July of the same year, when it was terminated by Akutagawa's tragic death. The controversy started when Akutagawa questioned, in the review section of Shinchō,[1] the artistic value of the story element in the novel. In his critique, Akutagawa referred explicitly to Tanizaki's recent works in which strange stories and complicated plots were characteristic features.

Tanizaki, on the other hand, had just written a strong denunciation of realistic novels and in particular of the autobiographical I-novel in which the author describes his own experiences or state of mind with little fictional mediation. This appeared in February 1927 in the first installment of Tanizaki's essays, which were then being serialized in Kaizō.[2] In his essay, Tanizaki stated that recently he had been interested only in fabricated "lies" rather than in the real experiences of the authors, in devious stories rather than in innocent ones, and in complicated, consciously structured stories rather than in simple, straight ones. He also declared his own intention to write stories as far removed from reality as possible, such as grotesque, fantastic or historical stories.

In the second installment of his essays in Kaizō, which appeared the following month, Tanizaki, referring to Akutagawa's comments on his works, challenged Akutagawa's doubt about the artistic value of the plot and story of the novel. Tanizaki states, after distinguishing the materials of the novel from its plot, that Akutagawa's criticism is based on his mistaken belief that Tanizaki's complex, elaborate stories reflect merely a personal preference, whereas they actually reflect Tanizaki's belief that interest in the plot is interest in the structure of the novel and in its architectural beauty.[3] One cannot say that there is no artistic value in these, Tanizaki argues. He says that to give up interest in the plot is to give up the special advantage of the novel; for the novel, compared to other forms of literature, can contain the most structural beauty.

Tanizaki states further that his love of strange materials and stories comes from deeper considerations than a mere interest in unusual ideas. In fact, he claims never to have created a fictional work out of merely fanciful or borrowed ideas, and that the plots in all of his works emerged from his deepest inner feelings and artistic concerns. Tanizaki adds that although Akutagawa teases him for being intoxicated with his own fascinating stories, a writer — and certainly he — cannot write anything unless he is in a state of fascination. He argues that an interesting plot makes the novel more readily understood by ordinary readers and that this is a positive factor in the novel.

In the April issue of Kaizō, Akutagawa specifically responded to Tanizaki's challenge and stated his ideas of the novel.[4] Presenting his argument in terms of a paradox which has since become famous, Akutagawa says that although he does not think that the novel which lacks a story-like story is the best, what determines the artistic value of the novel is not the story or the plot. Akutagawa states that novels which lack story-like stories are the closest to poetry. Although he does not think that such novels are the best kind, he thinks they are the purest kind of novel. Drawing an analogy with post-impressionist paintings, Akutagawa says that although all paintings are based on a basic design, there are paintings whose essential expressions are borne by their colors. He points to Jules Renard and Shiga Naoya as representative writers of pure novels without story-like stories. He calls them destroyers of the novel, comparing them to Cezanne as the destroyer of painting.

In the second section of the same essay, Akutagawa challenged Tanizaki's statement that it is the novel which, based on its plot, can contain architectural beauty most abundantly. Akutagawa says that if one talks of structural aesthetics, it must be drama that has much more architectural structure; besides, one cannot deny that haiku have the greatest structural beauty. Pointing to the structural complexity of the Tale of Genji, Akutagawa also takes exception to Tanizaki's statement that, compared to Chinese writers, Japanese novelists have historically lacked skills of construction. He then states that what determines the value of a novel is its "poetic spirit." Any philosophic ideas must be purified by the poetic spirit in order to be expressed meaningfully in the novel. Since the novel has the broadest capacity among the various forms of art as far as content is concerned, the depth of the poetic spirit in the novel becomes particularly important in determining its artistic value. He defines the poetic spirit as that of lyrical poetry in the broadest sense of the word, and claims that the poetic spirit is irrelevant to entertainment and vulgar interests.

Tanizaki immediately retaliated in the May issue of Kaizō. He says that it is useless and meaningless to try to present an absolute standard for the artistic value of the novel, a standard for good novels and bad novels. Art, like human history, develops and progresses, constantly breaking through the existing criteria for judgment and the existing concept of art. He says that at present, Japanese literature still suffers from the remnants of the bad influence of naturalism, and that writers as well as readers still consider easily written confessional novels to be profound or high spiritual art. He advocates the writing of novels with stories in order to rescue the novel from this situation.

Originally, Tanizaki argues, the novel emerged from the practice of storytelling, of telling interesting stories to courtiers and to the masses. Thus, such novels without stories as the Japanese confessional novels are exceptional and contradictory to the original concept of the novel. To regard novels with interesting stories as vulgar, cheap and unartistic, as contem-

porary Japanese literary circles do, is an abnormal phenomenon.
He then laments that in Asia the novel has been considered an
inferior form of literature, as something which is written for
women and children. The novel which can be understood by
common people, he argues, is better than the novel which cannot
be understood by them, so far as its artistic value is unchanged.
He then goes on to point out the contradictions which filled Akutagawa's statements and practice with regard to his own use of
story and plot, the contradictions in his use of such words as
"purity," "coarseness," "poetic spirit" and "lyrical poetry," and
his confusing evaluation of Goethe, Stendhal, Baudelaire and
Shiga Naoya with regard to the purity and poeticality of their
works. Dismissing his controversy with Akutagawa, Tanizaki
concludes that any good works are good, that good works are
produced as a result of severe training and the development of
skill, that only a master can produce masterpieces, and that
whether one prefers one kind of novel or another is a question
of the author's taste.

In the next (June) issue of Kaizō, Akutagawa responded to the
charges made by Tanizaki, in particular to those concerning his
contradictions, his confusion and the inconsistency of his statements. He does so by admitting the validity of Tanizaki's points
almost entirely, except on two counts. Akutagawa still maintains that "purity" determines the artistic value of the novel and
that what Tanizaki calls structural aesthetics exists in short
stories and in other forms of art as well.

Other than that, Akutagawa keeps a surprisingly low profile,
and the tone of the article is conciliatory rather than argumen-
tative. He calls Tanizaki a writer who can argue seriously
without holding a personal grudge, praises the grandeur of his
style and rhythm, and ends the essay with a reference to Lady
Murasaki's nasty comments about her contemporary rival-
writer, Seishōnagon, reminding him of the time when Tanizaki,
sitting with Akutagawa in an automobile on a snowy night, talked
with him as a friend about art. The next month Akutagawa committed suicide.[5]

The controvery between Tanizaki and Akutagawa aroused keen

interest in literary circles at that time, not only because it was
carried out between the two most active and promising writers,
but also because it was concerned with the question of the novel
at a time when Japanese writers, dissatisfied with the I-novel,
were searching anxiously for new forms. In the Taisho period
(1912-1926), Japanese writers, troubled by the weight of the I-
novel and confused by various Western influences, had become
extremely concerned with finding a concept of the novel which
would facilitate their creative expression. Yet it was Akutagawa's death, which deeply shocked contemporary writers, that
cast a new light on the controversy. His death was considered
to mark the end of Taisho literature, closing one phase in modern literary history. This is not only because what Akutagawa
said in this debate revealed his state of mind and the ideas he
had come to hold at the end of his life, providing an important
key to the understanding of his later works, but also because his
death made the controversy a symbolic event, terminating one
era of Japanese literature and opening the path to the new development of literature in the Showa period (1926-present), in
particular to proletarian literature.

The major issues in the controversy can be summarized as
follows:

1. What function does the plot or story serve in the novel?
In what way is the existence or nature of the plot or story related to the "purity" or vulgarity of the novel? Is the ideal
novel a popular, conventional novel whose major purpose is
storytelling for entertainment, or an art-novel, whose major
purpose is inner search?

2. Does the essence of the novel lie in the creation of a fictional reality or in the distillation of the poetic spirit of the author; does the novel aspire to poetry or story?

3. Tanizaki's argument pointed toward the creation of a
romance-like novel which creates a universe of its own, one in
which its own reality and order replace those of daily life.
Structure, therefore, becomes the most essential element in
creating the fictional reality of the novel. On the other hand,
Akutagawa was trying to break out of the strict, formal struc-

ture of the short story and to establish a formless fiction close
to lyrical poetry in which the author's poetic sensibility would
determine its artistic value.

4. Tanizaki's argument expressed his desire to move away
from describing and depicting, which is characteristic of the I-
novels, and toward creating and constructing; that is, he sought
to move away from the lyrical confession which characterizes
the high-minded novel and the I-novel. Tanizaki's position reflects the modern writers' loss of faith in the organic relationship between the author himself and the work, and their loss of
faith in the self as a literary subject. Dependence upon form
and style rather than upon content (particularly upon the self
as content) is indeed characteristic of modern literature.

Akutagawa's argument also reflects the modern loss of faith
in an organic relationship between the author and the work. Yet
Akutagawa tries to confront fully the chaos and formlessness of
modern life and the dissolution of the self, and searches for a
method to express the experience of this chaos itself, for a form
that will reflect the formlessness of life. What remains unchanged in the novel, Akutagawa argues, is the expression of the
poetic essence of life experiences.

5. It is evident that the arguments of both authors pointed
away from the realistic, social novel.

Tanizaki's stance is quite clear and marvelously consistent
with his previous concerns and future development. In 1927
Tanizaki was writing Tadekuu mushi (Some Prefer Nettles), the
work which terminates the first phase of his creative activity,
or which marks the beginning of the second phase. By this time,
Tanizaki had already dealt extensively with such major themes
of his early works as the fear of death, the sado-masochistic
pursuit of feminine beauty, the discovery of perversity or
cruelty in human nature, and the relation of art to these themes,
and had experimented with writing in a variety of forms and with
a variety of themes, including among his works realistic psychological novels, writings based on classical Japanese, Chinese
and grotesque stories, writings based on themes in Western stories, including especially those of Poe and Wilde, stories with

historical settings, and detective and horror stories. Nineteen twenty-seven was a historic year for Tanizaki, for he met, ironically through Akutagawa, Nezu Matsuko whom he later married and who became the model for the ideal woman in all his works. The discovery of his ideal woman, his decision to return to the classical Japanese literary tradition, and his move to the Kansai district all contributed in 1927 to the germination of the new seed for his literary development — the writing of romances containing a central myth of the ideal woman, cruel and unattainable.

Tanizaki had also by this time been subject to the strong influence of Western dark romanticism (especially Poe) and Edo kusazōshi, stories filled with violence and eroticism, and had wandered into the shadowy world of the Heian and medieval courts.[6] The controversy took place when Tanizaki, confident now of his own method and style, was shedding finally and absolutely the influence of naturalism and heading with his full energy toward the creation of his own world of romance and the realization in fiction of his visions of a romantic universe. It is only natural in this context that Tanizaki's arguments favoring the architectural structure of the novel, an autonomous world of "lies" independent from daily-life reality, and the necessity of plot and stories for the novel as fictional art, along with his anti-naturalistic and anti-I-novel stance, appear quite firm and unwavering.

Akutagawa, on the other hand, had been practicing in his own works most of the principles which Tanizaki advocated. He had meticulously avoided writing about himself or directly about his feelings, he considered the perfection of the work as a fictional work of art the most important purpose of his creation, and borrowing profusely from classical Japanese, Chinese and Western stories and legends, he had created an imaginative fictional reality removed from immediate daily life. Artificiality and complexity rather than natural simplicity and spontaneity of expression and structure are what characterize his work and what he consciously tried to achieve.

In fact, both Tanizaki and Akutagawa began their literary careers rebelling against the then-dominant naturalism and the

I-novels. Deeply immersed in Western decadent literature, these two truly urban writers were skeptical about the idealistic humanism of the Shirakaba group as well, a group which also rebelled against naturalism. Both of them, exploring the world of evil, the world of the ugly and the psychic realm of fear, devoted their creative energy to the practice and evaluation of the theory of art for art's sake. In this sense, both writers are representative of modern Japanese aesthetic literature.

Around 1924, however, Akutagawa reached a point of major crisis; in his previous eight years of amazingly fertile creativity, he had exhausted all the possibilities for his talent, intellect and artistic sensibilities. He felt his creativity had reached an impasse. His health deteriorated, and the conflict between his firm commitment to his family life and his desire to be free to lead a creative life exhausted him physically and psychologically. After 1924, Akutagawa's literature and views changed drastically. This artistic crisis coincided with a crisis in his personal life. In the same year, he met Muramatsu Mineko, a minor but brilliant waka poet and fell in love with her. About this poet, who was fifteen years senior to him, Akutagawa wrote in his last, autobiographical work, "A Fool's Life," that he had met for the first time an ideal woman who was also his match intellectually.[7] He says that he overcame the crisis by writing lyrical poetry, a work which was published in 1926 under the title Koshibito. In this work, Akutagawa, describing a man who wishes to throw away his family for the sake of love, pours out his sadness and the lyrical beauty of his feelings of love. What is significant is that this was the first time that Akutagawa dealt directly with his own feelings in a literary work. From that time, his writings turned drastically from artificial, well-constructed works to realistic and often autobiographical ones. In the last two and a half years of his life, he suffered from severe nervous tension, anxiety and deep melancholy.

With the growing deterioration of his health and the deepening of his nervous tension, he began to express a strong aspiration for life-force and for the healthy, whole personality represented by Goethe and Shiga Naoya. In particular, he admired Shiga

Naoya and his spontaneous attachment to and egotistic pursuit of
life, calling him a primitive, natural man.[8] The more strongly
Akutagawa suffered from self-pity, self-hatred and shame, and
the more he suffered from the sense of his own failure in life,
the more his concern shifted from art to life. The more he considered himself to be a failure in life who had not the strength
to live as he wanted, the more his faith in intellect and art di-
minished, and the more the tree of life, which symbolizes primitive vitality, became the center of his aspiration. In other
words, the arguments Akutagawa presented in the controversy
were his first theoretical defense of his conversion from art to
life, from the practice of art for art's sake to the writing of
I-novel-like "pure" novels. In particular, his denial of the significance of the story was a 180-degree shift from his own past
works, in which the use of the stories had enabled the author to
hide himself, to avoid dealing directly with his inner world as
well as with his relation to reality. In essence, it is not an ex-
aggeration to say that Akutagawa's major artistic concern had
been how to tell the story and the nature of the inner relation
between the story and the author.

Akutagawa's view that lyrical poetry or the poetic spirit is the
most significant determinant of the artistic value of the novel can be
understood properly only within this context. Thus, the controversy provides important documentation of the artistic development of both authors. What is the significance of the controversy
from the standpoint of the development of modern Japanese literature, and of world literature, and what is its significance from
the standpoint of theoretical concern with the novel as a genre?

It is usually assumed that Tanizaki, with his logical arguments, clear ideas and firm stance, was victorious in the controversy. As far as the disputants themselves are concerned,
this is definitely true; Akutagawa's "poetic spirit" is vague and
undefined, and as Tanizaki mercilessly pointed out, Akutagawa's
stance or theoretical arguments are unsustainable because of
the contradictory and obscure points he presents without sub-
stantiation. Above all, Akutagawa's points seemed to be a complete denial of his past achievements, while Tanizaki's argu-

ments were fully substantiated by his past works and would be
further substantiated in his subsequent lengthy creative activity.

The major weaknesses of Akutagawa's argument come from
the fact that Akutagawa's purpose in writing these essays was
to search for a new path that might open up the dead end of his
art, saving him from a stifling intellectualism and aestheticism.
At the time of the controversy, Akutagawa could state only the
change in his aspiration and express his new aspiration for life
and poetic purity, still vague and undefined, only in terms of
other writers and not in terms of his own artistic belief or theory.

Taisho literature, which started with a strong denunciation of
the Meiji I-novel, reached its peak of achievement in Tanizaki's
works and in Akutagawa's works prior to 1924, and in this sense,
Tanizaki's arguments present a theoretical justification for a
significant peak of achievement in the history of the modern
Japanese novel. The era of naturalism was decisively over, and
the novel was recognized as a fictional art form existing in an
autonomous universe separate from the direct expression of
life-experience. The strong tendency to moralism and ethical
concerns which characterized the Meiji novels — in particular
the naturalistic I-novels — was denounced most effectively by
Tanizaki, and the novel was recognized as the imaginative pursuit of beauty and the writer's own vision.

Tanizaki's enthusiastic rejection of high-minded, inner novels, such as the moralistic I-novels of confession and inner
search, and his advocacy of entertaining, "vulgar" and popular
literature represent one important direction which Japanese
novelists took in their struggle to overcome the narrow limitations of the I-novel. Indeed the Tanizaki-Akutagawa controversy
concerning whether the plot or poetic essence is the raison
d'être of the novel, their dispute concerning the "purity" and
"vulgarity" of the novel, reveals Japanese writers' concern with
the fundamental question of what the novel is. The question of
the relation between art and life was the central one in the Meiji
period (1868-1912), when the naturalistic novelists and the I-
novelists placed life above art. [9] The dispute over whether to
regard the novel as basically the art of storytelling and the

creation of a fictional reality (including the dreamworld) or to regard the novel as an expression of the poetic essence and distilled purity of the author's artistic sensibility can only be understood within the historic context of the Taisho writers' struggle to move away from the ethical and autobiographical I-novel. Their concern was, moreover, not restricted to Japanese writers but was shared by Western writers. The Tanizaki-Akutagawa controversy was developed by other writers into disputes over popular literature (tsūzoku shōsetsu), orthodox literature (honkaku shōsetsu) and the form of literature, disputes in which what the real novel should be was discussed in a wider, if not more profound, scope, integrating the questions of realism and of common readers.[10] Yokomitsu Riichi, in fact, later developed the concept of the popular novel — which he called, ironically, the "pure novel." Here the term "pure" is confusing, but what Yokomitsu meant by it was a "genuine" novel with plot, story and characterization, a novel that contains the dimensions of social and daily mundane life, as opposed to the narrow philosophic novels of inner search. Yokomitsu's "pure" novel is in fact close to the novel of social manners of the West.[11]

Akutagawa's return to the pure expression of inner feeling, to the novel without structure and story and the lyrical novel of inner search, seems in this context anachronistic, and indeed it may express only his recognition of the failure of his intellectualism and aestheticism (the alienation of emotional truth in art) and his aspiration to restore emotion and the truth of life experiences in art.

The question of realism, in what way art should reflect life, and the question of the audience were not included in the Tanizaki-Akutagawa dispute. This omission is a significant one, revealing the part played by their dispute in the development of modern Japanese literature in the Taisho and Showa periods.

The Showa period, whose literary activities are commonly regarded as having started with Akutagawa's death, is characterized by the rise of proletarian literature. With the proletarian writers' serious commitment to social change and the unification of literature and politics, society and the individual, the

I-novels as well as decadent aestheticism received a final, decisive blow. Regarded from the perspective of the development of Showa literature, including the postwar literary activities which started with the writers' self-reflection about their role in the war, the Akutagawa-Tanizaki controversy may appear to be merely an in-group fight of decadent bourgeois writers who were miserably alienated from society and the reality of life. Whether the artist tries to escape into the fictional world of another order (reality, dream) or tries to depend upon the poetic essence of her or his individual experience, both attempts express the alienation of the modern artist who has lost a vital and spontaneous relation to the reality of life and to art, and thus for whom an organic relation between life and art does not exist. Their concerns over plot and story, architectural structure and purity of spirit may appear to be irrelevant literary questions to the novelists who attempted to present the human and individual struggle for social change in the larger reality and in the flow of history.

Indeed, Miyamoto Kenji's brilliant essay entitled "Haiboku no bungaku" (The Literature of Defeat) was accepted as the final blow to the art of petty-bourgeois intellectuals.[12] Miyamoto Kenji analyzes the class nature of Akutagawa's literature, showing his fragile and sharpened sensitivity, his self-destructive defeatism, his self-pity and his desperation for happiness to be symbolic features of the infantile nihilism of sterile, bourgeois intellectuals. He sees Akutagawa's death as a symbol of the self-dissolution of bourgeois literature and intellectuals. Miyamoto argues that Akutagawa's dissociation from history forced him to mistake his personal ideas and feelings as something which could explain the world and human beings at large.

Stung by the attacks he too received from the proletarian writers, Tanizaki fastidiously retreated from the bundan and became more deeply immersed in his own world of romance. Both Tanizaki and Akutagawa came to be considered by proletarian writers as writers of the past, representative of a decaying capitalist class.

Akutagawa's conversion to the natural simplicity and purity

of the poetic spirit parallels the conversion of the Shirakaba
writer Arishima Takeo to proletarian literature. Akutagawa's
subsequent suicide also parallels Arishima's later disillusioned
declaration and suicide; in his sensational "Sengen hitotsu" (One
Declaration), Arishima declared the impossibility of transcending one's class background and then committed suicide.[13] Contemporary writers and intellectuals perceived Akutagawa's suicide as the defeat of bourgeois intellectualism and aestheticism,
and "vague anxiety," the term which Akutagawa used in explain-
ing the reason for his suicide, became symbolic of the mental
state of the Taisho-Showa writers and intellectuals who, alienated from social reality and from the masses, suffered from a
lack of faith and a sense of desperation.

Akutagawa's literary conversion and death do indeed indicate
his own denial of the aesthetic-intellectual attitude toward life
and art. They mark the end of the Taisho literary activities,
which were characterized by the writers' confidence in art and
in their ability to handle the fundamental contradictions and dichotomies in the novel — those between art and life, reality and
consciousness, transcendental aspiration and realistic imagination, and practice and realization — through intellectual and aesthetic manipulation. The balance which Akutagawa brilliantly
attained between the elements in each of these dichotomies in
"The Hell Screen" was completely shattered in his later works.
Akutagawa himself appears like a tormented protagonist in "The
Hell Screen," and his sudden conversion to Shiga Naoya and
Goethe seems almost like a purification ritual. Tanizaki's
grand, romantic dome also appears from this perspective to be
an illusory retreat.

The question of the structure, plot and story in the novel has indeed been a crucial question in twentieth century literature as
a whole. In the half-century since the controversy and Akutagawa's death in 1927, fundamental changes have taken place in
the form of the novel throughout the world, and these changes,
which have occurred largely since Proust and James Joyce,
have cast a new light on the controversy. From the novels of
Proust, Joyce and Virginia Woolf to the anti-roman works of

French authors, the novel without a story-like story has become
the dominant form of the novel in the twentieth century. At
present, no writers or critics can argue wholeheartedly that the
artistic quality of the novel should depend upon its architectural
structure and architectural aesthetic concept. The novel in the
twentieth century, responding to the shattering of the unified
view of the universe and of reality, reflects the fragmented inner
reality, as well as the writers' desperate search for a new
method to give shape to the "panoramic chaos" of both outer and
inner reality. The novel, contrary to Tanizaki's stress on architectural structure, has become the search for a method which
will recreate the unity of the fragmented self and relate the self
to life; life itself no longer has any comprehensible story of human life. Both Tanizaki's attempt to restore the story in the
novel and Akutagawa's attempt to reduce the novel to the poetic
essence of the artist's sensibilities were responses to this
philosophic and artistic problem which the modern novel faces.

Akutagawa's fundamental doubt about the story and about the
autonomous world of the novel as the replacement of poetic sensibility or inner reality can, from this perspective, be regarded
as doubt about the unity of the inner self of the narrator, the
storyteller, and of the author. In this respect, Akutagawa, far
from being anachronistic, emerges as an avant-garde thinker
who clearly foresaw the problems of the traditional nineteenth-
century novel and the directions which the modern novel would
take. In this sense, it can be said that the world novel approached the Japanese I-novel, which thus emerges as a most
modern sub-genre of the novel.

Yet the history of the novel proceeds further. The modern
inner novel, by turning exclusively on itself, reached the point
of self-destruction. Saul Bellow, a major contemporary novelist, for example, strongly advocates the restoration of the story
to the novel. While his own indebtedness to James Joyce is undeniable, Bellow argues that after Joyce, the novel became
warped by perpetually turning narcissistically to itself and re-
peating the futile question of what the novel is. In order to save
the novel from stifling itself, Bellow argues, the novel must re-

store its original character, that is, the story.[14] The question
of the story and the novel, of plot and expression, and the relations among the narrator, the I and the author thus remain basic
to the genre of the novel. It is because the Akutagawa-Tanizaki
controversy discussed these fundamental questions that their
dispute remains relevant to contemporary writers.

It was Akutagawa who, responding sensitively to the changes
of history, perceived keenly the limitations of his past works
and correctly sensed the end of his era as well as the future direction of the novel. On the other hand, Tanizaki, stubbornly
refusing to be affected by the changes in the times, insisting
anachronistically on his "decadent," "bourgeois" writings, created a magnificent world of his own literature. But now the
wheel has turned full cycle, and perhaps Tanizaki is again the
prophet.

The strong response of such major writers of modern Japanese literature as Tanizaki Junichiro, Akutagawa Ryūnosuke, Hagiwara Sakutaro and Mishima Yukio to Western writers of dark romanticism (such writers as Poe, Baudelaire and Oscar Wilde) can be readily understood in the light of their shared artistic concerns. Like their Western counterparts, the Japanese writers were concerned with the question of evil, the role of the grotesque and the ugly in art, and the relation of art to life, and they pursued these questions even after they moved away from the obvious influence of the Western writers. This is most evident in the Japanese writers of decadence and aestheticism, whose writing formed a major literary current from the late Meiji period (1868-1912) onward.

The writers of Western dark romanticism, particularly Poe and Baudelaire, explored the realm of the grotesque — psychic fear, the ugly, the irrational, and so forth — in their search for a means of transcending the romantic dichotomy they perceived in reality between body and mind, being and consciousness, and the outer world and inner world. Unlike the earlier romantic writers (Wordsworth and Emerson, for example), who envisioned a return to the original state of harmony or recovery from alienation through a return to nature and a rational scheme of education, such later romantic writers as Poe and Baudelaire, believing that nature and reality were unredeemably corrupt,

---

*A slightly longer version of this chapter appeared in, and is published here by permission of, Yearbook of Comparative and General Literature 27 (1978).

sought to attain the original unity through destructive transcendence, through delving into the heart of their alienation in
an exploration which could culminate only in self-destruction.
Paradoxically, therefore, their exploration of the dark psychic
realm was an endeavor for transcendence, an attempt to return
to the original unity envisioned as original nothingness.

The grotesque for these later romantic writers was at once a
symbol of the decadence of reality and consciousness and a
symbol of the imagination which could reveal this decadence in
its extremity. Yet at the same time, the grotesque was a form
of imagination which pointed toward the transcendence of the
decadence, a dark imagination which envisioned the original
harmony through self-destructive exploration of the realm of
the ugly, the fantastic (including the primitive and symbolic) and
the subconscious. For Poe in particular, the grotesque was a
part of his romantic ideology which understood, through a mythopoeic vision of man, nature and the universe, man's alienation
and his aspiration for unity.

The Japanese writers of aestheticism who were influenced by
the writers of Western dark romanticism did not necessarily
start as romantic writers. The "diabolism" of both Iwano Hōmei and the early Tanizaki was initially a part of their naturalistic endeavor to unveil the irrational, instinctive side of existence, while the early Hagiwara Sakutaro was concerned mainly
with exploring the depths of the wounded psyche. In the process
of their literary investigation of the alienated psyche — the
realm of the grotesque — however, they turned increasingly to
the search for a myth (a vision of a self-sufficient world of
dream) which would justify their exploration. Their ultimate
"return" to the Japanese cultural heritage and the archetypal
creative consciousness which underlies it can best be understood as the result of their aspiration for a larger metaphysical
and aesthetic framework which would explain their endeavors as
a drama of alienation and recovery. It is with regard to the romantic quest for a vision of destructive transcendence to which
this aspiration led that their exposure to and learning from
Western dark romanticism bears deepest significance.

From the turn of the century to the 1920s, the consciousness
in Japan of European literary and artisitic activities grew markedly, and such anti-naturalistic movements as art nouveau and
symbolism were accorded an especially favorable reception.
Yet during this time, Japanese artists and writers were developing their own world of aesthetic sensibility, producing a unique
world of fantasy and imagination which can properly be called indigenous. This period, occurring roughly ten to fifteen years later than
its European counterpart, can be called Japan's fin de siècle.

The emergence of Japanese aestheticism in the late Meiji to
Taisho periods (1912-1926) was vitally influenced by the active
introduction to Japan of the works of William Blake, Emerson,
the pre-Raphaelites, Water Pater, Aubrey Beardsley and art
nouveau, Gustave Moreau, and Oscar Wilde.[1] The works of
Baudelaire and Poe had already been introduced to Japan in the
nineteenth century and had been admired greatly,[2] but with the
introduction of this "new" European art and literature, Japanese
aesthetic writers became especially impressed with their significance. In this context, such writers as Kitahara Hakushū,
Hagiwara Sakutaro, Sato Haruo, Nagai Kafu, Tanizaki Junichiro,
Kinoshita Mokutaro and Hinatsu Kōnosuke, and such painters as
Takehisa Yumeji, Aoki Shigeru, Tanaka Kyōkichi and Fujimori
Shizuo, produced the aesthetic movement, which they regarded
as marking the arrival of the "real" modern period in Japan.
As in Europe, this was the period during which the aesthetic
concerns of art and literature were most closely related.

In the forty-first year of Meiji (1908), two groups of writers
and artists, Subaru (Pleiades) and Pan-no-Kai (The Pan Society)
were formed, groups which were to be the core of the aesthetic
movement. Subaru included such established writers as Mori
Ōgai, Ueda Bin, Yosano Kan and Yosano Akiko who had been
leading members of Myōjō, a group at the center of the romantic movement in the Meiji period. The most active members,
however, were the poets Kitahara Hakushu, Kinoshita Mokutaro
and Yoshi Isamu, all of whom had been dissatisfied with Myōjō's
optimistic romanticism. Reflecting the sharp impact of European decadent literature, these poets moved toward the explora-

tion of the grotesque, sensualism and exoticism, all of which
are evident features of dark romanticism. In addition to these
writers, Nagai Kafu and Takamura Kōtaro, both of whom had
just returned from abroad, and the painters Ishi Hakutei and Ya-
mamoto Tei, among others, joined the new organization. Subaru
was clearly an extension of the romantic movement fostered by
Myōjō, but in determining the direction of the new journal which
the group published (under the name Subaru), Ueda Bin's introduction of the French fin-de-siècle literature, later collected in
Kaichō-on, and of Walter Pater's aesthetic theories played a vital role.

Pan-no-Kai was composed of such young members of Subaru
as Kinoshita Mokutaro, Kitahara Hakushū, Yoshi Isamu, Tanizaki Junichiro and Ishi Hakutei. It was an art salon which, after
the fashion of Le Chat Noir, aimed at the integration of art and
literature. The members met at a restaurant on the banks of the
Sumida River in Tokyo and, talking about the literature and art
of Edo Japan (1600-1868) and of France, immersed themselves
in an atmosphere of decadence. Nagai Kafu at that time established the journal Mita Bungaku (The Literature of Mita), in which
he published translations of Western symbolist poems which
were later collected in Sangoshū (The Coral Collection, 1913),
a work which proved as influential as Ueda Bin's Kaichō-on. In
the forty-third year of Meiji (1910), Tanizaki published the
sensational "The Tattoo" in Shinshichō, a work which was
praised by Kafu as the harbinger of the new literature, and
a year later Hakushu started his own journal, Zamuboa (Shad-
dock), in which he published works strongly colored by exoticism and dandyism.

In considering the characteristic features of Japan's fin-de-
siècle art and literature, we might note first that it is an extension of the romantic movement in the Meiji period and started
as an anti-naturalistic movement, yet it was naturalist writers
themselves who turned to aesthetic literature and introduced
European writers of aestheticism. We can see in the Japanese
art and literature of aestheticism a fundamental merging of naturalism and romanticism, particularly dark romanticism. Sec-

ond, Japanese aestheticism was, culturally speaking, a reaction
to the Meiji goal of Westernization and modernization; it reflected a fundamental skepticism toward and criticism of progress, Western civilization and capitalist economic development.
Third, after an initial period of enthusiastic learning from European art and literature, most of the artists and writers of aestheticism returned to Japanese and Oriental culture and philosophy, moving in some cases toward a reactionary nationalism in
their rejection of Western culture and in their exaltation of the
Japanese tradition. Most typically, they developed a nostalgic
aspiration for the characteristically erotic and grotesque art
and literature of the Edo culture which had developed in the two-
and-a-half centuries of Japan's cultural "isolation" prior to the
beginning of the Meiji period in 1868.

Yet their "Edo taste" was only a way station in their search
for a cultural archetype and spiritual roots; such major writers
of the aesthetic school as Tanizaki and Hagiwara Sakutaro, and
the painter Aoki Shigeru, even tried to return to the primordial
origins of Japanese and oriental culture and aesthetic sensibility, attempting to create their own myth that would integrate life
and death, the self, nature and art. After elaborating briefly
these three characteristic features of Japanese aestheticism, I
would like to turn to a discussion of Hagiwara Sakutaro here,
and to Tanizaki Junichiro in Chapter 5, to illustrate the way
in which the ideas inherent in dark romanticism played a significant role in Japanese aesthetic literature.

Soon after the Russo-Japanese War of 1904, Japan reached its
peak of naturalism in literature with the works of such writers
as Shimazaki Tōson, Tayama Katai, Tokuda Shūsei, Iwano Hōmei,
Shimamura Hōgetsu and Chikamatsu Shūko. These writers,
deeply influenced by de Maupassant and even more by Zola, established the genre of the I-novel, which is basically autobiographical and confessional. The confessional novelists' attempt at the
naturalistic unveiling of the self often approached the destructive, masochistic exposé of the inner self inherent in the tradition of Western dark romanticism. Here was the basis for the
affinity that Japanese writers of naturalism felt toward the "di-

abolism" of Poe, Baudelaire and Wilde.

As was briefly discussed in Chapter 1, Iwano Hōmei, a most articulate proponent of Japanese naturalism, although he called himself a neonaturalist and thereby distinguished himself from the first generation of Japanese writers of naturalism, was one of the most committed translators and introducers of Baudelaire and Poe; calling Baudelaire Poe's masterpiece, he explained European aesthetic literature as emerging from a core formed by the writings of Poe and Baudelaire.[3] Hōmei considered the self as the absolute goal of his literary, religious and philosophic pursuit. Regarding Satan as representing the worst self, he pursued evil and the ugly (artificial beauty or the rejection of natural beauty), and delved into the realm of psychic fear and dread opened by his self-destructive pursuit of pleasure. Although he was concerned with the masochistic exposé of his own perverse, evil nature, and with the ruthless pursuit of desire and pleasure, a pursuit which often resulted in the unethical and sadistic exploitation of others, his persistent, unsentimental presentation of himself gains an existential dimension and becomes an expression of the sinfulness of human nature itself. His underlying aspiration for transcendence through evil brings his "mysterious semi-animalism" close to the idea of destructive transcendence in such writers as Poe and Baudelaire.

The link between naturalism and aestheticism is evident in the works of other writers as well. Nagai Kafu had, under the strong influence of Zola, already established himself as a naturalistic writer when he turned to writing the so-called "Sumidagawa [Sumida River] Stories" after his return from the United States and France, stories which showed his "Edo taste." Although such later writers of aestheticism as Tanizaki and Sato Haruo started their literary careers by attacking naturalism, they too were baptized in the "diabolism" of Japanese naturalism and in essence developed it further. In this respect, Japanese aesthetic literature, although it was an extension of the earlier romantic movement and began with an attack on the then-dominant naturalistic literature, became the major link between naturalism and dark romanticism.

As a part of the national modernization enterprise in the Meiji era, Japanese writers were deeply concerned with modernizing the self by actively learning from Western art and literature. The self-conscious effort to produce modern literature in Japan initiated by Tsubouchi Shōyo and Futabatei Shimei reached its first stage of achievement in the early years of the twentieth century with the appearance of the confessional naturalistic I-novel, including works by such writers as Tayama Katai and Shimazaki Tōson. Tōson and Katai were the product of learning from the West, and at the same time they typically represented those who came from the rural areas of Japan to Tokyo with the ambition to be "successful" in the new Meiji society. The writers of aestheticism and Natsume Sōseki,[4] by contrast, were typically from Tokyo and, with their urbane sophistication, sneered at Tōson and Katai's aspiration for success, uncritical worship of the West, and ethical pursuit of life. In essence, aestheticism was a reaction to Meiji utilitarianism and the thrust of modernization. The atmosphere of fin de siècle itself — the artists' separation of art from morality, their extreme sensuality and their pursuit of the grotesque — reflects the artists' basic reaction to Meiji utilitarianism. Although in Meiji Japan, unlike European society at that time, there was neither a firmly established bourgeois class nor a religious orthodoxy to form the core of middle-class morality, the thrust for modernization, backed by utilitarianism, created a similar isolation of artists, evoking in Japan as well as in Europe a strong sense of crisis. It was only natural that the artists' attempt to restore art in a hostile industrial age, their exploration of the senses and of beauty, led them back to the classical culture which existed prior to the Meiji period.

The Edo period in particular was the period when Japanese culture, cut off from the outside world, reached a state of ripeness and produced its own decadence; violence, cruelty and eroticism characterize late Edo literature especially. At the same time, the aesthetic writers were already far removed from Edo, and Edo culture was as exotic to them as Western culture. Their Edo taste was synonymous with their exoticism. Edo presented to them an exotic world of the senses, removed in

time and space, yet linked with a strange affinity to the European
world of the end of the century in which beauty and the senses
were also explored, and in which Orientalism, reflected for example in the influence of Edo art — ukiyoe especially — on the
French impressionists, was apparent. Although theirs was an
escapist attempt to retreat into a world of taste and for some
writers this atmosphere was no more than one in which they
could be drunk and left no serious impact, for such writers as
Tanizaki, Hakushu and Sakutaro, the rejection of Meiji culture
and the discovery of Gothic themes in both Western dark romanticism and Edo culture forced them to pursue further their
search for the origins of their aesthetic sensibilities and their
cultural home. Kafu's return to Edo, Natsume Sōseki's return to Zen Buddhism and the Chinese philosophy of Taoism,
Tanizaki's return to Heian culture, Sakutaro's return of the
wanderer to a mystical home called Japan, Kawabata's return
to the Kojiki and the aesthetic tradition, and Mishima's metem-
psychosis all represent the writer's attempt to return to the
source and to establish a myth that would recreate a self-sufficient world of the senses. All of these writers tried to restore
the original unity by exploring the psychic realm of fear, the
world of sensuous beauty and eroticism, and the world of the
grotesque. It is in relation to their effort at the creation of myth
and the restoration of original unity through destructive transcendence that we can see the most fundamental impact of Western romanticism. A comparison of the works of Sakutaro with
those of Poe can help to show this with particular clarity.

Hagiwara Sakutaro (1886-1942), Japan's leading modern poet
and one of the first to establish free verse, started his poetic
career under the strong influence of Kitahara Hakushū, Kambara
Ariake (a symbolist poet), Poe, Baudelaire, Nietzsche and Dostoevski.[5] He admired Poe in particular, and his world of poetry
is highly reminiscent of Poe's. Sakutaro began by defining
himself as a diseased man, and his world was perceived through
nerves sharpened to abnormality by his sickness. It was a
world in decay, and at its center a great void opened its mouth,
evoking a sense of fear of life. In confronting this nothingness,

the poet confronted his own diseased face, his own double.

At the bottom of the earth a face appears
A lonely, diseased man's face appears

In the darkness at the bottom of the earth
Stems of grass begin to emerge waving
Rats' nests begin to appear
Numerous hairs entangled in the nests
Begin to tremble
From the lonely, diseased earth of winter
Around the winter solstice
The roots of thin blue bamboo begin to grow
Begin to grow
That looks truly pitiful
Looks smoky
Truly, truly looks pitiful

In the darkness at the bottom of the earth
A lonely, diseased man's face appears

> ("A Diseased Face at the Bottom of the Earth";
> collected in Tsuki ni Hoeru [Howling at the Moon],
> 1918; my translation.)

The lonely, diseased poet wanders in the universe of "flowing time, darkness and the silent moment,"[6] driven by a fear of the unknown and led by the light and shadows that flicker in his subconscious, following the footsteps of fate toward a final vision that awaits him beyond reality.

To the poet who confronts the loneliness that turned into a "faceless woman" clad in a red dress,[7] to the poet who confronts his own soul in the depths of despair and nothingness, there appears gradually a recovery of something spiritual, something transcendental, a recovery which could be achieved only through the destruction of his own body. To recover the spiritual by delving deeply with sharpened sensibilities into inner darkness — a world of fear, loneliness and sterility — to attain transcendence through extreme commitment to the abnormal, grotesque and destructive, is a central idea of dark romanticism. During Sakutaro's later period, his sense of fear,

loneliness and the sterility of life became systematized as his
sense of the loss of the original home, and recovery through the
destruction of his body became his journey of return to his original home. This process of systematization into the loss of the
original home and its recovery is the process of his return to
his Japanese cultural origins and is indeed the process of his
myth-making.[8] Finally, he reached the idea of eternal return
through spiral descent into the depths of the poet's soul. Poe's
poet in Eureka, whose grotesque and arabesque imagination
brings the entire universe to its primordial unity through his
suicidal and centripetal concentration on himself, is fundamentally akin to the poet of Sakutaro.

Sakutaro, like Poe, tried to express his vision of transcendence and the process of attaining it through the music
of words. Words, by destroying their own meanings, grasp
and express what exists beyond words, thus creating an inner landscape. The evocative power of words' musicality,
the inner landscape where darkness and dawn, dream and
reality, mingle is the world of purgatory for the poet. "The
Rooster," a poem which Sakutaro wrote inspired specifically
by Poe's "The Raven," illustrates the depths of his empathy
with Poe's world.

Before the dawn
A rooster cries outside the houses
Its voice long vibrating.
It is the voice of mother
     Calling from faraway nature in the lonely countryside
Tō te rō   Tōru mō   Tōru mō

In the cold bed in the morning
My soul flutters.
Surveyed from the space between the shutters
The scenery outside looks shining bright
Yet before the dawn
A melancholy creeps into my bed
Crossing over the misty tips of tree branches
It is the voice of a rooster
     Calling from faraway nature in the lonely countryside
Tō te rō   Tōru mō   Tōru mō

Beloved, beloved,
Behind the cold screen in the dawn
I sense a vague fragrance of chrysanthemums
Like the scent of diseased spirits

The fragrance of white chrysanthemums rotting unnoticed
Beloved, beloved,

Before the dawn
My heart wanders in the shadows of the cemetery
I cannot bear this pale pink air
Beloved,
Mother.

Come in haste and extinguish the candle
I hear the sound of the storm
      That blows across the far horizon
Tōru-mō   tō-te-kā

> ("The Rooster"; collected in Aoneko [The Blue
> Cat] 1924; my translation.)

Sakutaro himself explained that in writing this poem he was inspired by "The Raven" and that he tried to practice the principles of poetry-writing Poe described in "The Philosophy of
Composition."9 The use of a mysterious animal, the use of the
refrain, the use of melancholy as a theme, and the evocation of
mental scenery by the use of sound and its repetition are all
reminiscent of "The Raven."

   Dawn, the time of the poem, is appropriate for presenting a
special condition of consciousness in which reason is suppressed
and the memory of the dream haunts the psyche. The faraway
scenery which the poet glimpses through the shutters is his own
psychic scenery, evoked most vividly when reason is suppressed.
In Poe's poem, the time is midnight, the polar opposite of daytime, yet the dawn reminds us of Poe's state of dreaming consciousness, the condition of the mind just prior to sinking into
sleep. The decline of rational thinking is expressed through the
sense of decay that pervades the poem, and a strongly sensuous
state of consciousness emerges with the sense of decay. Yet
most fundamental in making the poem close to "The Raven" is
the evocation of something which is lost, something which is

buried deep in the psychic realm. In Sakutaro's poem, the beloved and mother are put together, making "faraway nature in
the lonely countryside" the primordial origin of life, the original
home of the poet. Both in Sakutaro's poem and in Poe's poem,
the longing for a deceased lover is turned into a longing for
metaphysical existence. What Sakutaro saw in "The Raven" was
"transcendental memory," which is what his own poetry always
seeks to recapture. Although in Sakutaro's later works an extreme "Japanism" which rejects Western elements can be found,
his return to Japanese culture was his attempt to return to the
spiritual archetype, an attempt which exists as an essential core
of dark romanticism.

   In the post-World War II period, we can see further evidence
of the significance of dark romanticism and the profundity of its
influence on Japanese literature in the writings of Mishima Yukio. The Japanese writers of aestheticism, who form the mainstream of modern Japanese literature, reveal the links between
traditional Japanese literature and the ideas and aesthetics of
dark romanticism by their conscious effort to associate their
literary endeavors with traditional Japanese literature. In each
case their introduction to and learning from Western dark romanticism played an important role in their rediscovery of the
Japanese literary tradition. This is nowhere more clear than
in the case of Tanizaki, which is the subject of the next chapter.

The works of Edgar Allan Poe were introduced to Japan relatively early in the Meiji period (1868-1912); the translations of
"The Black Cat" and "The Murders in the Rue Morgue" in the
twentieth year of Meiji mark the introduction of Poe to Japan.[1]
Ever since that time Poe has been one of the most popular and
influential Western writers in Japan. During the Meiji period
the critics and writers who played an influential role in introducing Poe include Lafcadio Hearn, Natsume Sōseki, Ueda Bin,
Iwano Hōmei, Baba Kocho, Hirata Toboku, Tayama Katai and
Nagai Kafu.[2] Among them, Lafcadio Hearn and Uedo Bin played
decisive roles in laying the foundations for the acceptance and
understanding of Poe's writings.

Hearn, in his lectures at Tokyo University, said that the
uniqueness and true value of Poe's works lies in his imaginative
exploration of fantasy, psychic terror, the realm of the shadow,
and the mysteries of the universe. Hearn pointed out Poe's lack
of didacticism or moral instruction and concluded that the value
of literary works does not depend upon their moral content but
upon their truth and power of suggestion. Hearn also talked
positively of the contribution Poe made to poetry by introducing
new concepts of rhythm and sound.[3]

Ueda Bin, a student of Lafcadio Hearn's and the translator and

*This chapter first appeared in Comparative Literature, XXIX:3 (Summer
1977), 221-240. It is included here, slightly revised, by permission of Comparative Literature.

editor of the most influential collection of Western poems, Kaichō-on, introduced Japanese readers to Poe's influence on
Baudelaire, Mallarmé, and such later English romantic poets as
Rossetti, Swinburne, and Thompson.[4] These two introductions
determined the way Poe would be understood in the future by
Japanese writers. Poe's works are most typically opposed to
realistic or naturalistic literature, and Japanese literature in
the Meiji period was dominated by naturalism. Tanizaki once
remarked that "if you do not write a naturalistic novel, you are
not a writer."[5]

Hearn's emphasis on Poe's exploration of the psychic realm
and on the elements of mystery and grotesque fantasy in his
works, together with Ueda Bin's association of Poe with the
French symbolist poets, provided new insights and opened a new
literary realm for writers discontented with naturalism. Hearn
himself was writing fantasies and ghost stories, drawing his inspiration from Japanese folk literature and legend, and casting
new light on the tradition of the supernatural and the grotesque
in Japanese literature in an era of overwhelmingly didactic,
practical, and naturalistic writing. The influence Japanese
poets received from Baudelaire, the symbolist poets, and the
English writers of the aesthetic school cannot be overempha-
sized. It is in this context, that is, in relation to the symbolist
writers and English writers of the aesthetic school like Oscar
Wilde, that Poe was most typically understood and admired by
Japanese writers.

Yet the study of Poe in the Meiji period was limited largely
to introductory remarks and the translation of his works, and
understanding of them remained superficial. In the Taisho period (1912-1926) writers who were "influenced" by Poe began
to reflect his influence in their works. This period was one of
reaction to naturalism and to the confessional I-novels; it was
characterized by two dominant literary movements, one of the
Shirakaba group and the other the so-called aesthetic school.
These movements — and the philosophic and aesthetic ideas underlying them — were almost diametrically opposed. The Shirakaba group sought a new sense of life in the limitless expan-

sion of the self and of human possibilities, while the aesthetic
school was committed to the pursuit of the beautiful, even to the
point of sacrificing social and moral integrity. Yet they were in
agreement that literature is an art form and that style, structure, words, and images are at least as important as the content
of literary works. Perfection in a work as art, together with or
in place of philosophic depth, was a professed goal of most of
the writers of this period; this was especially true of the writers
of the aesthetic school who were most strongly influenced by
Poe. Among them Sato Haruo, Hagiwara Sakutaro, Akutagawa
Ryūnosuke,[6] and Tanizaki Junichiro openly acknowledged their
indebtedness to Poe, and their works show the depth of his influence. In particular, the relationship between Tanizaki and
Poe seems to present a unique case for comparative study.

Students of Tanizaki usually agree that, like other Taisho
writers, he began his career under the spell of the West: the influence of Poe, Baudelaire, and Oscar Wilde, among others, is
reflected in many of his early works. It is agreed, however,
that the influence of the Japanese literature of the seventeenth
and eighteenth centuries, especially the erotic and sadistic stories in Kusazoshi and Kabuki plays, was also strong. According
to the orthodox view, the influence of the Western writers became superficial by the end of the Taisho period. Drawn to both
East and West, Tanizaki, after a period of severe internal conflict between the two attractions, turned completely to the world
of classical Japanese literature and made a conscious artistic
endeavor to link his later works with his Japanese heritage.[7]
My purpose here is to consider whether the Western influences
were indeed superficial and to examine Poe's influence on Tanizaki's later development, when he attempted to create his Japanese Byzantium.

Tanizaki Junichiro, one of the major modern Japanese writers,
was born in 1886 in the old section of Tokyo and died in 1965 at
the age of seventy-nine. He left behind thirty volumes of collected works which include novels, plays, tales, essays, and
three versions of his translation into modern Japanese of The
Tale of Genji. Such works as A Fool's Love, Some Prefer Net-

tles, The Makioka Sisters, The Key, and The Diary of a Mad Old
Man were translated into English, and some were long-standing
best sellers in the United States. The Western reader will re-
member him best for the controversy aroused by The Key (1956),
the sensual story of a perverted old man who schemes to throw
his wife into the arms of his young assistant in order to arouse
his ebbing sexual interest. In The Diary of a Mad Old Man and
Seventy-Nine-Year-Old Spring, written after The Key, Tanizaki
turns to the theme of perverted eroticism. These erotic books,
dealing with man's carnal desire and desperate effort to retain
his waning sexual force in old age, have been criticized for approaching pornographic literature.

Most of his works, in fact, were controversial, and critics do
not agree in their assessment of them or of Tanizaki himself as
a writer; they do agree, however, on the perfection of his novelistic skills in creating a self-sufficient, polished world of beauty.
In most of his works, especially those of his middle period, Tanizaki fastidiously excluded the social, economic, and political
life of Japan, creating a literary space untouched by the forces
of life in modern Japan. Often drawing material from Japanese
history or old Japanese legends, he created a "pleasure dome"
which is "out of space, out of time."

It is only natural that proletarian writers and such existen-
tialist writers as Oe Kenzaburo criticize the lack of basic ideology and relevance to modern existence in Tanizaki's works.[8]
On the other hand, critics like Ito Sei argue that to regard the
conditions of the flesh, such as erotic desire for life, as a determining factor in human life is an ideology in its own right,
and defend Tanizaki as a writer whose major theme was man's
struggle to attain the sense of life at the risk of moral and social integrity.[9] With critical assessment so polarized and many
critical questions unresolved, Tanizaki will no doubt continue to
be the subject of many critical studies in the future.

Tanizaki's creative works can be divided roughly into three
periods; the first ends with Some Prefer Nettles in 1928,[10] and
the third starts with The Key in 1956. It is in the first period,
from the forty-third year of Meiji to the third year of Showa

(1910-1928), that Western influences, including that of Poe, were most evident; we can find many themes, expressions, descriptions, and stories reminiscent of Poe and of such writers as Baudelaire, Wilde, Zola, and Thomas Hardy.[11]

Some critics have emphasized the influence of Wilde on Tanizaki, underestimating that of Poe.[12] The importance of Wilde's influence is undeniable. Tanizaki tries to separate art from life, placing art above life.[13] Because of his characters' antimoralistic and antisocial pursuit of sensual pleasure, justified for the sake of artistic creation, the term "diabolism" has been widely applied to Tanizaki's early works. Yet Tanizaki's diabolic aesthetes do not suffer from the severe remorse or pangs of conscience experienced by Dorian Gray. In Tanizaki's works, there is no struggle against conscience, against a firmly established social and religious orthodoxy.

In Taisho Japan there was no orthodoxy of religion; nor was there a fully developed and established bourgeoisie against whose moral principles and hypocrisy writers had to rebel. Above all, the writers lived in the protected literary circle of the bundan, free to experiment with any new foreign ideas. Tanizaki's famous and quite autobiographical work, "The Sorrow of the Pagan Outcast" (Itansha no Kanashimi, 1917), in which the hero sadistically ignores the affections of his family and friends in order to be true to his artistic sensibility and creative urge, appears to be the puerile rebellion of an adolescent; likewise, the masochistic self-torture which he calls "the sorrow of the pagan outcast" appears quite sentimental, since the orthodoxy against which he rebels at the risk of self-destruction is in fact quite obscure.

Instead, Tanizaki's heroes' diabolic pursuit of sensuous pleasure proves to be a distorted effort to attain a sense of life through the pursuit of unattainable feminine beauty, the pursuit of the absolute. Throughout Tanizaki's works, the search for a sense of life through the masochistic pursuit of an unattainable woman is a major theme. Tanizaki's heroes feel a deep sense of alienation that spurs them to perverted efforts to recover from it.[14] Tanizaki's grotesque expresses these efforts to

overcome alienation: it is not merely an exercise in decadent
aestheticism. Indeed, the grotesque that expresses the heroes'
pursuit is an appropriate style. In Tanizaki, as well as in Poe,
the grotesque does not refer merely to this perverted pursuit,
but also to the narrative form or perspective, which is ironic
and tragicomic. Furthermore, Tanizaki developed, in his later
period, his own myth of eternal woman, a myth that justifies the
heroes' grotesque efforts at self-recovery. By developing his
own myth, Tanizaki created his own world of romanticism. In these
respects, Tanizaki's works are fundamentally similar to Poe's.

The major themes of Tanizaki's early works are the fear of
death, the sadomasochistic pursuit of feminine beauty, the discovery of perversity or cruelty in human nature, and the relation of art to these themes. As a young man, Tanizaki himself
suffered from a strange nervous condition manifested in sudden
seizures of fear, especially fear of trains. In many of his tales,
he describes this as a fear of persecution, a fear of madness and
death. The narrator of "Kyōfu" (The Fear, 1913) explains that
his heart starts beating rapidly the minute he enters a moving
vehicle. The drumming of his heart increases in speed and intensity, and he feels as if all his blood was rushing to his head,
with his body about to burst into pieces or his brain into madness. This immediately reminds us of the descriptions in Poe's
"The Imp of the Perverse" and "The Tell-Tale Heart," where
the narrators burst out into self-destructive confessions of
their crimes, urged on by the ever-growing sound of their hearts.

In "Seishun monogatari" (My Adolescent Days, 1932), Tanizaki says that he could not exalt death or madness as did Taka-
yama Chogyu, a romantic writer of a decade earlier; instead,
when he read Poe, Baudelaire, Strindberg, and Gorki, anxiety and
fear permeated his nervous system, distorting his senses and
his emotional responses to things. The fear of the explosion of
his body and brain could be ignited at any time and place by the
slightest sensory stimulus, for it had no concrete external
source. He calls the period in which he suffered from this fear
a period of inferno. In many of his tales he describes it in
terms of the dizziness felt when standing at the verge of an

abyss, a sensation of extreme fear and pain that might culminate
in the total loss of his sanity.

The fear is clearly that of death and persecution, yet Tanizaki,
unlike Poe, gives death itself a very small role in his works.[15]
Furthermore, the fear of death is actually the fear of his own
urge toward self-destruction. The fear, therefore, can be called
a "pleasurable pain," and its source is entirely internal. The
hero's urge toward self-destruction is indeed the work of what
Poe called the "imp of the perverse." In fact, to evoke this state
of pleasurable pain, of the abysmal terror of self-destruction,
is the purpose of the protagonists' diabolic actions in almost all
of Tanizaki's works and is their major theme.

This sensation of pleasurable pain is directly related to the
other themes of this period, the discovery of the perversity or
cruel love of destruction in human nature and the sadomasochistic pursuit of feminine beauty. Many of Tanizaki's tales
were obviously inspired by Poe's crime and detective stories,
tales in which the heroes commit, with the utmost cruelty,
crimes that are almost gratuitous. These tales include "Gold
and Silver," "The Criminal," "An Incident at Yanagiyu," and
"The Cursed Play."[16]

Many devices and techniques used by Poe appear in these
tales, including the Dupin-narrator relationship later popularized
in that of Sherlock Holmes and Dr. Watson. In most cases, the
heroes' extreme sadism, the analytical precision with which
they murder and hide the corpse, and their observations on
criminal psychology vividly reveal their fascination with evil
and gratuitous cruelty and their concern with making murder a
work of art. The discovery of one's own perversity is related
to the theme of the double; Tanizaki wrote several tales, such
as "A Story of Tomoda and Matsunaga," in which he dealt. explicitly with the double and doppelgänger.[17]

Yet the sadism of the heroes is often masochistic. In "Ha-
kuchūkigo" (The Devil at Noon, 1918), the hero, after witnessing
a grotesque murder carried out by a beautiful woman, offers to
be murdered by the same woman. He asks a friend to witness
the scene of his own cruel death. "Hokan" (A Harlequin, 1911),

a masterpiece of the early period, is the story of a man who
takes uncontrollable pleasure in humiliating himself and in
pleasing others by allowing them to control and manipulate him.
His effort to exist only in the consciousness of others, in which
condition the pain he feels gives him a strong sense of his own
self and body, is a classic case of masochism. The hero feels
a strong sense of himself, a unity of consciousness, by existing
only in the other's image of himself.

Tanizaki's grotesque world of perversity is obviously similar
to Poe's. In the latter's crime stories, the heroes commit sadistic, gratuitous crimes which are often followed by self-
destructive confessions. Such crimes appear in "William Wilson,"
"The Tell-Tale Heart," "The Black Cat," "The Cask of Amon-
tillado," and "The Imp of the Perverse." In "The Black Cat,"
the hero perceives the ominous otherness in the cat's eyes and
murders it brutally. The same pattern appears in "The Tell-
Tale Heart," in which the hero is provoked to cruel murder by
the old man's vulture-like eye. The heroes of "The Black
Cat" and "The Imp of the Perverse" explain their acts of
perverse evil as the result of the human impulse for self-
torture.

> Yet I am not more sure that my soul lives, than I am that perverseness is one of the
> primitive impulses of the human heart... This spirit of perverseness, I say,
> came to my final overthrow. It was this unfathomable longing of the soul to vex
> itself — to offer violence to its own nature — to do wrong for the wrong's sake
> only — that urged me to continue and finally to consummate the injury I had in-
> flicted upon the unoffending brute. [18]

The act of evil for evil's sake is as masochistic as it is diabolic: the pure evil is directed against himself, to vex his own
soul so that he can be immersed in the immediacy of pain and
terror. In the spontaneous experience of pain and terror, the
nonreflecting consciousness kills the reflecting consciousness
and thus the hero is immersed in the sense of himself, of his
immediate body and subjectivity. The criminal action is an extreme method the hero adopts to cultivate artificial sensuous
intoxication through self-torture. Murder is an attempt to
eliminate the split in his consciousness caused by the ominous

eye, to restore the wholeness of his consciousness.

In "The Premature Burial" and "The Pit and the Pendulum," the heroes, by their own imagination, induce sensations of the utmost terror and pain of death. "A Descent into the Maelström" and "MS. Found in a Bottle" also describe the heroes' experience of the ecstasy and terror of self-annihilation, their experience of an abysmal descent into nothingness. Thus, both in Poe and Tanizaki, the diabolism is actually directed toward the heroes themselves as a method of inducing pain and ecstasy and of intoxicating the reflecting consciousness in the immediacy of pain.

In Tanizaki, the themes of the discovery of perversity in human nature and the masochistic desire for self-destruction are intertwined and are, furthermore, related to his other major theme, the pursuit of the femme fatale. "Bushu-ko hiwa" (Secrets of Lord Bushu, 1931), set in medieval Japan, is the most successful dramatization of the relations among these themes. One night in his youth, Lord Bushu was taken by a devilish old lady to the attic of a castle. There, women were preparing severed enemy heads to be brought before the lord of the castle for identification. In the dark room filled with a nauseating odor, he had the sensation of looking deeply into an abyss which had suddenly opened in his mind and felt dizzy with terror and expectation. The young boy was particularly struck by the beauty of the hands of one beautiful young girl, hands which handled the heads. A faint smile appeared on her face when she held an especially ugly head, one without the nose, and looking at her, he felt himself in an extreme state of excitement that led him to a hitherto unexperienced ecstasy. The ugliness and the grotesqueness of the severed head brought out the sublimity in the girl's cruel beauty, and he found himself wishing earnestly that he were that severed head. He later finds that the beautiful wife of his master is secretly planning to remove her husband's nose as an act of revenge. Discovering this secret wish of the lady, Lord Bushu swears to be her servant and succeeds in rendering her husband an ugly cripple without a nose. He has intense moments of ecstasy when he imagines the man with an ugly, noseless face making love to a beautiful woman.

Here the sadism of the lord is actually masochistic, and it becomes clear that the three major themes of this early period — the fear of death, the discovery of the abyss (the perversity of one's own nature), and the fear of absorption in it — are directly related to Tanizaki's heroes' masochistic pursuit of the femme fatale. Indeed, the pursuit of the femme fatale is itself, for Tanizaki, a theme which deals with man's urge for self-torture and self-destruction. In "Akuma" (The Devil, 1912), the hero is tortured by a physically attractive and cruel woman, while at the same time threatened by a mysterious, devilish man who swears to take revenge on him because of his relationship with her. Although extremely frightened by him, the hero continues his self-humiliating pursuit of the woman. In "Zoku akuma" (The Devil: A Sequel, 1913), he encourages the man to murder him and is indeed murdered by him.[19]

Both the woman and the man are devils, yet the true devil is the "imp of the perverse," his self-destructive urge. Both are only agents of his inner desire, and he deliberately manipulates them to torture himself. In all of Tanizaki's stories in which the fatal woman is the main theme, the heroes are involved in drawing out the diabolic nature of beautiful women, thus molding them into ideal women, black-widow spiders which devour males after sexual ecstasy. The creation of the cruel, beautiful woman is the externalization of the hero's inner desire, and in actuality, she is his puppet. This can be seen most readily in "Chijin no ai" (A Fool's Love, 1924).

The hero of the novel falls in love with a Western-looking waitress and encourages her to be more bold in displaying her beauty and sexual attraction. She begins to have many love affairs, yet the more cruel her treatment of him becomes, the more ecstatic the pleasure he finds in being with her. The creation of the fatal woman in order to be tortured by her is also the main theme of such other major works of the early period as "Shisei" (Tattoo), "Jyotaro" and "Suterareru Made" (Until Forsaken). In the latter period, such works as "Shunkinsho" (A Portrait of Shunkin), "Ashikari" and Futen rojin nikki (The

Diary of a Mad Old Man) are only extensions of these early works.

Tanizaki's heroes, however, do not pursue beautiful women for the sake of erotic fulfillment. Rather, they pursue an unattainable absolute, the symbolic essence of feminine beauty. In the early period, the beauty is typically revealed in human flesh, but it is human flesh as an objet d'art which refuses normal erotic communication: Tanizaki's heroes find the essence of feminine beauty in women's feet.

In "Tattoo," the author says that the beautiful is the strong and the ugly the weak. The heroes long for the beauty that rejects them absolutely as ugly and weak, precluding any possibility of normal human relationships. Thus, beauty is elevated to the position of an absolute, an almighty existence. This is inevitable, for the pursuit of beauty, like the commitment to evil, is self-torture. Tanizaki's characters are involved in such fetishism, besides the involvement in women's feet, as licking a handkerchief dirtied by the woman's mucous, drinking a loved one's urine, and so forth. The pursuit of the unattainable beauty and the pursuit of the ugly are essentially the same.

Tanizaki separates art from life and from morality (goodness) in order to associate beauty with evil. In "Kirin" (Unicorn, 1910), which shows the strong influence of Oscar Wilde, Tanizaki presents a Chinese emperor who is torn between his aspiration to become a virtuous ruler and his desire to become a slave to his beautiful and brutal empress. He finally yields to the empress, whom he calls the devil. The pursuit of pleasure and beauty must lead to the pursuit of evil, for the true pleasure the heroes seek is that of self-persecution. The fear of death described by Tanizaki's heroes is based on their psychic dread of life, their sense of alienation; their masochism is a means of objectifying their fear. Yet Tanizaki's hero is the creator of the sadistic persecutor; she is the externalization of his inner desire and is almost his double. Thus he is the schemer responsible for the whole situation: he is the persecutor as well as the victim. In this sense, Tanizaki's hero becomes a god, the creator of his own, self-contained world.

In both Tanizaki and Poe, art plays a significant role in this

grotesque endeavor to restore the sense of life. We have seen
that the creation of an ideal fatal woman is itself an art. In
"Tattoo" (1910), a sadistic young tattooer, who enjoys watching
the pain he causes his customers, finds an innocent young girl
with beautiful feet in whom he recognizes hidden powers of evil.
Pouring all his psyche into his art, he tattoos on her back an
enormous female black-widow spider, thus transforming her
into a diabolical woman. She then declares that the tattooer will
be her first victim. Here it is the tattooer's art that turns the
innocent girl into a diabolical woman, thus fulfilling his secret
masochistic desire to be devoured by a beautiful and cruel
woman. Art is both the secret agent for creating evil and the means
of inducing a masochistically ecstatic state of consciousness.

The similarity to Poe's art here is obvious, although in Poe's
case the diabolical women do not have the same fleshly eroticism. Poe's dreamers create their own "bower of dreams,"[20]
the "arabesque" room, by decorating it with their art of interior
decoration. The arabesque room is meant to induce a dreaming
consciousness in the inhabitant's mind; there he indulges in his
grotesque dreams of transcendence by destroying his own and
his lover's physical being or sanity. The agents of the hero's
grotesque imagination, evoked by his art, are Poe's vampiric
women with supernal beauty.

The similarity and difference between the concepts of art of
the two authors can best be illustrated by comparing Tanizaki's
"The Golden Death" (1914) with Poe's "The Domain of Arnheim";
"The Golden Death" is almost entirely based on Poe's tale. In
both tales, the narrator tells of his friend, extravagantly rich
and poetic in nature, who attempts the creation of an earthly
paradise. In both tales the narrator's visit to the paradise
forms the climax, and in both paradises the narrator finds that
the original nature has been transformed by art, creating an extremely bizarre and bewildering earthly paradise, that is, a
grotesque and arabesque one. It was both Poe's and Tanizaki's
pleasure dome, which their art, by correcting nature, created.
For both writers, art proves to be superior to nature; it is not
nature but art that saves the heroes.

In Poe's "The Domain of Arnheim," the narrator's visit to the paradise strongly suggests his actual dreaming. The river journey is actually an inner journey, the imaginative fulfillment of his dream. At the end of his journey, the "arabesque canoe" which had taken the narrator to the inner gate of the paradise descends rapidly into a huge amphitheater. This tale, like "The Fall of the House of Usher" and in fact like most of Poe's tales, is a dramatization of the myth he presents in Eureka. Eureka presents Poe's myth of the fall of man and nature from the Original Unity — primordial nothingness — and their return through self-annihilation and the destruction of earthly reality. The poet in Eureka is endowed with the power to initiate the return movement to Original Unity. The task of Poe's artists is to dream of glorious, "golden" death, to convert the void into a space filled with meaning.

The grotesque and arabesque are for Poe a means of entering into a darkly radiant world of dreams through destruction of the body and of reality. As Poe's keen irony dramatizes in his tales, this attempt at grotesque transcendence appears mad and comical from the perspective of rational intelligence. Poe's ironic grotesque presents the grotesque, transcendental hero as both tragic and comic, as both Eureka's archetypal poet and an insane, perverted man.

In "The Golden Death," the end of the hero's dream is also death. Yet the purpose of his art is not to cause death itself, but to bring about a state of extreme sensuous intoxication, so extreme as to risk self-destruction. Tanizaki's paradise is more voluptuous and erotic than Poe's, filled with the statues of centaurs, animals, and beautiful naked women. In the midst of the ecstasy created by the effect of the paradise, the hero dies, covering his entire body with golden powder. He himself becomes a most glorious, shining part of his paradise, a work of art.

The narrators of both tales are objective observers who witness the heroes' grotesque endeavors to create their own paradises. While Poe's narrator gradually becomes involved in the drama of the hero and at the end becomes almost his double,

Tanizaki's narrator remains a rational man who escapes from
the intoxicating effect of the paradise. Although he calls the
hero a great artist, the narrator maintains the distance between
the rational reader and the grotesque hero. In Tanizaki too, the
dual or ironic point of view which regards the hero both as absurd and mad and as a positive artist is present.

Indeed, both Poe and Tanizaki frequently use the uninvolved,
third-person narrator to describe the hero's grotesque effort.
In Poe's stories the uninvolved narrator becomes involved.
Thus, at the climax, the hero's drama is experienced by the narrator as his inner experience. In the works in which Poe uses
a first-person narrator, the hero is split between a rational self
and an irrational one; the narrator-hero, representing the rational self, describes the grotesque drama of the irrational self,
a drama which the narrator-hero says that he himself finds difficult to comprehend. This skillful use of the narrator is a device to express the ironic, dual perspective inherent in Poe's
grotesque; the serious and rational appear comical and absurd,
while the mad and perverted appear tragic.

Although Tanizaki uses the uninvolved third-person narrator
with great skill, the tales narrated by the hero himself do not
always maintain the ironic point of view successfully. The
reader is called upon to take the hero's grotesque drama seriously and with sympathy, which immediately raises the question
of the drama's social, moral, and ideological relevance. It is
only in The Diary of a Mad Old Man that Tanizaki, dramatizing
man's tragicomic struggle for life, uses the ironic perspective
successfully. In this work he reveals an almost terrifying spirit
of irony and self-mockery. In his middle period, however, Tanizaki turned to the world of dream and imagination in his effort
to create a self-sufficient romantic world, one that could give
structure to his hero's grotesque pursuit of a sense of life.

While Poe had a myth that justified the poet's grotesque endeavor at destructive transcendence through his art, Tanizaki
had no such cosmic myth. Tanizaki's heroes, therefore, are not
transcendental heroes, but mad aesthetes who indulge in sensuous ecstasy to the point of death. Poe was a romantic who per-

ceived the deterioration of the isomorphic relations between the
order of mind and that of the body and who believed in the power
of imagination to transcend the phenomenal world to reach a
higher level of reality where the split between subject and object is eliminated.

Tanizaki, on the other hand, did not yet have his own myth to
explain metaphorically his view of the universe — his view of
the source of man's alienation and of the life and task of the artist and his vision of the ideal reality. Although in his youth he
defined himself as a romantic writer who believed in the "poetic
intuition" which perceives the world beyond phenomenal reality
(a world he grasped in Platonic terms),[21] it is difficult to call
Tanizaki's early works romantic in the absence of a myth which
creates a self-sufficient world of dream and legitimizes the
theme of grotesque recovery from alienation. While Poe's
mythopoeic thrust to create his own universe resulted in the
creation of the beautiful, mathematically balanced universe of
Eureka in which the poet is finally absorbed, Tanizaki had to
depend on his skill of expression to convince the reader of the
validity of his hero's grotesque endeavor. Asking the reader to
hold in abeyance the question of morality, Tanizaki sought to
appeal only to the reader's aesthetic sense. In this endeavor,
the novel was not quite an appropriate form, and in the middle
period his works gradually moved toward the world of romance.

While Poe's exploration of the sadomasochistic attempt to
attain a sense of life and of the endeavor in grotesque art to induce dreaming consciousness presents features of human experience that are meaningful and interesting from the existential-
phenomenological point of view, Poe dramatized them in his own
fantasy world. He also had a myth that justified them externally
as legitimate endeavors for man's return to Original Unity.

Tanizaki's middle period starts with his awareness of the
need to create a self-sufficient world of dream and beauty in
which the question of morality and relevance to reality will be
temporarily suspended. Without such a world, his exploration
of grotesque eroticism might prove to be merely sensational.[22]

This problem concerned all of the writers of the grotesque.

Until the middle of the nineteenth century, the grotesque had been considered pejoratively, for it explored the realm of the ugly, the fantastic, and the subconscious, including man's fears and secret desires. During the romantic age, when artists saw the grotesque aspects of objective reality, the grotesque came to be regarded as closely related to the artist's reaction to and conception of reality.[23] Even then, the grotesque was approved only half-heartedly; it was only in the modern period that the grotesque became recognized, through the works of Dostoevski, Kafka, Faulkner, Pinter, and Beckett, among others, as a highly significant symbol, style, form of imagination, and structural basis for literary works. Poe, by placing the origin and function of the grotesque in his romantic myth, was the first writer to clarify the link between Gothic terror and the romantic quest, thus integrating Gothic literature into the tradition of Western romanticism. The idea of grotesque, destructive transcendence occupies the central place in his myth.

Tanizaki's turning to the world of classical Japanese culture reflects the same concern as that of the writers of the grotesque with the legitimacy of the grotesque world he creates. It is, like Coleridge's adoption of the medieval ballad form, a device to draw a magic circle around the hero and his exploration. It also reflects his mythopoeic desire to create his own dreamworld, which first became evident at this time.

Some Prefer Nettles, the novel that marks the end of Tanizaki's first period, already presents his effort to draw a magic circle, to create a myth of ideal feminine beauty that would enable him to pursue the theme of the masochistic search for a sense of life as the theme of man's search for unattainable ideal beauty. In his early writings, beautiful, diabolic women were the object of the hero's desire and the hero wanted to be tortured by them. Tanizaki described the essence of such women as "white flesh." In this period, the woman is a living creature with white flesh, and it is the beauty and pleasure of the flesh itself that intoxicates the hero. Yet gradually, this white flesh is transformed into a white woman, an eternal woman who becomes the object of the hero's aspiration.[24]

The eternal woman is first of all unreachable. In "Ningyo no nageki" (The Sorrow of the Mermaid), Tanizaki says that the mysterious beauty of the mermaid, a beauty that absorbs the whole existence of the hero, is fully revealed in her immense, unfathomable eyes. Her "divine orbs" look as if they are gazing at eternity from the depth of her soul. The reader will be reminded of Poe's description of Ligeia's eyes, eyes which make the hero feel the approach of the full knowledge of eternity. The mermaid is unattainable for human beings, but she is the only source of excitement for the hero, who is tired of all the pleasures of this world. This unattainable beauty gradually takes a more distinct form in Tanizaki's later works as both the beauty of eternal maternity, from which the hero is alienated, and that of the classical Japanese court lady hidden behind a thick screen.

By identifying the fatal woman as a mother figure and transforming the hero's masochistic longing for the fatal woman into man's longing for his lost mother, Tanizaki explains the origin of the hero's alienation and gives universality and human relevance to his hero's masochistic drama. Poe's longing for his mother and for a mother figure is well known. So is Tanizaki's attachment to his own mother, whom he describes as a beautiful woman. Yet unlike Poe, Tanizaki's creation of eternal motherhood and its beauty is a conscious literary device; Tanizaki as a man evidently did not suffer from a mother complex.[25] The essence of unattainable feminine beauty is symbolized in a persona of a mother figure.

At the same time, Tanizaki came to identify ideal beauty with the beauty of the classical Japanese court lady, whose white face glows faintly in a dark, screened room like the fluorescent glow of fireflies at night. Glimpsed only momentarily, she is inaccessible, a dream woman existing only in one's imagination and separated in time and space. Although the essence of her beauty is also whiteness, it is no longer white flesh, but whiteness itself. Tanizaki's fatal woman thus emerges as an archetypal Japanese court lady as well as an archetypal mother.

There is no doubt that Tanizaki rediscovered the beauty of Japanese culture and literature,[26] yet the claim that Tanizaki,

abandoning his Western influences, returned to the classical
world is misleading. Instead, Tanizaki created his own
dreamworld and eternal woman, as exotic to him as their
Western counterparts, out of classical Japanese culture. The
court life he presents in "The Mother of Captain Shigemoto"
(1949) and the medieval life in "Secrets of Lord Bushu" are
distinctively Tanizaki's own creations rather than historically
accurate representations. Tanizaki himself explains enviously
in "Ave Maria" (1923) that the myth of the eternal woman
and the worship of woman do not exist in Japanese culture.[27]
Thus he creates his own goddess to rule over his self-sufficient dreamworld, a mythical world or one which functions
as a substitute for myth.[28] The eternal mother as goddess, as
the symbolic essence of his dreamworld, is most vividly expressed in "The Mother of Captain Shigemoto," the masterpiece of his middle period. Captain Shigemoto's mother, who
has lived in his dream, finally appears at the end of the
novel shining faintly in the darkness with a circle of light
around her. Tanizaki's return was not to classical Japanese
culture but to the primordial and infantile area of human
consciousness, to the realm of the subconscious and dreams.

Tadekuu mushi (Some Prefer Nettles, 1928) explains how
this autonomous dreamworld is created. The protagonist
Kaname is torn between his attraction to a Eurasian prosti-
tute, who powders her legs to make them completely white,
and his father-in-law's old-fashioned, doll-like mistress, who
is carefully groomed to suit the old man's anachronistic
taste. In this transitional novel, the hero is torn between
his desire for white flesh and his longing for whiteness, the
eternal beauty of woman.

With his mistress, Ohisa, Kaname's father-in-law lives an
aesthete's life in complete retirement, recreating a type of life
of old Edo. They frequent the Bunraku theater, and Kaname,
while watching the white face of a crying doll move faintly
across a distant stage, comes to realize that the essence of
Ohisa's beauty is that eternalized by the Bunraku puppet.
Tanizaki writes:

The Ohisa for whom his secret dream searched might not be Ohisa at all, but another, a more Ohisa-like Ohisa. And it might even be that this latter Ohisa was no more than a doll, perhaps even now quiet in the dusk of an inner chamber behind an arched stage doorway. A doll might do well enough, indeed.[29]

After this novel, Tanizaki turned to the world of classical literature and beauty and recreated his ideal feminine beauty in historical figures and in historical settings. Such masterpieces as "Yoshinokuzu," "Ashikari," "A Portrait of Shunkin," "Mōmoku monogatari" (The Story of a Blind Man), "The Mother of Captain Shigemoto," "Yume no ukihashi" (The Bridge of Dreams) were written one after another.

In these works, the desire for white flesh disappears almost completely (although still lurking below the surface), and the hero's longing for the essence of feminine beauty is dramatized as his longing for an unattainable mother figure or for a superior woman with classic Japanese beauty. The hero's self-torture, born out of his longing for the unattainable, is intense, yet by fathoming this pain, the hero obtains a deep, soul-satisfying pleasure, a complete ecstasy. The eternal women in these stories are only extensions of the beautiful and cruel women of supernal beauty who tortured the heroes in the early works. Thus Tanizaki created his own world of romance by creating his own romantic myth of supernal beauty. Tanizaki also developed stories of sadomasochistic torture in historic Japanese settings, using the rich tradition of the grotesque in Japanese literature.

Poe's supernal beauty is also unattainable. Poe's myth of the poet's return to the original unity presents a drama of the poet in search of the beauty which exists only in the original paradise, the origin of life itself. Poe's ideal woman is doomed to die. Both Ligeia and Eleonora, whose beauty symbolizes man's original state of harmony and his aspiration for it, die and thus become unattainable for the heroes. They may even have existed only in their dreams. Following their aspiration for supernal beauty, the heroes enter the path to self-annihilation, returning to the original condition of nothingness.

Supernal beauty is attained only through self-destruction. The

grotesque in Poe is a symbol of decadent human nature and reality, the result of the Fall, as well as a symbol which points
toward transcendence of the decadent. In Tanizaki too, the grotesque serves not merely to induce sensuous pleasure, but as a
means of entering his dreamworld, of returning home. It is a
means for the hero to assure his sense of life, a sense which he
cannot obtain in the modern, industrial world. The origin and
function of Tanizaki's grotesque, too, are legitimized by his creation of a romantic world of dream.

Some Prefer Nettles is often considered a dramatization of the
conflict between Tanizaki's attraction to the beauty and culture
of the West and those of the East. With this novel, the period of
Western influence on Tanizaki appears to end, and since his major works all explore the world of classical beauty, critics argue
that the Western influence on Tanizaki was not lasting. Rather,
however, the novel dramatizes the shift of the hero's pursuit of
white flesh to whiteness itself, a shift from the world of reality
to the world of romance, to the self-sufficient world of romantic
dream. Poe's influence on Tanizaki appears, then, not merely
in Tanizaki's early choice of the themes that were to characterize his literary career, but also in the creation of the romantic world that began with this shift.[30]

Tanizaki was fascinated by the Gothic themes presented in the
writings of Baudelaire, Wilde, and Poe, such as the ties between
love and cruelty, pleasure and pain, and domination and humili-
ation, and tried to dramatize them in his own language and in
the natural settings of Japanese life. Tanizaki's later turning
to the world of classical beauty did not mean that he had dis-
carded these themes and Western influences. On the contrary,
he developed these same themes more fully and uniquely within
the tradition of Japanese culture.

More importantly, Tanizaki developed the Gothic themes into
romantic themes: Tanizaki's insistent dramatization of man's
sense of self-estrangement from "home," of his vision of and
aspiration for eternal femininity, and of his grotesque, desperate
effort to regain it, finally results in the creation of a self-contained, romantic world of his own. Based on Japanese tradi-

tion, Tanizaki created his own literary space and his own myth
of the ideal woman to enable himself to develop his Poesque romantic theme of the self-destructive pursuit of a sense of life.

Tanizaki's literary world develops, therefore, from a mere
description, however interesting, of man's perverted effort to
attain a sense of life, a world that reflects his Edo taste or
Gothic taste, to a romantic world in which man's alienation from
the original harmony and his struggle to regain it become a major theme. The grotesque is not only integrated into his romanticism, but also emerges as a positive, although paradoxical,
symbol which points toward the ideal reality. Poe's influence
on the formation of his world is significant — especially Poe's
concept of supernal beauty, his hero's tragicomic drama of
search for it and the role of the grotesque in this drama.

Toward the end of his life, Tanizaki returned to present reality from the world of romance and seemed to resume his earlier
pursuit of the theme of erotic desire for white flesh, especially
in The Key and The Diary of a Mad Old Man. Yet this time the
heroes are old men nearing death who have already lost their
sexual power. Their longing for white flesh is symbolic and not
physical; the white flesh is almost a symbol of desire for life
itself. Their longing for erotic desire is actually a longing for
a life-giving force.

In Tanizaki's later works, eros, life, and death are linked to
each other; life can be experienced only as a sense of life, and
in man's pursuit of a sense of life, he encounters the terror of
death. Eros is a beautiful, sublime, and grotesque life-force,
which brings life to death. In the old men's desperate, masochistic, erotic desires, Tanizaki presents man's tragicomic,
grotesque yet sublime struggle for life. This is essentially the
same struggle Poe dramatized in his tales of the grotesque and
systematized in his romantic myth. Tanizaki proves in these
novels that the themes which preoccupied him in his early days
were indeed his own. Tanizaki's early exposure to Poe's world
of "negative romanticism," with its central concept of grotesque
transcendence, cannot be irrelevant to the ultimate development
of his own world of romanticism in the Japanese literary tradi-

tion. While Tanizaki's Japanese romantic world is unique, it is
not incompatible with the Western romantic tradition. Thus Tanizaki emerges not as a "pagan outcast," but as the legitimate
heir to both the Japanese literary tradition and to the Western
tradition of romanticism, in both of which the grotesque plays
an essential role.

With the rise of proletarian literature in the late Taisho period, Tanizaki's aesthetic world became the target of criticism
and he responded by isolating himself further from Japan's social reality, retiring even more deeply into his own romantic
world. In the new Showa literature, the artists' concern over
the relation between politics and literature gave a new vitality
to their concerns over the relations between the self and art and
art and reality. The Taisho period writers tried to separate art
from morality, and the artists tried to separate themselves
from intellectuals. In the new Showa era, however, art became
concerned with social issues again, and the separation of art
from intellectual and social concerns became impossible. Both
modernist literature and proletarian literature, to which I turn
in the following chapters, sought to make art once again a reflection of social reality and the modern predicament.

DISEASE AND MADNESS IN JAPAN'S
MODERNIST LITERATURE: YOKOMITSU RIICHI'S
"MACHINE" AND THE SHORT STORIES
OF KAJII MOTOJIRO

The introduction of avant-garde European art and literature to Japan began around the ninth year of Taisho (1920).[1] At that time, the poets and writers who were associated with such journals as Shinkō Bungaku (New Emerging Literature) and Aka to Kuro (The Red and the Black) began actively to develop the Dadaist and expressionist movements in Japan, paving the way for the New Perceptionist movement (shinkankakuha) led by Yokomitsu Riichi. The Japanese avant-garde movement was closely related to nihilistic decadence and revolutionary anarchism. Dadaist art, combining individual decadence and revolutionary class consciousness, became engaged in rebellion against and destruction of established art and indeed of the entire social system. Such representative Dadaist writers as Tsuboi Shigeji, Kawasaki Chōtaro, Hagiwara Kyōjiro and Tsuji Jun all believed their art to be the forerunner of revolution. The manifesto of Aka to Kuro reads:

What is poetry? What is the poet? Throwing away all the concepts of the past, we declare baldly, "Poetry is a bomb! The poet is a black criminal who throws a bomb at the thick walls and doors of the prison."[2]

The so-called terrorists of the literary circle, regarding the reality which surrounded them as a prison, tried to destroy the social system and the poetic concepts which were fostered by it.
    Their creative and revolutionary élan was expressed in their

spirit of negation and commitment to destruction:

Our existence is negation itself! Negation is creation! Creation is nothingness!
...Negate! Negate! Negate! Let us pour all our force into negation! Only then
can we exist![3]

They considered artistic creation to be a form of action, and
their negation and destruction were directed at both the establishment in art — "class art" — and the social system — capitalist imperialism — which sustained it.

The avant-garde movement was divided into many small
groups because the writers and artists, basically anarchistic,
naturally tended to be quite individualistic, yet most of the
groups remained close to the Marxian socialist proletarian literary movement. Considering themselves to be terrorists engaged in class struggle within the literary circle, they shared
with the proletarian revolutionaries the feeling that the reality
of the machine culture created by capitalism was oppressive to
art and human life, and both shared the common purpose of destroying the oppressive class system and the art which served
as its "running dog."

Both the avant-garde art movement and the proletarian movement received a great blow from the Kanto earthquake of 1923.
Shinkō Bungaku and Aka to Kuro, along with Tanemaku Hito (The
Sowers), which had been established in 1921 as the first journal
for proletarian literature, had to cease publication. By 1925,
when the new Peace Preservation Law was passed to provide
added legal sanction for limiting radical activities, the anarchists had clearly parted from the Marxists, and with the defeat
of terrorism, avant-garde art seemed to have lost its revolutionary élan. In the thirteenth year of Taisho (1924), a year
after the earthquake, two new journals which were to be the
center of early Showa (1926-present) literary activities were
established. One was Bungei Sensen (Art and Literature Battlefront),[4] a journal which sought to establish a new united
front for proletarian literature, and the other, established by
Yokomitsu Riichi, Kawabata Yasunari, Nakagawa Yoichi and

others, was Bungei Jidai (The Age of Art and Literature),[5] a
modernist journal which took a leading role in the so-called New
Perceptionist movement.

Bungei Jidai started without any consciously formulated ideological or methodological manifesto, except to state that it was
committed to the development of a "new art and literature,
based on a new life," as Kawabata stated in the first issue.[6]
The members of the group which published the journal were very
close to the Dadaists and expressionists of DAMDAM and MAVO,[7]
and to other avant-garde writers who had been active before the
earthquake. The fact that the New Perceptionists emerged from
the Taisho (1912-1926) avant-garde movement is reflected in
Kawabata's article "The New Directions of the Newly Emerging
Writers," in which he attempted to explain "the theoretical basis of New Perceptionist expression."[8] The elements he considered vital in the New Perceptionist movement are reflected
in the four parts into which he divided the essay: (1) the emergence of the new art and literature, (2) the New Perception,
(3) expressionistic epistemology, and (4) Dadaistic expression.
In the second issue of Bungei Jidai, Yokomitsu wrote, " I recognize futurism, cubism, expressionism, Dadaism, symbolism,
structuralism, and a part of actualism as belonging to the New
Perceptionism."[9]

Although Yokomitsu, Kawabata and others had not yet established their own literature, they were sure that their literature
would be the totality of the new avant-garde art in that it would
reflect the perception of the new age, absorbing the results of
the theoretical and methodological experiments of its forerun-
ners. Yokomitsu's "Atama narabi ni hara" (The Head and the
Stomach, 1924), published in the first issue of Bungei Jidai,
contains the famous line describing a rapidly moving express
train, "The small station was ignored like a pebble," and this
line alone was taken by writers and critics as a stylistic revolution.

New Perceptionism soon lost its coherence as a movement
because it had lacked a firm theoretical structure from the
start, but the lack of internal cohesion became particularly apparent when some members left Bungei Jidai to join the pro-

letarian literary movement. Yokomitsu, who was seriously concerned with the validity of Marxian dialectics as a means of grasping reality, tried to show that the New Perceptionism was as radical as Marxism in its epistemological method and insisted that its art was not bourgeois or antidialectical.[10] Despite Yokomitsu's effort to bridge the gap between Marxism and New Perceptionism without changing his original theoretical stance, however, the journal could no longer accommodate the writers who were inclined toward proletarian literature, and it ceased publication after the May 1927 issue.

While the proletarian literary movement, led by such writers as Aono Suekichi and Kurahara Korehito, continued to develop actively, leading to the formation in 1928 of the Japanese Proletarian Artists' Federation (NAPF), those of the young modernist writers who were not basically Marxist formed in the same year a new group to publish the journal Bungei Toshi (The City of Art and Literature). Joining such writers as Abe Tomoji and Funabashi Seiichi was the young Kajii Motojiro,[11] whose dozen short stories stand as the crystallization of the modernist aesthetics of Japan. Although Nakagawa Yoichi, a New Perceptionist, later joined the group, it differed from the New Perceptionists in the stand it took against proletarian art. The manifesto of the group, written by Abe Tomoji, reads as follows:

On a plain from which old things disappear
without leaving any trace, we technicians
will make the plan for a new city materialize.
We will build this truly strong, healthy and
multi-angled, three-dimensional city. [12]

Declaring its anti-Marxist position openly, the group supplied the basis for the formation of the Shinko Geijyutsuha (New Emerging Art School) in 1929. Although the anti-Marxist stance of Yokomitsu and Kawabata became more apparent after the so-called debate on "formalism" carried out between the New Perceptionists and the Marxists (represented by Nakano and Kunahara), they did not join the New Emerging Art School. Instead, they began to publish their own journal, Bungaku (Literature),

in 1929, through which they continued their basically aesthetic,
art-for-art's-sake literary activities.

Bungaku, with Poetry and Poetics[13] and Poetry-Reality,[14] new
journals for avant-garde poetry, took the role of introducing new
artistic and literary ideas and movements from Europe; Poetry
and Poetics was concerned mainly with surrealism, while
Poetry-Reality published Itō Sei's translation of Ulysses, and
Bungaku published a translation of Proust's A la Recherche du
Temps Perdu. Kajii's first important work, "The Lemon" (1925),
and most of his works which were later collected in The Lemon
(1931), were published in Poetry-Reality.

The translations of Joyce and Proust had a significant influence in Japan's literary circle, especially on Yokomitsu, to
whom they suggested a new direction after his initial, experimental stage as a New Perceptionist. Itō Sei had already written
several essays in which he advocated highly sophisticated literary expression, and he was establishing himself as a new theo-
rist who considered the novel as basically a literary method. In
a series of essays which were collected in New Psychological
Literature,[15] he criticized the New Perceptionists' impressionistic description of outer forms and phenomena, and suggested they should move to a more direct expression of inner
psychology. At the same time, Yokomitsu, moving away from
New Perceptionism, was writing an essay entitled "Poetry and
the Novel," an essay which was later revised into his famous
"On the Pure Novel."[16] In it he argued that literature must present an autonomous world of human experience, a world including inner psychological experience and experience in human
relations.

Among the avant-garde writers whom Poetry and Poetics actively introduced were Rimbaud, Valéry, Proust, Eliot and in
particular such surrealist poets as Eluard, Breton and Aragon;
the journal focused on their exploration of the subconscious and
their use of automatic writing and stream of consciousness.
Yokomitsu's "Kikai" (Machine, 1930) was the major outcome
of his shift from New Perceptionism to psychological realism.
With Kawabata's "Suishō genso" (Crystal Fantasy, 1931) and

Hori Tatsuo's "Sei kazoku" (The Sacred Family, 1930), it is
among the first and most successful products of Japanese modernism, which reached its maturity after going through initial
stages of anarchism and struggle against Marxian proletarian
literature. While "Machine" was received as a sensational
achievement by such critics as Kobayashi Hideo and Itō Sei and
was to become one of the most influential works of the decade,
Kajii's works, although they were among the most brilliant
products of the modernist movement, were received enthusiastically only among his close friends. Even among them, Kajii's
works were generally considered to be unique but highly personal writings, writings which reflected, in essence, his disease-
sharpened sensibilities.[17] While Yokomitsu was always at the
forefront of literary activities and was always influential, Kajii,
quietly perfecting and nurturing his literary world, lacked social
recognition to the end. In Kajii's works, however, we can recognize one extreme form of decadent aestheticism which, purified as visionary imagination and combined with the method of
inner realism, resulted in an achievement which fully parallels
that of Yokomitsu.

Both "Machine" and such works by Kajii as "The Lemon,"
"Under the Cherry Tree," "Copulation" and "Instrumental Fantasy,"[18] tracing the manner in which extremely sharpened,
"abnormal" sensibilities build a solid wall to defend against an
aggressive, threatening outer world, deal with an estranged inner world of "madness." "Machine"[19] is the story of a young
man from a remote area of Japan who, working under exploitative conditions at a small, family-operated factory in Tokyo,
gradually develops a persecution complex. The factory produces such products as name plates, and the owner of the factory, a middle-aged, "hen-pecked" man, is constantly experimenting with ways to improve the chemical treatment of metals.

The protagonist, who swears his loyalty to the owner, becomes involved in a "dangerous" secret experiment which would
place the factory in a better position in this highly competitive
and unstable small industry. Doing so awakens his suspicions
of two fellow workers, Karube and Yashiki, each of whom he be-

lieves is involved in stealing his "secrets" and those of the factory, and he comes to believe that they suspect him of stealing their secrets and those of the factory. In this way, a triangular relationship of suspicion is created. Each becomes involved in a highly tense psychological play, trying to outdo the others and to trap them into revealing their evil intentions, first allying with one and spying on the other and then reversing the alliance. Mutual hatred and a desire for revenge bring them to physical confrontations in which each hits the others and is himself beaten.

In the center of the factory, and in fact in the center of the protagonist's mind, is a "dark room" where the experiments are carried out, a room whose key is kept by the master himself. Eventually the protagonist gains access to the room and, becoming concerned that the others may go there as well, keeps trying to catch them at it. When he himself enters the room, he becomes earnestly involved in experimenting with chemicals whose poisonous effects corrode his skin and mind. In fact, working at the factory is itself like yielding to the gradual, corrosive effects of a poison.

Once in the slot, I found my skin and my clothes wearing out under the corrosive attacks of ferric chloride....[20]

The factory is constantly in a state of financial crisis. The protagonist blames this on the master's "failings," one of which is his habit of losing money — especially the earnings of the factory from which the salaries of the employees are to be paid. The protagonist's involvement in the experiment in the dark room is partly due to his sincere wish to help the master improve the financial situation of the factory and partly due to his desire to obtain the "secret" that would also rescue him from the intolerable work at the factory. Yet the more he frequents the dark room, the more deeply he becomes haunted by suspicion and fear of persecution, and the more deeply he becomes locked in the paranoiac relations with the other two, creating a psychological hell with no exit.

The night when the master loses all of the earnings for which the workers had worked without sleep and under intense psychological pressure, they turn to drinking. The next morning, the protagonist finds that Yashiki, the more clever of the other two, had mistakenly drunk poison (ammonium dichromate) and was dead. The protagonist suspects that Karube, the other worker, might have killed Yashiki to prevent him from stealing the secret, yet for the same reason he suspects that he himself might have been the murderer. The story ends with his loss of himself:

Perhaps I murdered him. I knew better than anyone where the ammonium dichromate was. Before drunkenness overtook me, I kept thinking about Yashiki and what he would be doing somewhere else the next day, when he would be free to leave. And if he had lived, would I not have lost more than Karube? And had not my head, like the master's, been attacked by ferric chloride?

I no longer understand myself. I only feel the sharp menace of an approaching machine aimed at me. Someone must judge me. How can I know what I have done?[21]

Since the story is told by a first-person narrator, the situation is regarded only through the perspective of the protagonist. As the story progresses, the reader begins to suspect that the tense psychological situation that exists among the three may simply be the product of the protagonist's fantasy, and at the end, the reader is left sharing the protagonist's suspicion that he himself may be the murderer. By following the protagonist's understanding of reality — of his situation in the factory — the reader is actually looking into the deranged inner world of the protagonist. Affected by the poisonous chemicals of reality, the protagonist steadily becomes mad as the alienation of his inner world from the outer reality deepens and he loses his grip on himself. The more deeply he looks into his "dark room" — a metaphor for his inner world — for the purpose of finding a way to recover from the alienation, the further his madness progresses. Once this process is initiated by the "law" of reality, there is no way to arrest it or escape from it. The law is that of the "machine," the machine which controls not only the physical reality of those who live in it, but their very minds as well. The protagonist gradually becomes a part of the machine. The protagonist discovers this soon after he starts living in the factory:

The discovery that in the tiniest things a law, a machine, is at work came to me as the beginning of a spiritual awakening.[22]

The protagonist is, of course, a modern man suddenly placed
in a modern machine-culture which exploits the body and the
mind of both the capitalist and the laborer; as the protagonist
notices, the owner of the factory has long been affected by the
poisonous chemical fumes of "the dark room." Yet the protagonist may be interpreted more specifically as a modern intellectual who has lost the way to relate himself to the new industrial
reality and thus lost himself as well. His sharp observation,
cleverness and skill tend to support this understanding. His
struggle is that of an intellectual who believes that he has the
key to the secret to save himself and others from destruction
in a hostile society, yet the very method he employs for the purpose — coiling into the dark room in search of the secret —
deepens his alienation from reality and thus hastens his collapse
into madness; the "experiment" he carries out there is a "dangerous" one which eventually leads to his self-destruction. Although the work lends itself to symbolic interpretation, however,
it also presents realistically the condition of the exploited laborers in capitalist Japan. Yokomitsu is successful thus in integrating the socio-historical reality into his story of the psychological distortion of modern existence.

The atmosphere of the factory — reality — is filled with a
sense of threat, immediately evoking the protagonist's fear and
anxiety. His psychological play with the others — one of persecution and victimization — is the result of his sense of threat
and his struggle against impending destruction. The more he
struggles, however, the more deeply he becomes caught, and in
the end, he reaches a state of total despair at the height of madness.

Using the madman's point of view skillfully, the story dramatizes the growing alienation of the protagonist in a threatening
modern civilization. The protagonist believes until the very end
that he is the only sane person, while the others are madmen or
criminals. The sense of superiority with which he views the
others brings out both the pathos and the irony of the situation.
Oppressed and insulted, he is a victim — and is consequently
mad — but the reality which surrounds him and is responsible
for his madness is more insane and pernicious than he is. The

irony of the sanity-insanity paradox inherent in the madman's point of view reveals the tragic condition of modern man. The oppressed and the insulted turn on and attempt to destroy one another. The protagonist's deadly serious, "mad" involvement in the psychological play among them and his despair at the end is at once tragic and comic.

The dramatization of a sense of fear and anxiety, and of a sense of impending destruction, is also the central theme of many of Kajii's short stories. At the beginning of "The Lemon," one of Kajii's earliest works, the protagonist explains:

An incomprehensible, ominous lump was oppressing my heart constantly. Shall I call it anxiety or hatred — it was like a hangover after drinking — just as drinking every day will inevitably bring a period of hangover, such a period came to me.[23]

The protagonist, who suffers from a lung disease which makes him constantly feverish, starts reacting to his surroundings with sharpened sensibilities. A penniless college dropout, he is in search of some "luxury," some sensuous indulgence that, however momentary, can convert his drab, everyday life into a gorgeous, colorful world, thereby transforming his ennui into excitement.

Such things as colored-glass marbles, pieces of amber, perfume bottles with rococo designs and fireworks attract his sharpened senses. One day he comes across a fruit shop on a dark, shabby street corner in Kyoto. The light shining on the piled-up fruits makes their radiant colors stand out in the surrounding darkness. The protagonist describes their beauty as being like the sudden coagulation of a flow of music in allegro time. Finding lemons — not usually sold by the small, local stores — among these fruits, he buys one. The coolness of the lemon and its simple color seem to dispel the melancholy and anxiety which had been weighing on him. Its refreshing fragrance seems to bring new energy to his body, whose lungs had never inhaled fully.

Walking on the street with the lemon in his pocket, the protagonist feels as if he were a French poet strolling the streets

of Paris in dandy's clothes. He feels powerful, happy and proud.
When he enters Maruzen, a bookstore specializing in foreign
books and his favorite place, he finds the perfume bottles, the
books on the painters he most admires, and in fact the entire
atmosphere of the store oppressive. He takes the lemon out of
his pocket, and, making a "fantasy castle" by piling up books,
places the lemon on top of it. He then walks out of the store,
leaving the lemon there, creating a quiet yet tense feeling around
itself, absorbing into itself the inharmonious colors of the books
around it. He feels like a villain who has left a great bomb in
the bookstore and believes that within ten minutes the lemon
will explode.

"The sense of incomprehensible anxiety" from which the protagonist suffers is the result of the separation of the self from
being, which creates ontological doubt about the meaning of the
self. "The Lemon" was written soon after the Kanto earthquake,
a few years before Akutagawa committed suicide, leaving only
his sense of "vague anxiety" to explain his death.[24] The same
decade saw the collapse of the intellectualism and culturalism
of the Taisho period along with the rise of the proletarian movement on the one hand and the spread of a decadent atmosphere
and sense of desperation on the other. The source of the protagonist's "anxiety" is his decadence, yet by cultivating "pure
senses" to transcend the decadence in which he feels himself
enwrapped, he is attempting the transcendence of decadence
through decadence. The lemon is a metaphor for his pure sensibility, and what Kajii envisions is the transformation of the
world by it.

The pure senses which are cultivated also experience external
objects in the same way they do the self, breaking the barrier
between object and subject. A certain inner condition is created in
which the inner and outer reality mutually permeate each other,
the soul coming out of its confinement to live among things,
while things become animated to serve as metaphors for the
condition of the soul. Kajii's stories, presenting a "landscape
of the heart," are paintings of the sensibilities in a distilled
state, and they come quite close to being poetic prose. Kajii's

fantasy — "a certain state of the soul" — is a lyrical condition of correspondence and becomes transcendental when it reaches its extremity.

In both "Kei no shōten" (The Ascension of K, 1926) and "Yami no emaki" (The Scroll of Darkness, 1930), the narrator-protagonists envision clearly the spread of the shadow into which they will eventually be absorbed. Kajii's heroes are extremely frightened by their impending absorption into the shadow, but their spark of life flares up only when they encounter it; only then, envisioning absorption into the darkness as the beginning of a new life, can they escape from the ennui and despair of everyday life. In "The Ascension of K," K tells us that his spirit has become sharpened and pointed with the progress of his disease and that he has begun seeing "shadows" as things of substance:

K said that there is nothing more strange than the shadow.... If you gaze at it intently, there appears a creature in the shadow. It is nothing but your very self.[25]

To enter the darkness is to identify oneself with the creature in the shadow, one's doppelgänger. The narrator imagines that K, who has committed suicide, must have left his body to be united with the self in the shadow, and that he must have ascended to the moon.

The narrator-protagonist of "The Scroll of Darkness" tells us:

I have lived long at a sanatorium in the mountains. There I learned to love darkness.[26]

He then paints verbally the "landscape of darkness," which is a metaphor for "the biting loneliness and fear" of a sick man living close to death. Every night he strides with a passion into the "landscape of darkness," for in order to step into the darkness, one needs a "passion for despair." One day, a man suddenly appears before him on the mountain path and then, step by step, disappears into the darkness. He sees himself disappearing into the darkness and feels that it is he himself who is standing in the darkness with only a small, faraway light illuminating his existence.

The protagonist in "Aru kokoro no fūkei" (The Landscape of

the Heart, 1926) is obsessed with gazing. He explains:

To gaze, that is to become something. A part of my soul — or all of it — becomes identified with something.[27]

Turning into a "pure gaze," he envisions a landscape which is a metaphor for his heart in correspondence with the transcendental realm. He sees a pale light in the landscape of darkness painted by his gaze; it is an insect, his soul, emitting a phosphorescent light in the darkness.

At this point, Kajii's imagination becomes that of a visionary whose condensed and purified sensibilities transform the outer reality. His imagination projects his inner condition on the outer world, and at the moment of perfect projection, both the inner decadence, despair and anxiety and the outer drab, everyday reality are transcended.

In "Sakura no ki no shita niwa" (Under the Cherry Tree, 1929), a surrealistic fantasy, the narrator, envisioning the beautiful, ethereal cherry blossoms sucking their nourishment from the rotten corpses buried beneath the tree, perceives life and death as inseparable. He imagines a procession of crystalline liquid absorbed from the corpses by the fine roots of the tree moving slowly, "like a dream," through the capillaries of the tree to the flowers. The mysterious serenity of the cherry blossoms at their peak, like the serenity of a "rapidly turning top" or "the fantasy which is evoked by well-played music," is the result of the passion of copulation whose end is death. One day, the protagonist sees at the shore of a river the corpses of winged insects.

When I saw this, I felt my heart struck. I experienced the cruel joy of a pervert who digs up a tomb to taste a corpse. . . . I need a catastrophe. Only when balanced by one do my images become clear. Like a devil's, my soul is thirsty for melancholy. Only when the melancholy is perfected in my soul will I have peace.[28]

The vision of a union of the grotesque and the beautiful, of death and life, is clearly the product of the most decadent aesthetic sensibility, of a "diseased sensibility." The world of fantasy which is created by the protagonist's ability to "see through" the inner realm belongs to the realm of madness, the realm of abnormal sensibility; yet as in the case of the deranged imagination affected by the poisonous chemicals in "Machine," the diseased, decadent imagination aspires to transcend the initial, threatening human condition.

Yokomitsu and Kajii conceived of the fear caused their protagonists by their helplessness before impending annihilation as a universal ontological problem. "Machine" reflects a specifically capitalist exploitative condition which is governed by the law of the machine, and Kajii's "abnormal sensibilities" are specifically referred to as stemming from his disease and from the anxiety and loneliness which resulted from his sense of impending death. Their protagonists' sense of threat, inner confusion and desperate struggle to escape, however, reflect the condition of the modern Japanese of the late Taisho and early Showa periods, a time characterized by the rise of imperialism, ruthless police repression, economic depression, and the failure of anarchism and socialism.

The police repression threatened all avant-garde literary activities, not just those of the proletarian literary movement. It was a period characterized by anxiety. The writers of the period wavered between proletarian literature and decadent modernist literature, experimenting in every possible way in their search for a method and an ideology which would reflect the new human situation.

In addition to the ideological conflict between Marxism and modernism, a conflict which affected most of the writers in one way or another, the questions of form, expression and language raised vital issues for the writers of this period. Neither proletarian writers nor modernist writers could be satisfied any longer with the easy identification of the writer with the work — the I-novelists' conception that regarded literature as self-expression. Akutagawa's escape into a well-constructed world of stories had revealed only the futility of intellectual aestheticism as a response to the new human condition. Possibly as much as for any writer of the period, Yokomitsu's literary ac-

tivities reflected its conflicts and questions. After extensive experiments with language (which he called the struggle with his
native tongue), expression and form during his New Perceptionist period, he shifted toward "the pure novel" of realism with
"Machine," the first major result of his search for a new direction. Yokomitsu's ironic use of the dramatic confession creates
a dual perspective — irrational and rational or an involved inner
perspective and a detached critical perspective — leading to the
integration of the inner psychological novel with the realistic
social novel. Although Yokomitsu's theory of the pure novel
called for creating works which would present just such an integration of the psychological and the social novel, "Machine"
achieved this objective far more successfully than the works
written consciously according to the dictates of the theory, most
of which proved to be much more inclined toward the novel of
social manners.

Kajii, who admired Shiga Naoya and tried to combine modern-
istic perception with realism and plain language, was also in the
forefront of the search for a new literary method. The transcendental vision which Kajii's heightened sensibility revealed
is conveyed by plain language, and his presentation of his inner
landscape attains a simplicity and unaffectedness close to that
of Shiga Naoya's I-novels. His works can properly be called
verbal paintings. Like "Machine," Kajii's works use the
stream-of-consciousness method to delve into the psychic
realm of the protagonist. Although "Machine" is not an I-novel,
but a dramatization of an intellectual's understanding of the human condition, by incorporating the most characteristic techniques of the I-novel — first-person narration, the use of a single point of view presented by the narrator-protagonist, direct
description of the inner reality of the protagonist, and the use
of plain language and realism — the work draws the reader into
the inner world of the alienated hero, subjecting the reader to
the same feeling of sympathy for and closeness to that world as
that created by the I-novel.

Kajii's short stories, on the other hand, are written in a form
basically akin to that of the I-novels in that the author intends

to present a certain state of his own consciousness, a state
which he attains at a certain moment in his life; yet the highly
distilled (although realistic) description of that state itself becomes a metaphor, imparting a poetic character to the works.
Kajii's works are the best examples of the modern lyrical novel.
If "Machine" is a successful example of the use of psychological
realism to dramatize the understanding of social life and abstract ideas, Kajii's unique short stories are successful examples of the use of inner realism and stream of consciousness
to create a new reality which transcends both immediate inner
and outer reality. He achieves this by projecting the subconscious onto the outer reality. Thus, following the protagonist's
stream of consciousness or "gaze" reveals not only his inner
reality, but the inner nature of phenomenal reality as well. The
phantasmagoric visions created by Kajii's "diseased sensibility," by his decadent, Baudelarian sensibility, are the results
of his "gazing" at reality. His visionary imagination is attained,
therefore, through his conversion into a pure gaze. The excitement the protagonist experiences at the moment of vision stems
from a heightened sense of reality, from a renewed sense of life.

In the works of both Yokomitsu and Kajii, the basic method of
realism achieves a symbolic representation of the human condition. The modernist perception of the human soul as diseased,
as estranged from itself and existing in a threatening environment, is dramatized by inner or psychological realism. In the
context of Japanese literature, their achievement meant the
transcendence of the I-novel through the use of I-novel techniques.

When Shimamura, the hero of <u>Yukiguni</u> (Snow Country, 1937), hears that Komako, a rural geisha, writes down in her notebook the names of the characters in the novels which she reads and rough outlines of the plots, he calls it a waste of effort. Yet he soon regrets dismissing her action so readily, for he knows that her action is one of maintaining her "cleanness," that it reflects an unconscious effort to keep herself from the inevitable corruption that awaits country geishas. Komako does steadily become corrupted before the eyes of the reader, but the inevitability of her corruption is all the more tragic because of her unusual cleanness, which forces her to do useless things neatly.

It is a totally useless thing, a meaningless act which will not have any consequences, for an uneducated country geisha to keep records of the various, mostly third-rate, books which she reads at random. Yet Shimamura sees in her wasteful action the wastefulness of life itself and her unconscious defense against it. Just as to keep a diary of the insignificant life of a rural geisha is meaningless, so are his endeavors in life and his dilettante art criticism.

Shimamura is a critic of the Western ballet, an art form which he has never seen and possibly will never see. Yet he has chosen this subject precisely because it is unrelated to his life, so that he can escape from the sense of wastefulness of his endeavors in life and art. His very attempt to escape into a fantasy world of art, however, seems to him a wasteful effort

to avoid a confrontation with life, an effort whose only consequence will be to reveal more strongly man's attachment to life.

In fact, the sense of waste occupies the central position in his
view of life and art and is the main theme of the novel as well.
Shimamura, like Komako, is nothing but a powerless being before the inevitable corruption — the all-consuming power of
death — which negates life completely. The recognition of this
force of annihilation renders Shimamura incapable of acting and
living vigorously with hope. Life itself is an extraordinary
waste, and the effort to find rational meaning in it is as fruitless
as Komako's keeping her diary. Yet both Shimamura and Komako keep their bodies tight trying not to lose their balance,
not to let themselves be swept away by the tide of corruption.
Her instinctive tidiness and Shimamura's cynicism and dilettantism are unconsciously and consciously adopted attitudes,
masks to cope with the wasteful reality of life and to fortify
themselves from the force of self-annihilation.[1]

Shimamura is a traveler, a "homeless" man, who goes from
place to place without specific purpose, climbing mountains
precisely because it is purposeless.

Shimamura had come down from these mountains, as the new green was making
its way through the last of the snow, to meet Komako for the first time; and now,
in the autumn climbing season, he found himself drawn again to the mountains he
had left his tracks in. Though he was an idler who might as well spend his time
in the mountains as anywhere, he looked upon mountain climbing as almost a
model of wasted effort. For that very reason it pulled at him with the attraction
of the unreal.[2]

He is also a typical sukimono, a man of the senses. Like the
hero of the Ise monogatari (Tales of Ise) and the shining
Prince Genji, he is a sensitive appreciator of beauty and a
gentle lover, detached, yet susceptible to sensuous pleasure.
He expects nothing from his love affairs except the joy they
bring and promises nothing through his love; yet his tenderness stems from his sympathy for fellow beings doomed
to sink into nothingness. Thus he is a dilettante artist and
a self-imposed outsider in the traditional manner of the
Japanese sukimono.

Unlike Basho and Nichiren, Shimamura is not a stoic activist-
outsider, not an artist or religious mystic with a firm sense of
purpose and an ideology to separate him from the primary life
of the senses and to save him from a sense of waste;[3] nor is
Shimamura a self-destructive sufferer-outsider like Dazai
Osamu or Hagiwara Sakutaro, each of whom tried to transcend the emptiness and wastefulness of life and art by
pushing the sense of his own powerlessness to its extremity.
While Kawabata's later hero, old Eguchi, comes close to the
latter type, Shimamura is a lukewarm lover, an uncommitted
artist, a nonideological philosopher of life and a morally
ambiguous social outsider; he is more properly a successor to
Genji and such artist-monks of medieval Japan as Kamo no
Chōmei and Yoshida Kenko. Although he finds life too wasteful
and tiring to attempt to rationalize or moralize it, he has not
lost his capacity to appreciate life sensuously. Although he
lives without hope, he continues to wander, unconsciously seeking an essential life-giving force to restore his sense of life.
A yearning for life undeniably lies behind his consciously adopted
outsider-dilettante posture. In actuality, Shimamura is torn between his sense of the waste of life and his unceasing longing
for a sense of life. Komako evokes his lurking desire for life.
    Although Shimamura feels akin to Komako in her detached
resignation from life, he sees in her unstained cleanness the
undomesticated vitality innate in the original life-force. He
sees her cleanness as indistinguishable from the clear cool air
and the mountain green of the snow country. During his visit
there, Shimamura loses his physical desire for a woman when
he sees an unclean geisha sitting against the mountain green.
After dismissing her he climbs the mountain, where he meets
Komako. Entering an old Shinto shrine in a dense cedar forest
with him, she seats herself on a primeval, moss-covered rock.
Her neck reflects the dark green of the cedar forest, and Shimamura, sensing the harmony of Komako's cleanness and nature's sacredness in the primitive silence of the mountain, feels
his sexual desire for a woman's body purified completely.

Later, the sound of Komako's samisen, vibrating in the mountain air as if corresponding to cosmic music and bringing out the loneliness and vitality of nature, fills Shimamura with a sense of awe.

A chill swept over Shimamura. The gooseflesh seemed to rise even to his cheeks. The first notes opened a transparent emptiness deep in his entrails, and in the emptiness the sound of the samisen reverberated. . . . Taken with a feeling almost of reverence, washed by waves of remorse, defenseless, quite deprived of strength — there was nothing for him to do but give himself up to the current, to the pleasure of being swept off wherever Komako would take him.

Komako looked up at the clear sky over the snow. "The tone is different on a day like this." . . . The notes went out crystalline into the clean winter morning, to sound on the far, snowy peaks."[4]

Komako is a curious mixture of vitality and the sadness of life, evoking simultaneously Shimamura's aspiration for the restoration of a sense of life and for the purification of his desire for life. In fact, Komako and the purity of the snow country are always inseparable.

When Komako removes her geisha makeup in front of the mirror in Shimamura's room, her clean skin is revealed and merges into the mountains and the whiteness of the snow in the background, while her bright red cheeks shine in the center. In the tableau created by the mirror, the reality fades away gradually, and the symbolic essence of Komako's cleanness and nature fuse into one another to create Shimamura's dreamworld. The snow shines with fluorescent whiteness in the depths of the mirror; yet Shimamura sometimes feels that the black mountain also shines this way on starry nights.

Black though the mountains were, they seemed at that moment brilliant with the color of the snow. They seemed to him somehow transparent, somehow lonely.[5]

Komako is not only harmonious with nature's unstained cleanness, but also with its cosmic loneliness and darkness.

Komako's unspoiled freshness and cleanness evoke Shimamura's longing for something which does not exist in his life but which exists in his memory, in his dream. In many of Kawabata's novels, this undefined object of yearning takes the slightly clearer form, although still symbolic, of a lost first love, usually an older woman. Like all of Kawabata's "clean" women, Komako inspires the hero's hidden longing for some original state of innocence, a state which lives vaguely in his memory as one of unity, happiness and unstained beauty. Shimamura's longing for a clean woman expresses his longing for the archetypal woman, Mother, as a life-giving force.[6]   For Shimamura, woman's original beauty and purity are symbols of the original condition of life, of the home from which he is now alienated. Kawabata's love story, therefore, despite its realistic presentation, recounts the symbolic journey of his hero in search of the essence of life and nature. In this sense, Shimamura is not an aimless wanderer, but a romantic dreamer and quester who wanders in search of the lost original unity. The snow country is a symbol of this original unity, and Komako is a temptress who tempts Shimamura, despite his pretended resignation, to undertake the journey to the snow country. The opening scene vividly expresses this theme of inner journey:

The train came out of the long tunnel into the snow country. The earth lay white under the night sky.[7]

When Shimamura passes through the dark tunnel and enters the world of whiteness, he enters a symbolic world dimensionally different from the world of daily life. It is a world of dream, one of the whiteness of night, and a cold world where nature imposes itself in strange silence. The essence of this world and of his entry into it are expressed in his discovery of Yōko's beauty in the unreal world he glimpses through the window glass.

In the depths of the mirror, the evening landscape moved by, the mirror and the reflected figures like motion pictures superimposed one on the other. The figures and the background were unrelated, and yet the figures, transparent and intangible, and the background, dim in the gathering darkness, melted together into a sort of symbolic world not of this world.

It was then that a light shone in the face.... It was a distant, cold light. As it sent its small ray through the pupil of the girl's eye, as the eye and the light were superimposed one on the other, the eye became a weirdly beautiful bit of phosphorescence on the sea of evening mountains. [8]

Yōko's beauty appears unreal and ethereal in the twilight, where everything is blurred and melts into the transparent beauty of a symbolic and transcendental world. Her beauty brings out the silence of nature in the twilight, and her face exists in the center of the silence, reflecting the wildfire of nature. The wildfire in Yōko's eye glows within the darkness and silence of the winter snow country, her eyes passionately longing for them. The world of beauty and reverie in which woman's beauty and nature's beauty are fused into one another, the symbolic world glimpsed through the "other-worldly power of his mirror" of the train window, is the transcendental world into which Komako leads Shimamura.

The impression [of the light off in the mountains that had passed across the girl's face] came back to Shimamura, and with it the memory of the mirror filled with snow, and Komako's red cheeks floating in the middle of it.... Always ready to give himself up to reverie, he could not believe that the mirror floating over the evening scenery and the other snowy mirror were really works of man. They were part of nature, and part of some distant world. [9]

The strange flame in Yōko's eye and Komako's burning red cheeks appear again at the end of the novel as the glow of the Milky Way, as a crystallized symbol of man's cold passion and longing for eternity and the essence of life. The winter night, lit by the glow of Yōko's eyes, reveals the darkness and coldness of the ultimate world of nothingness to which man will eventually return. The snow country then, with its coldness and whiteness, is also the transcendental world of death. The snow country is where Komako's "fiancé," traveling on the same train as Shimamura, comes to die.

The opening scene of the novel, in which the two enter the snow country together, metaphorically reveals that Shimamura's inner journey to the world of dream, of original unity, is an inner journey to the world of death. This world is, however, glimpsed only momentarily through the glass, a mirror that reflects the observer's inner world. The world of the snow country into which Shimamura journeys is a world of dream, a world where reality and unreality, the conscious and the subconscious, life and death, are fused into a dim, phosphorescent, symbolic other-world. The fusion of reality and dream, of phenomenal nature and symbolic nature, are recurrent themes in Kawabata's novels.

Komako, through her love for Shimamura, comes to experience the terror of hoping, of attachment to life, and becomes aware of the possibility of her mental corruption. She emerges as the essence of passion for life. Yet at the end of the novel, Komako regains her original independence and will to continue to live neatly and with unsentimental detachment. She is ready to carry the agonizing burden of a hopeless existence by becoming the protector of Yōko's purity. Yōko, as Shimamura has seen, is the essence of Komako herself. Crystallized forever at the end of the novel as the purity of insanity, Yōko is a more symbolic and abstract presentation of Komako's purity, a purity which evokes man's longing for the original essence of life.

Although Shimamura appears to be a cynical realist and dilettante who is incapable of love, his cynicism and dilettantism are a mask, a consciously adopted attitude which enables him to abandon the everyday world of conventional life and to retain the possibility of his inner journey to the essence of the universe. Like Kawabata's old men, young Shimamura lives constantly near the abyss of nothingness, desperately yearning for a sense of life.[10] Shimamura's dilettantism is a defense against the terror of nothingness, the fear of confrontation with the abyss of life. Although he sees the nothingness in life and the nothingness which awaits him in death, he is not a nihilist who denies life and the dreamworld completely. Rather, he is an ambivalent artist-hermit who, knowing the futility of resisting the transience of life, tries to attain the real feeling of life itself. Simultaneously, he aspires to eternal simplicity, a state

of vitality and innocence, one which will negate the agony of
dark attachment to life. He recognizes the absolute distance between this state, absent in life, and his actual life.

There are moments in the novel, however, when Shimamura
does attain a sensory experience of the unity between the sense
of life and the eternal essence (beauty) of the universe. Climbing a mountain one day, "seduced" by the fresh smell of leaves,
he sees two butterflies flutter away and become gradually absorbed into the transparent nature, their yellow turning to white.
Shimamura feels strongly the existence of a large bosom of nature which both gives him a vivid pleasure in life and accepts
and absorbs him as it did the butterflies. Likewise Komako's
beauty and purity in the colorless color of nature evoke this
sense of harmony as well as the sense of life. The world of the
translucent silence of the mountain bosom is at once the mother's bosom and a world of cosmic nothingness: the world of
death and nature become one as the home to which he will ultimately return.

Indeed, the snow country constantly reminds him of death.
The snow country is cold and its earth frozen. Komako's hair
is cold and her skin impresses Shimamura as unusually cold.
When Shimamura watches the steady corruption of Komako as
her cool determination to live neatly begins to fade, he reflects
upon his fantasy world of criticism of the Western ballet and
reexamines cynically his plan to translate and publish some
critical works. At that time, winter is approaching in the snow
country, and as each day grows colder, he watches the insects
in their death agony.

It was a quiet death that came with the change of season. Looking closely, however, Shimamura could see that the legs and feelers were trembling in the struggle to live. For such a tiny death, the empty eight-mat room seemed enormous.[11]

Shimamura sees himself, Komako and all living creatures in
this dying insect. Everything in nature lives and dies. The
butterflies flutter away into the whiteness of nature, tiny lives
absorbed harmoniously into a vast space. Yet the return to nature is also the agonizing lonely death of the insect in a vast,

hostile space. Shimamura feels both aspects of the return: the bosom of nature, the snow country, is cold nothingness as well as the mother's bosom. Yet it is in either case the setting for man's homecoming.

Komako's cold hair and body contain her warm, burning blood, and her transparent, cold white skin contains her peony-red cheeks. The mountains are green under the darkness and whiteness of the snow. They contain life and man's passion for life. While the snow country is a world of silence, of original nothingness, it is also the transcendental dream-world that contains the original innocence of life. In the last scene, the cold glow of the Milky Way, at once crystal clear and phosphorescent in the darkness, becomes the all-inclusive symbol of Shimamura's yearning for unity, of his passion for life and of his loneliness and desperation. The darkness of the sky is the death to which his cold passion for life will lead. In the darkness of the universe, he experiences the eternal loneliness of life.

In the crystalline glow of the Milky Way in the dark sky, in nature's wild flame of twilight fire reflected in Yōko's eyes, and in Komako's red cheeks burning with passion for life in the coldness and whiteness of the snow, Shimamura sees his own passion and yearning for life and his own loneliness identified with the cosmic loneliness of the silent, primordial world of nothingness. The vastness and the brightness of the Milky Way seem to absorb the entire earth and Shimamura himself. The fire on the earth of the snow country corresponds to the radiance of the dark sky. The earth and the sky, man and nature, merge in their darkness and brightness into one vast cosmos. The world of primordial unity is the terrifyingly cold yet voluptuously tempting and ecstatic world of death. At its center, Komako stands with the sensuous yet symbolic serenity of a Noh mask.

The Milky Way came down just over there, to wrap the night earth in its naked embrace. There was a terrible voluptuousness about it. Shimamura fancied that his own small shadow was being cast up against it from the earth.

The light was dimmer even than on the night of the new moon, and yet the Milky Way was brighter than the brightest full moon. In the faint light that left no shadows on the earth, Komako's face floated up like an old mask. It was strange that even in the mask there should be the scent of the woman.

And the Milky Way, like a great aurora, flowed through his body to stand at the edges of the earth. There was a quiet, chilly loneliness in it, and a sort of voluptuous astonishment.[12]

While beauty is the central preoccupation and sole medium in Shimamura's search for spiritual unity, he is not himself a creator of eternal beauty, nor does he negate his life in search of it; art is not for him a substitute for life. Rather, for Shimamura, art is an expression of man's consciousness of his own alienation and of man's aspiration for unity. Art itself embodies man's ambivalent desire for life and its transcendence, the dichotomy between life and eternity.

Behind Shimamura's attachment to beauty lies his essential ambivalence between attachment to life and detachment from it. Shimamura is attracted to Komako's corruptible purity, just as Genji was attracted to Yugao because in her sad and innocent beauty Genji found the sadness of the transience of life itself.[13] Genji's feeling of aware, the feeling stemming from man's awareness of the disparity between the reality of life and its ideal vision, expresses the ambivalence of man's desire for and detachment from life. For attachment to beauty evokes yearning, both for life and for what is absent in life as well. While beauty, therefore, launches Shimamura on his symbolic journey in search of the essence of unity, the transcendence of life, it is at the same time beauty that brings him back incessantly to life. Beauty is the embodiment both of man's desire for life and of his aspiration to transcend life. Like Genji and Kamo no Chōmei, Shimamura goes back and forth between attachment to life and detachment from life, between the world of the senses and the world of purity and silence. This conflict between the desire for life and its transcendence into the world of art and death appears throughout the works of Kawabata and forms the central theme of his Gothic novel, Sembazuru (Thousand Cranes, 1951).

Kikuji, the hero of <u>Thousand Cranes</u>, is, like Shimamura, an obscure character, an indecisive, cynical young man. Although he is disgusted with his late, wealthy father who loved women and art, he is perceptive enough to see the despair, born of attachment to life, behind his father's endless involvement in sexual affairs. Kikuji knows well that this same desperation can make women demoniac, as is the case with Chikako, one of his father's mistresses, and that it is what drove his father to the serene world of tea and the eternal beauty of tea utensils. Kikuji's destiny is to have inherited this desperation of his father, together with his house and his mistresses.

The curse of the house left for Kikuji after his father's death symbolizes his fate. Kikuji's house retains his father's tireless desire for life and his lustful obsession with sexual pleasure, as well as his despairing longing for spiritual consolation and the purgation of his desire in eternal beauty. It retains as well his mother's quiet resentment, resignation and despair, all reflecting her waning life-energy, and Chikako's demoniac, vengeful jealousy, reflecting her crude attachment to life. In other words, the house contains hatred, unsublimated frustration (desire and jealousy) and the unfulfilled longing for spiritual salvation. The house contains the curse of human life. The birthmark of Chikako which Kikuji glimpsed in his infancy is at once a symbol of the ugliness of the body and of human desire, of demoniac frustration and of man's obsession with life. The ugly mark on Chikako's breast symbolizes her lack of essential femininity, her lack of sexuality as well as of maternal tenderness. Kikuji is a child symbolically fed by the breast with the ugly mark. Chikako's lack of sexual fulfillment and loss of sensuality convert her into a maniacal spirit of revenge obsessed with power, and thus she becomes a poison which drains man's erotic life-force and spontaneous desire for life.[14] Yet the mark's ugliness is that of man's obsessive love of life itself.

After his father's death, Kikuji gradually comes to realize that he is the legitimate heir of the curse of the house. Chikako starts controlling him, and through her he is drawn into the world of tea, away from which he had consciously kept himself. At Chikako's tea ceremony he meets Mrs. Ota, one of his father's former mistresses, and he starts having an affair with her. Before long he becomes almost identical to his father — Mrs. Ota often mistakes him for his father — and he is drawn into the ambivalence which lies between the sensuous world of women and the eternal serenity of tea.

Although Chikako's greedy attachment to life and the purifying serenity of tea are contradictory to each other, Chikako and tea are inseparable. Because Chikako's birthmark makes those who perceive it aware of the grotesqueness of life, they are drawn to the world of tea. At the tea ceremony, Kikuji is introduced to a young girl named Inamura, whom he is to consider as his potential bride. Her unstained beauty, innocence and cleanness evoke his longing for something which is lacking in his life; he is reminded of his alienation from feminine tenderness. She makes him aware of his present corruption, the ugliness of Chikako and the frustration of his father.

And yet he felt that he was wrapped in a dark, dirty, suffocating curtain.... The dirtiness was not only in Chikako, who had introduced them [Kikuji and the Inamura girl]. It was in Kikuji too.[15]

The Inamura girl is, like Yōko, the ultimate of purity, and Kikuji is separated from her by an absolute distance.

From the time of Chikako's tea ceremony, Kikuji is no longer a cynical observer, but is trapped in the duality of his aspiration. Through Mrs. Ota, he comes to know the deeply satisfying tenderness of a woman, that of the eternal Mother. Yet her femininity has been distorted by the poison of Kikuji's father and Chikako; her feeling of guilt drains her vital life-energy, making her a melancholic woman. She is a dream-mother who, tired in this world, wanders like a ghost. Like Yugao in The Tale of Genji, Mrs. Ota's vitality is drained by the obsessive desire for life, jealousy and vengeful spirit of others; Mrs. Ota fades away as the morning glory fades in the daytime.

Chikako, Mrs. Ota and tea all symbolize the world of Kikuji's father. His involvement in tea and tea utensils as artwork was antithetical to his attachment to life.

"Beautiful," said Kikuji, as if to himself. "It wasn't Father's nature to play with tea bowls, and yet he did, and maybe they deadened his sense of guilt."[16]

The more Kikuji himself is drawn into the swamp of human desire, the more urgently he longs for eternal beauty and spiritual serenity to purify his desire. The Inamura girl and her handkerchief motif of a thousand cranes become a symbol of his dreamworld of innocence and purity where the power of the grotesque birthmark cannot reach. Yet it is the grotesque birthmark itself that evokes man's aspiration for the cleanness of the Inamura girl. It is Chikako who brings Kikuji to Inamura.

"If we are to be friends, I can't help thinking we would have done better to have someone besides Kurimoto [Chikako] introduce us. I should apologize to you."

She looked at him suspiciously. "Why? If it hadn't been for Miss Kurimoto, who could have introduced us?"

It was a simple protest, and yet very much to the point. If it had not been for Chikako, the two would not have met in this world.[17]

The tea ceremony where the two meet through Chikako embodies this duality of man's consciousness. It inspires man's aspiration for purity and beauty, the world symbolized by the Inamura girl, but at the same time it makes man conscious of the existence of the ugly birthmark of life. The Inamura girl and Chikako are both the essence of tea.

Even the seemingly timeless tea utensils have stains of human desire. Beneath man's aspiration for eternal beauty, there is always the curse of desire, and it leaves a stain on the artwork man creates. Mrs. Ota's Shino cup, whose beauty is contained in its eternal serenity and which seems to transcend any owner's life, is contaminated by man's grotesque desire. Both Mrs. Ota and Fumiko believe that the brownish stain on it is Mrs. Ota's lipstick stain.

The rim might have been stained by tea, and it might have been stained by lips.

The color of faded lipstick, the color of a wilted red rose, the color of old, dry blood — Kikuji began to feel queasy.

A nauseating sense of uncleanness and an overpowering fascination came simultaneously.[18]

Kikuji too, although he is consoled by the cup's serene beauty, is reminded vividly of Mrs. Ota's sensuous body whenever he sees it. When he touches it, he becomes subject to the illusion that the Shino piece is Mrs. Ota and is terrified and guilt-stricken by the persistence of his sexual attachment to her. He thinks of Mrs. Ota as a perfect work of art and the Shino cup as a perfect woman.

This duality of the beauty of art and the duality of man's aspiration for the beauty of art are central to the search of Kawabata's dilettante heroes. They are dilettantes because art exists for them between man's life and his dream of transcending life, to neither of which they are thoroughly committed. These dualities also appear in Maihime (The Dancer, 1951). Yagi, the main character of the novel, explains that the darkness of the Fujiwara period is reflected in the strange sensuousness of the Fujiwara Buddhas. Although Buddhas represent man's desire for spiritual salvation, for eternity, the statues of Buddha made during the Fujiwara period are, according to Yagi, also symbols of the mysterious, sensuous beauty of woman. Yagi says that the essence of the Fujiwara religion was perhaps the worship of woman. The sensuous and mysteriously tempting Fujiwara Buddhas reflect both the dark but gorgeous erotic life of the Fujiwara men and their aspiration for emancipation from desire.

The same duality appears in the mask of Jido, the Noh mask in Yama no oto (The Sound of the Mountain, 1954). The mask had been treasured by an old man who died a grotesque death during his sexual orgy with a geisha. Although the mask crystallizes the purity of a boy before his sexual maturity, it is, like the Shino cup, strangely sensuous. Shingo, the hero of the novel, is almost tempted to kiss the mask. The mask reflects Shingo's aspiration for his ebbing life-force, as well as his aspiration for the prefall condition, the original maternal beauty which is sexual and sexless simultaneously. Kawabata seems to say that art exists in this interval, between life and eternity, between man's erotic desire for life and his longing for eternal beauty. As will be seen below, these contradictory desires are both related to death; Kawabata's heroes come to realize that their ultimate struggle is with death, the negation of life and the condition for return to the original unity.

In Thousand Cranes, Kikuji, annoyed by his entanglement in the swamp of desire and determined to free himself from his father's curse, decides to give up tea and to sell his house. Fumiko, moved by similar feelings, sells her mother's house and breaks the Shino cup with her mother's lipstick stain. Fumiko's escape from the curse of human desire, however, takes the form of complete withdrawal from life, perhaps into death. By the time Kikuji realizes that he can be released from his darkness by Fumiko's cleanness, Fumiko has already become unreachable, crystallized as the purity of death. At the end of the novel, Kikuji finds himself left with Chikako.

In The Dancer, Namiko, Yagi and their daughter Shinako suffer from the conflict between life and art, between the desire for life and the transcendence of desire achieved through art. Yagi, a demon of observation, is keenly aware that aspiration for art is nothing but man's sentimentalism, his longing for a dreamworld, and prefers to dwell in a world devoid of illusions and false hopes, the world of the devil.

Namiko, although she is a naturally sensuous woman, is trapped in the ambivalence of her desire for life and art. Terrified by the demoniacal way Yagi manipulates her, Namiko finds her spontaneous erotic force waning. She abandons her professional aspiration as an artist and is reduced to teaching ballet to children for tuition. The money she earns goes to Yagi; Yagi lives, materially as well as psychically, off Namiko's life-energy. Life and art are interdependent — with the waning of life-energy, artistic intuition also fades away. Yagi is Chi-

kako in that his basic frustration in life, his lack of erotic, in-
stinctual gratification, has turned him into a demon of revenge
and destruction. Yet Yagi is also, like Shimamura, affected by
the darkness of life, the force of nothingness that has drained
his youthful appreciation of sensuous gratification.

Both Chikako and Yagi can destroy the spontaneous life-energy
of others, but because they depend on the innocent for their live-
lihood, they themselves will be destroyed as well. They cannot
convert nothingness into a full meaning in itself by their commitment to evil. Aware of their own powerlessness and secret
longing for spiritual consolation, they suffer from eternal loneliness. Yagi quotes the medieval monk Ikkyu's statement that
to enter Hades is more difficult than to enter the world of Buddha. Even evil cannot restore the sense of life, and Yagi himself fails in his attempts at transcendence through evil.

In The Sound of the Mountain, Shingo cannot accept with detached resignation the fact that he is an old man who is in the
process of losing his sexual power and is steadily approaching
death. He despairs over his lost masculinity, which is the symbol of the life-force, but at the same time, he feels only disgust
over his friends' grotesque obsession with youth, sex and life.
The more closely he approaches the state of sexlessness, the
more strongly he becomes aware of his aspiration for a pure,
tender, beautiful woman, such a woman as he once loved but was
not granted. Such a woman appears repeatedly in his dreams,
an object both of longing and of sexual desire. The dream
woman symbolizes his sexual gratification as well as the purification of desire, ideal love and supernal beauty.

The object of Shingo's aspiration is his wife's elder sister,
long dead, for whom he had yearned as a young boy. The woman
is clearly a mother-figure, but his frustrated longing for her is
often confused with his feeling for his daughter-in-law, Kikuko,
who still retains the cleanness and purity of a physically imma-
ture, not yet sexually ripened woman. In one of his erotic
dreams, his wife's dead sister and Kikuko become fused as
the sensuous dream woman for whom Shingo has been longing. Here again, longing for maternal essence and longing

for the purity of virginity are fused.

Shūichi, Shingo's son, too deeply wounded by life to be saved by Kikuko's purity, becomes involved in a sadomasochistic affair with a war widow. Shingo watches Shūichi's spiritual paralysis and increasing corruption with terror and disgust. His son has lost hope for life and is spiritually desolate, yet Shingo knows that his son's desperation is ultimately the same as his own. Shingo is unable to do anything for his son or to take care of Kikuko's unhappiness. He is equally powerless to prevent the misery and corruption of his daughter, Fusako, or the destruction of his son-in-law. His inaction makes him an irresponsible father, one who is unable to take care of the problems in his children's lives. His indecisiveness stems from his sense of man's powerlessness, his basic feeling that man is essentially helpless against others' desperation and before the force of annihilation.

He cannot, however, give himself up to his desperation, cannot be what Shūichi calls a free man; nor can he be a demoniac pursuer of the sense of life in his remaining years. Shūichi is irritated by his father's sentimental longing for harmony, innocence and purity of spirit. At the same time, he hates the family system, perceiving the family as a decaying social and ideological unit that prevents man from openly confronting the human condition. He becomes deliberately destructive, even to the extent of calling Kikuko a free agent, yet in the depths of his mind, he keeps longing for Kikuko and is supported by her unstained life-force.

Although Shingo is appalled by the spiritual paralysis of his daughter and son, by their grotesque attachment to life, he knows that they are struggling against the darkness of life itself and their own sense of the terror of destruction. The basic frustration in life which underlies their grotesque cruelty and destructiveness makes Shingo pity them, yet his pity is self-pity as well. The terror he perceives in their corruption and desperate attachment to life is the same terror Shingo perceives in his friends' grotesque obsession with life and sexuality, and it is the very terror he constantly feels in himself.

A screeching of insects came from the garden. There were locusts on the trunk of the cherry tree to the left. He had not known that locusts could make such a rasping sound; but locusts indeed they were.

He wondered if locusts might sometimes be troubled with nightmares.

A locust flew in and lit on the skirt of the mosquito net. It made no sound as he picked it up.

"A mute." It would not be one of the locusts he had heard at the tree.

Gripping the shutter, he looked toward the tree. He could not tell whether the locust had lodged there or flown on. There was a vast depth to the moonlit night, stretching far on either side.[19]

The grotesque screech of the locusts and the ominous silence of the one he picks up express Shingo's state of consciousness exactly.

Shingo gradually comes to realize that his aspiration for primal beauty and primordial sexual unity is an aspiration for ultimate unity with nature — that it is an aspiration for death. Nature and the seasons supply the essential images and structural unity of the novel. Shingo's sense of his old age and approaching death is felt within the seasonal changes. The novel starts at the end of summer, when signs of the coming autumn are already apparent. A big sunflower reminds Shingo of the masculinity which he is about to lose. Unlike the seasons with their cyclical return, man is subject to the passage of time. Shingo feels the approaching end of his life as a man in his tragicomical struggle against it. The reader is reminded of Shimamura, who watches the silent death agonies of the insect at the end of the summer season. The novel begins with Shingo's occasional loss of memory, a loss caused by a disease from which he had suffered earlier, and it is filled with Shingo's obsession with death and dream. The loss of memory is a frightening reminder of his approaching death, but it is at the same time a state of delirious forgetfulness, a passage to his dreamworld. In his dreams, a world of oblivion, he experiences curious sexual satisfaction, recalling vividly his archetypal woman of love and beauty. The

dreamworld is one of fused consciousness, a state of consciousness that is vague — infantile or senile — yet sensory.

Shingo's nostalgia for his lost sexuality and his desire for life
evoke the terror of death; yet the sense of death leads him to a
delirious world of memory, giving him the feeling almost of returning to his home and forgotten childhood experiences. The
soundless sound coming from the mountain, from the mysterious
depths of nature, is also coming from the internal realm of oblivion buried deep in his subconscious. It reveals the terrifying
void that awaits him; but at the same time, nature's silent
depths, from which the sound comes, link the primordial darkness with the depths of his own subconscious, the original home
from which he had long been separated.

Then he heard the sound of the mountain.

It was like wind, far away, but with a depth like a rumbling of the earth. Thinking that it might be in himself, a ringing in his ears, Shingo shook his head.

The sound stopped, and he was suddenly afraid. A chill passed over him, as if
he had been notified that death was approaching.

As he closed the shutter, a strange memory came to him.[20]

Thus he attains a moment of epiphany, an experience of the unity
of life and death, of the terror and ecstasy of death. Death,
which seemed to him a horrible void, an antagonistic negation
of life, is converted into the original core of existence, the primordial nothingness from which he was born and to which he
will return. Shingo also perceives this all-inclusive nothingness in the bell of the temple. The novel ends with Shingo's
suggestion to his family that they all return to his homeland in
the country to see the autumn leaves. In fact, the homecoming
is the thematic scheme of the novel, ironic as well as symbolic.[21]

Kikuko's purity and innocent beauty, like the eternal virginity
of the mask of Jido with its sensuous but sexless beauty, evoke
Shingo's aspiration to be absorbed into nature, to return to the
original nothingness. Akin to Komako and the Inamura girl, Kikuko is the Mother and the virgin. Shingo's aspiration for ma-

ternal femininity, sexual as well as sexless, felt as his erotic
desire for life and desire for innocence, is unified with his
desire for the ecstasy of self-annihilation. Man's erotic
force unites life and death. This theme, at the heart of The
Sound of the Mountain, is developed even more fully in the
experiences of old Eguchi in Nemureru bijyo (The House of
the Sleeping Beauties, 1960).

The obsessive attachment to life of Kawabata's characters and
their paradoxical disgust with this obsession has been one of the
crucial themes of Japanese literature.[22] In The Tale of Genji,
Genji, Fujitsubo, Kaoru and Ukifune, all of them floating between
their attachment to life and sexual fulfillment on the one hand
and the attraction of death and spiritual serenity on the other,
sink gradually into a state of desperation. The worldly and successful Genji and Fujitsubo constantly aspire for the serenity of
the eternal world of death and in turn suffer from a lack of true
erotic fulfillment. Kaoru, who is introspective and religious,
constantly thinking of abandoning the world of the senses, is
drawn into the dark agony of sexual longing for Ukifune, while
the naturally sensuous Ukifune abandons her life for death and
the spiritual other world. The eroticism of Genji is gorgeous
but dark. Yugao, who symbolizes the death-aspiration in Genji,
is a melancholic woman without sexual vitality, while Kokiden
and Lady Rokujyo, aggressive, frustrated devils, represent the
obsessive spirit for life. Rokujyo's vengeful spirit and Kokiden's desire for power are the prototype of Chikako's birthmark.

If these obsessed spirits of life supply the basis of the action
(they are the only doers in The Tale of Genji), the heroes, who
are torn between their contradictory desires for life and death,
are tragically deprived of action. Even Murasaki, who arrives
at a higher realization of this duality of human desire, can only
endure. In the end she too becomes the victim of the vampiric
spirit of sexual frustration.

Kawabata's "dilettante" characters are also unable to act, to
participate in life with enthusiasm, yet they are constantly
drawn to life through their erotic force. Although they despair

over man's essential powerlessness before the force of annihilation — all the more because of their awareness of it — they continue to aspire for the essential life-force which combines beauty and erotic creativity. Life in the world is sterile, yet death does not promise them anything. Kawabata's characters, trapped in this desolate space between life and death, set out on a journey in search of their "home."

Their attitude is basically akin to that of the wandering artist-priests of the medieval age, men such as Kamo no Chōmei and Yoshida Kenko. They were hermit-monks as well as dilettante artists. Chōmei, the author of Hōjyōki (An Account of My Hut, 1212), was a sukimono, a dilettante artist who, seeing nothingness in everything but only ominous silence in death, tried to make his perception and sensibility of the nothingness of life the source of his sense of life. Kenko, the author of Tsurezure-gusa (Essays in Idleness, 1331), who considered art as susabi, an idle divertissement, a temporary escape from the desolation of life, was also a dilettante artist-monk. While Chōmei clung to the end to his lyrical subjectivity, Kenko was aware of the fact that his attachment to his sense of aware, his lyrical lamentation over the evanescence of life, itself created an ugly obsession with life. Kenko, whose sentences seem short and fragmentary compared to the eloquent lyricism of Chōmei, finally had to sink into silence itself.[23] It is only in Zeami's yugen, which places the source of spiritual and aesthetic revelation in the "ma" interval of non-action and silence, that this terrifying void is filled with meaning, is converted into a spiritual and aesthetic essence. While Zeami's "ma" is attained through a stoic commitment to art, Kawabata's idea of art as essentially an expression of the artist's dual consciousness of sensuous attachment to life and spiritual longing for eternal nothingness is close to Chōmei's.[24]

The dual use of silence in traditional Japanese aesthetics as an ominous negation of life and as a mysterious core of meaning also appears in The House of the Sleeping Beauties. This novel explores the world of decadence by presenting the drama of a man who transgresses into the world of taboos in his search

for a sense of life.[25] Old Eguchi, the hero of the novel, is a
"grotesque" hero who dares to restore his waning life-energy
and to attain, if momentarily, a true sense of life. Consequently,
he ventures into the world of decadence, into the realm of eros
and death. Eguchi visits a strange house of prostitution near the
sea to make love symbolically to sleeping beauties. He finds
lying down next to sleeping virgin girls like sleeping with dolls.
They are like dead bodies, but are curiously the essence of life
as well. Eguchi feels that sleep is, paradoxically, life itself.
Furthermore, he thinks that sleeping with the sleeping beauties
is like sleeping with a secret Buddha. The girls are ominously
silent, devoid of human feeling and traces of life, but mysteriously suggest a secret knowledge which he faintly feels he had
in the past. Through the girls, Eguchi is led into the world of
memory and oblivion buried deep in his subconscious, there to
regain the secret truth of life; yet this world of oblivion and
memory, the world of dream, is also the world of death. Eguchi comes to the verge of death through being with the girls and
in fact the novel ends with a girl's actual death, probably caused
by Eguchi himself.

Cut off from the outside world, the house is a suitable entry-
way to man's inner world; it is buried in the darkness of the
outer world, yet inside, one always hears the sound of the sea.
The dark, closed, "secret" room buried in the universal darkness of the outer world is a place for experiencing directly the
essence of life itself, the essence of eros. The house suggests
man's subconscious existing in the midst of primordial nothingness, of the primordial sea, the source of life-giving force and
of death.

Eguchi is always attracted by small, light-colored nipples,
while dark, wide nipples appall him. Yet he is sexually aroused
by dark-skinned, dark-nippled girls and is almost driven to take
the virginity of one forcibly and even to strangle her. Dark nipples, symbolically akin to the birthmark on Chikako's breast,
represent the agony of erotic desire and ugly attachment to life,
and they arouse his desire. Yet this desire for life leads him
to a desire for death, either of the girl or of himself, for erotic

fulfillment. Light-colored girls, on the other hand, while shining dazzlingly white, lack sexual vitality and are isolated from full participation in the creative and destructive force of eros, from life itself.

Ultimately, however, Eguchi comes to realize that light-skinned girls and dark-skinned girls are inseparable, just as life and death are inseparable. Not only does he dream of a deformed baby born from his daughter, but the breasts of his mother by which he was fed are associated with blood. In one of his dreams, he recalls his mother, of whom he thinks as his first woman. During his first night at the house, Eguchi smells the milk-smell of a nursing baby coming from the body of a young, light-skinned girl. His aspiration for the light-skinned girl, the innocence of life, is revealed as his aspiration for his mother. On another occasion, he perceives a thick, heavy smell emanating from a dark-skinned girl, which he considers the smell of life itself; yet his seemingly contradictory aspirations come to be joined by images of his mother. The memory of his mother's breasts and the smell of her milk become mixed with the image of her withered breasts and the smell of blood that covered them at her death. His first woman, after fulfilling her erotic function of giving and nourishing life, died withered and ugly. The mother's life-giving force and life-nourishing milk are ultimately converted into a death-giving force and the blood of death. The memories of his mother make the light-skinned girl and the dark-skinned girl one. All life is one continuous movement toward death. While virginity seems to shine eternally white as a symbol of the innocence of life, the dark power of sensuality — the creating and perpetuating force of life — brings death, the return to innocence, through its full participation in life. Milk and blood, birth and death, are bound together inseparably.

It was natural that when Old Eguchi thought of his mother as the first woman in his life, he thought too of her death.

"Ah!" The curtains that walled the secret room seemed the color of blood. He closed his eyes tight, but that red would not disappear.[26]

The secret room which Eguchi enters in his attempt to restore his life-energy becomes a death chamber sealed with a red curtain of blood. Erotic desire is the vital life-force which consumes life itself. Eguchi, on the verge of his loss of sexuality and of his death, comes to realize fully the paradoxical oneness of life and death, of ugliness and cleanness, and of his erotic desire for life and his aspiration for death. He experiences the grotesqueness and ecstasy of life and death as the ultimate, all-inclusive experience of man as an erotic creature. Eguchi is an extension of Shingo and, in fact, of Kawabata's young dilettante heroes Shimamura and Kikuji as well.

Shimamura, Kikuji and Shingo, although they nourish the same desire, are hesitant to commit themselves to the pursuit of it. Shimamura and Kikuji leave Yōko and the Inamura girl untouched, for they know the girls' purity is unattainable and that they exist only in their dreamworld. Shimamura and Kikuji are susceptible to the regenerating and consoling power of eros and thus are constantly brought back to human reality. Shingo's longing for youth, purity and femininity is also sexual, yet his pursuit is carried on only in his inner world of imagination and dream. Although Shingo often crosses the boundary into the world of taboo in his dreams, he remains a respectable social existence in his actual life. Standing at the abyss of hell, he still meditates on the difficulties of entering it.

Eguchi, on the other hand, pursues his secret longing even at the risk of his moral integrity. His visits to the secret house to make love to sleeping beauties are journeys into the world of profanity in pursuit of his erotic desire for life; yet old Eguchi knows himself that he is in search of his dream and memory and not the actual body of a woman. Although he treads a step further into the world of decadence than the other characters, he does not confuse reality and dream, and he comes to realize that the ultimate unity can exist only in death.

Unlike Shūichi and Yagi, who try to enter the world of evil in order to recover from alienation, Shimamura, Kikuji, Shingo and Eguchi realize the almost absolute distance which lies between themselves and the original maternity. They find that by daring to eliminate this distance, they must delve into the depths of their subconscious and there enter the realm of taboo and death.

The dark winter's night of the cold snow country and the overwhelming darkness which surrounds the secret room of The House of the Sleeping Beauties make the cold glow of the Milky Way and the dazzling whiteness of the virgin body of the child-like girl shine out. Everything is dark and empty, yet nothing is empty. In the darkness of the room, the cell of his subconscious, Eguchi constantly hears the sound of the sea, the sound of the eternal depths and silence of nature. Just as oblivion, senility and sleep are the passage to death, they are also the passage to the secret truth of life itself. At the end of the novel, Eguchi, who had been caught in the interval between eros and death, meaning and nihility, plunges into a final commitment to life: lying between the light girl and the dark girl, dreaming of his Mother's milk-smelling and blood-stained breast, he impulsively kills the dark girl. Like his senile friend Fukura (who is in hell), the girl is dragged into the fathomless obscurity of the darkness of the outside, while he lies ever closer to the shining beauty of the light-skinned virgin girl. At this point he is in a delirious state, one almost of madness or true senility.

Shingo and Eguchi succeed in attaining a moment when the horrible silence of death imparts a symbolic meaning to life. The sound of the mountain and of the sea, coming from the depths of silent nature, fills them with the certainty of their sensory existence. The world of death which they experience sensorially is the world of erotic death. It fulfills their aspiration for eternal maternity, beauty and sexual fulfillment simultaneously.

From the perspective of social existence, Kawabata's dilettante heroes are indecisive people, non-doers possessing what the author of The Tale of Genji calls lukewarm hearts, and dilettante appreciators of art. In terms of human relations, Kawabata's characters are symbolically impotent. Their erotic love of women does not result in communication; nor does it take them out of their involvement in themselves or out of their symbolic and internalized involvement with love and beauty. Kawabata's characters, isolated and powerless, are swept along by the senseless force of life. They are alienated from self and life, but are at the same time imprisoned in self and life. There is no losing oneself in another's body or transcendence of the self into a common social and humanistic realm. The secret house which Eguchi enters is a symbol of the self; by symbolically making love to sleeping girls he withdraws deeply only into his own self, his own world of imagination.

Kawabata's heroes are neither saints who accept the world of death with religious resignation, nor committed artists who sacrifice their personal happiness in conventional terms for the pursuit of immortal beauty. In the tradition of sukimono and of the dilettante-artist monks, they live with the ambivalence of human desire in the space between life and death, between sensuous desire and eternal beauty. Yet their dilettantism and social obscurity eventually enable them to transgress spiritually into the profane and sacred world of erotic taboos — incest and necrophilia — experiencing death through erotic fulfillment. There, in their imaginative commitment to the erotic force of life, they envision death as the extension of man's desire for erotic fulfillment in life and for unstained primal beauty. Beauty and art connect life and death by embodying man's dual aspiration for life and for its transcendence, that is, for eternity.

Envisioning death as the original essence of life, Kawabata's heroes accept entry into it as a terrifying yet sensually ecstatic homecoming. Eguchi, in his moments of fused consciousness when dream and reality mingle, becomes almost pure, transcendental consciousness itself. At these moments, the universe (reality) exists as the harmony of life and death, man and nature, in their ecstasy and terror, beauty and ugliness. What Kawabata's characters envision in death is a primordial unity of reality and consciousness, a unified state of dreaming consciousness.

The liberation of women was one of the basic concerns of the Meiji intellectuals who struggled with the question of modernizing the self, and thus the women's liberation movement has a long history in modern Japan. Women's concerns, however, were generally left to women intellectuals and treated separately rather than as a part of broad social movements. Similarly, women writers were classified separately (as "female-school writers"), and their literature was considered a special category related only tangentially to the central activities of modern Japanese writers.

Heirs to a long tradition of women's literature in Japan, modern Japanese women writers tended to focus on emotions and psychology, while women's status in a modernizing society was excluded from the principal literary currents. Japanese proletarian literature, which reached its peak at the beginning of the Showa period (1926-present), was no exception in this regard. Such major writers as Kobayashi Takiji paid only scant and superficial attention to the questions of women, and in general, the theoreticians who were concerned with the questions of laborers, peasants and intellectuals in revolution ignored women.[1]

Miyamoto Yuriko, a leading proletarian writer of the first half of the Showa period, stands out in this context as an exceptional figure, as a writer who placed women's concerns at the

*This chapter originally appeared in the Bulletin of Concerned Asian Scholars 10:2 (April-June 1978), pp. 2-9, under the title "Literature, Ideology and Women's Happiness: The Autobiographical Novels of Miyamoto Yuriko," and is published here by permission of the Bulletin.

center of her literature and integrated them with the socialist
movement of her time. She began her writing career as an idealistic humanist who was disturbed by the alienation of elite intellectuals from the masses; yet in her attempt to grow into a
real intellectual, liberated from the conditioning forces of her
bourgeois background, she came to realize that being a woman
imposed an obstacle as great as any other she confronted. She
came to believe that overcoming the class nature of her philosophic and aesthetic ideas and becoming a truly liberated woman
were both crucial to living a rich and meaningful life. She saw
the family and marriage systems as feudal institutions preserved
in the interests of modern capitalism and considered them to be
the primary forces oppressing women. At the same time, she
noted the failure of women intellectuals to grasp the class nature
of their ideas and their cynical and reactionary retreat into false
femininity. For Yuriko, being a humanist meant being a feminist
and communist revolutionary, and the humanist, feminist and revolutionary struggles were necessary truly to liberate human beings.

Miyamoto Yuriko was born into an upper-middle-class, intellectual family in 1899 and died a committed and major communist writer in 1951. She accepted historical incidents as personally significant events and grew from a bourgeois humanist
into a humanistic communist, from an intellectual observer into
a committed fighter, from the bright, overprotected daughter of
an elite family into a liberated woman, and, above all, she grew
into a fine fiction writer who combined history and individual experience in literature. Her art is a mirror reflecting the complex history of Japan and the inner life of the Japanese artist
who lived through it.

She dealt with three major concerns throughout her life, concerns which she considered central problems or conflicts to be
resolved. They are the questions of consciousness and practice,
women's happiness and creativity, and politics and literature.
Focusing on her ideas on women, this chapter examines how
these central problems and her consciousness of them shaped
her creative works and are reflected in them.

A precocious writer, Miyamoto Yuriko published her first

novel, Mazushiki hitobito no mure (A Flock of Poor Folk), in Chūōkōron in 1917, when she was only eighteen years old.[2] It appeared with a strong endorsement by Tsubouchi Shōyō, who observed that she was endowed with keen perception and an ability to think originally, qualities that are clearly shown in this first novel. The novel is about an ojōsan (an honorable daughter) from Tokyo who visits the remote agricultural village owned by her grandfather. The protagonist, observing the details of the poor peasants' lives, is appalled by the injustice of the system of landownership as well as by the distortions which absolute poverty creates in human psychology and character. In her sincere attempts to help the poor peasants, she meets only vicious greed and apathy on the part of the peasants and cynical arrogance from the village elite. Although the work is filled with youthful sentimentalism, Yuriko's treatment of the protagonist's deep self-reflection and self-analysis when she confronts the absolute defeat of her upper-class humanism is impressive. The novel ends with the protagonist's determination to find something, however small, which could be shared with the peasants and her determination to grow into a person who understands life.

What principally characterizes the novel is the author's tendency toward introspective self-searching, together with her idealism and strong faith in human goodwill, characteristic traits which were to stay with her the rest of her life. Reflecting the strong influence of Tolstoy and such writers of the Shirakaba group as Arishima Takeo, she expresses in this work a youthful and hopeful belief in the union of consciousness and practice, and her determination to contribute to human welfare. In this respect she differs from the naturalist writers and urban intellectuals of the late Meiji period (1868-1912), whose discovery of the deep chasm between themselves and the peasants, and of the evil of a system which separates people so absolutely merely led them to an overall pessimism and desperation about human nature.

Soon after the appearance of this novel, however, Yuriko was confronted by a serious contradiction between her consciousness and her practice, a contradiction which emerged not so much

from social conditions as from her personal life. In 1918 she
accompanied her father, a prosperous London-trained architect,
to New York, and while studying at Columbia University she fell
in love with Araki Shigeru, a scholar of Oriental linguistics fifteen years older than she. Although she was passionately in love
with him (he appears as the character Tsukuda in the novel Nobuko), the marriage was important for her in other respects too
because it would allow her to be independent from her family,
assuring her a new start in life. She saw it as a way to live as
she wished, to develop her feelings and sensitivity, and her husband declared his commitment to help her do so. Yet in her
marriage, to which her parents objected unyieldingly, she found
herself still trapped by the feudal institution of the family. The
family pressure she had felt as a daughter was replaced by even
heavier pressure in her role as a wife. She went through an agonizing and futile struggle with her mediocre scholar-husband,
a security-seeking, emotionally cold man, and she concluded
that the occupation of housewife, with its emotional and mental
inactivity, petty hypocrisy and banality of thought, is totally detrimental to human creativity. She realized that she would have
to sacrifice her imagination and creativity as a writer unless
she were to be reborn as a different woman or unless society's
attitude toward women were to change. She discovered from her
four years of marriage that a woman becomes emotionally and
psychologically vulnerable to her husband, and at the same time,
paradoxically, that the "security" of the wife's role justifies and
maintains relations between man and woman on the basis of the
family institution rather than on the basis of real human involvement in each other.[3]   Her experiences in marriage were soon
to become the basis of her first masterpiece, Nobuko (1923),
which, like all of her subsequent novels, is highly autobiographical in nature, reflecting the experience and realization of a
particular phase of Yuriko's life.[4]

Unlike many women, Nobuko did not think she could change her life situation by
finding a new love, for then she would just be moving from one man to another
and would still be someone's wife. It was not that she disliked her married life
because she compared Tsukuda with someone else. It was because of the many

difficulties that the incompatibility of their personalities created and because she
could not accept the differences between men and women in the way they fulfill
themselves in marriage, differences which are accepted generally. Either she
would have to be reborn as a different woman or the common social ideas of sex
life would have to change in certain respects for her to remain married without
problems.
To be perfectly honest, she could not claim to be free from apprehension about
her independent life in the future. She could not imagine that Tsukuda was un-
aware of her subtle weakness. No matter how eager Nobuko was for her independence, he saw through her weakness, thus allowing her to act as she liked,
like a spoiled child, and called her his "baby."

Yuriko-Nobuko[5] also discovered the hypocrisy of intellectuals
who argue for ideals but have no intention of living according to
them. She determined to live according to her beliefs, distinguishing bourgeois intellectualism from revolutionary intellectualism, and paid a high price to put this into practice. The
traumatic experiences during the four years of what she called
her "swamp period" convinced her finally that any ideas which
were not substantiated by her personal life were meaningless.
She set out to establish her own life-style and to live according
to her own ideas.

Nobuko-Yuriko's problems were not only those of a unique
woman artist who could not be confined to the traditional role of
a wife, but also those of an awakened modern woman whose ego
could not submit to the ego of the husband. Nobuko's insistence
on her modern woman's ego, however, was not directed toward
the denial of marriage or heterosexual love during this period.
It meant only that she had the strength to break her marriage
when she realized that her husband's personality was not compatible with hers and that marriage to him would prevent the
free and full development of her ego. In this sense, Nobuko can
be said to be the first novel which dealt with the question of the
modern female ego with full seriousness, parallel to the pio-
neering treatment of the male ego in such Meiji novels as Kokoro and Hakai.

When Yuriko became a communist after living for three years
in the Soviet Union, she was forced to confront the social and
political implications of her belief that consciousness can be in-

tellectually meaningful only when it contributes to a concrete
change in life which facilitates one's inner growth. Subject to
the heavy censorship of her writings and the strenuous experiences of trial and imprisonment after her return to Japan, her
health deteriorated, and she suffered at one point from a complete loss of vision. During these years, when she was not al-
lowed to write freely, she committed herself to leading a study
group composed of women and to writing essays on women,[6] as
well as to writing letters to her second husband, a communist
who had been sentenced to life imprisonment.[7] These years
required a firm commitment; many writers, subject to great
pressure and actual physical torture, declared, some truly and
others superficially, that they had given up their communism,
while a majority of the writers wrote nonpolitical works or fell
silent. All suffered from self-doubt, self-pity, cynicism and
desperation. Yuriko, with Kobayashi Takiji, who was brutally
murdered by the police, stand truly heroic in this context.

In Nobuko, the protagonist's decision to give up her husband
and go against the desires of her family was for the sake of her
personal growth and happiness. Although well aware that her
action would invite criticism as an egotistical act, Nobuko felt
at that time that marriage was detrimental both to women's happiness as individual human beings and to their creativity. It was
necessary to be independent from men, emotionally as well as
economically, in order to secure a room of one's own. Yet Nobuko's solitary life makes her experience the frightening loneliness and emptiness that exist in life without love. She comes
to reconsider whether marriage itself is the problem or whether
it exists in deviation from an ideal form of marriage.

In Futatsu no niwa (The Two Gardens, 1947), an autobiographical sequel to Nobuko, Yuriko traces her life after her divorce
to her decision to visit the new Russia. Although she was now
writing novels steadily and enjoying a newly independent life as
a professional writer, she (Yuriko-Nobuko) suffered from loneliness and a sense of sterility which came from the absence of
total involvement in human relations. After the divorce, she

lives with Motoko, a woman translator, and comes to realize the
prejudice to which single women are subject in a male-oriented
society and the distortion in their characters which women suffer because of it. They force themselves unnaturally to behave
like men, yet they are more vulnerable than married women,
more conscious of themselves as sexual objects, and cannot liberate themselves from sex. Her relationship with her friend
Motoko gradually comes to resemble that between lovers, and
Nobuko feels it to be a psychological burden.[8] She feels that
single women tend to become alienated cripples, deprived of
proper objects of love, and realizes that a satisfying male-
female or sexual relationship is necessary for women's happiness. Thus she comes to reject the androgynous existence
which she once thought necessary.[9]

Nobuke describes two incidents which occurred during this
period as decisive in her determination to step into a new life.
One is the affair of her mother, then fifty-two, with her son's
thirty-two-year-old tutor. The unfortunate love affair, which
ended in her mother's bitter disappointment, illustrated the
tragic fate of women who could not find the correct channel for
their passion and self-growth in the feudal family system.
Nobuko-Yuriko came to realize the impossibility of love's transcending differences of age and environment, given the existing
warped male-female relationship. At the same time, she found
herself appalled by her mother's romanticism, so miserably removed from reality, by the easy cynicism concerning love and
men which her mother adopted and by her mother's quick return
to a bourgeois life after her brutal disappointment. There
Nobuko-Yuriko saw a lack of the true passion which might have
enabled her to develop the full possibilities of happiness and the
meaning of life in love, even though defeated.[10] Above all, Nobuko hated the hypocrisy of the intellectual who talks of beautiful
ideas yet is a cowardly egotist in daily life.

She sees as well the traps created by women's vulnerability
to romantic love. Women desire to be romantic heroines, finding happiness only in being loved by men. They spend all their
psychic energy in loving and lose the capacity to see that they

are only catering to an illusory ideal of femininity created by men. She sees in her mother both passion misused and the lack of a true commitment to love. This realization leads Yuriko to explore love relations which are not based on romantic love.[11]

The second decisive incident was the suicide of Akutagawa Ryūnosuke in 1927. The Two Gardens describes the profound shock brought by his death, a shock which resulted in her decision to go to Soviet Russia.

If indeed to grow in class awareness is the only correct way to live in history for a member of the bourgeoisie, how does such growth take place?
"Do you know?" Nobuko sat next to Motoko, who was proofreading, and continued, "I know that there is a limitation in Aikawa Ryonosuke's [Akutagawa Ryūnosuke's] intellect...but how does the 'class transformation' occur in such individuals as you and I?"

She knew that among those who are identified as members of the proletarian school, writers who did not come from the working class or were not living in poverty, with the exception of such theorists as Shinohara Kurato, would be ignored. In fact, her own writings were indeed ignored by them.

Nobuko felt, however, that whether or not she was recognized by them, she had things to say as a human being and as a woman, and that she could not wipe out her own way of life. If she could stop her way of life somewhere because she became hung up on some theory, why had she thrown away the life with Tsukuda, pushing his pleading face away with her own hand...? "I think I will go to Soviet Russia. I would like to live there. I would like to see with my own eyes and experience with my own body everything there, good and bad."

(The Two Gardens, p. 263; my translation)[12]

Yuriko received Akutagawa's death as the tragic self-dissolution of a bourgeois intellectual fundamentally alienated from life itself, as the total defeat of his intellectualism and aestheticism. She was chilled by the thought that she herself might follow his path if she continued to live as a detached intellectual writer. Interestingly, her future husband, Miyamoto Kenji, made his critical start by writing a brilliant and influential essay "The Literature of Defeat," in which he analyzed the class nature of Akutagawa's sensitivity, anxiety, desperation and aesthetics.[13] At the time, Yuriko was already an established writer, while

Kenji was a very young man, fresh from the countryside, vacillating between politics and literature as his life's work (today he is chairman of the Japan Communist Party).

What particularly shocked Yuriko-Nobuko was Akutagawa's deep loneliness as a man. Akutagawa, firmly tied to his family, with a gentle, homemaker wife and bright children, was desperately lonely, starved for love. He fell in love with a woman whose intellect matched his own, but gave her up for the sake of his family. His sentimental overflow of emotion when he finally did so, and the pathetic sincerity of his subsequent writings in which he describes his own feelings and sense of defeat, moved her deeply. There she saw a sensitive man burdened by obligations as a father and provider which drained his energies and damaged his fine sensibility. She recognized that Akutagawa's anxiety and sterility as a detached bourgeois writer would also be her fate and that she too would be a victim of the institution of the family, deprived of love. Here she gained a new insight in her struggle; it was not only women but men as well whose creativity was stifled by their efforts to cope with an oppressive reality. A vital love of life, of a life committed to active thinking, writing, acting and loving, sprang up in her. In order to complete and enrich her life, she needed a liberated man. Human liberation, not merely women's liberation, was necessary.

Her concern with meaningful male-female relations deepened when she met Miyamoto Kenji and married him. This was also the point at which she actually joined the Communist Party, although she had already become a communist in Russia, begun to write proletarian literature, and been engaged in active organizing work — particularly among women — since her return. After living together for only a short time, both of them were arrested. Kenji was sentenced to life imprisonment, and their twelve-year separation began. Although she learned through her passionate love for this brilliant ideologue who was ten years her junior that women's happiness and creativity, supported by faith in life and in love, are truly compatible, this fortunate union was by no means earned easily.

In "Koiwaike no ikka" (The Family of Koiwai, 1934), Yuriko

describes the wife of a communist forced to go underground. The
wife, although uneducated, is endowed with natural intelligence
and strength of character developed through a life of poverty.
She is firmly committed to her husband and works hard to maintain the family under the unusual circumstances, supporting and
taking care of her parents-in-law and her children. She is the
epitome of the strength and endurance with which traditional
women are usually supposed to be equipped. Although she is the
actual center of the family, she develops a curious sense of isolation and lack of purpose when her husband finally decides to go
underground. She is an ideal wife for an activist, supplying
abundant moral support, yet she knows clearly that an unbridgeable gap has been created between her and her husband, who
were united only as partners in a homemaking enterprise. The
story ends as the wife, appropriately named Otome (young
maiden), realizes that there will be a day when he will not return home unless she herself joins the movement with equal seriousness and commitment. The story describes the growth of
this maiden into an independent participant in life, and this
growth is treated as an essential factor in true love-relations.
Later, in Banshū heiya (The Banshū Plain, 1946), Yuriko deals
with the question of ideological differences between husband and
wife and concludes that the sharing of ideology and political actions is also essential.

Yuriko's relationship with Kenji was deeply satisfying. Con-
tradicting her previous insistent stance, she changed her name
from her maiden name Chūjyō to her husband's name Miyamoto
and assumed positively the role of daughter-in-law and sister-
in-law in his family. This evoked criticism and disgust among
women writers and intellectuals, for she appeared to be pro-
tecting his male ego.[14] Although we may discern in her attitude
the concern of an older woman and established writer to eliminate any source of inferiority complex which her young husband
might have, to see in it a willingness to assume the traditional
role of a woman would totally miss the point. Although she believed that what she was doing was right, however, she later
came to realize that she was indeed trying to protect her hus-

band's male ego and was thereby creating another fraudulent
male-female relationship.

In Banshu heiya, which deals with her love for Kenji and is set
in the days around the end of the war, Yuriko presents her protagonist, who is unshakably certain of her love for and commitment to her husband, as naturally attached to his family. Her
concern with and understanding of the women in his rural,
lower-middle-class family is alive, devoid of any intellectual
aloofness, and filled with genuine love. In this novel, the protagonist achieves a genuine tie between herself and the working
class and peasant people from whom she is separated by education, class and cultural-social background.

What made this possible, twenty years after Nobuko, was
her understanding of the common fate which women in the
Japanese family system share and her commitment to proletarian revolution. When the protagonist of Banshu heiya,
Hiroko, hears that her brother-in-law was among the vic-
tims of the Hiroshima holocaust, she visits her husband's family in Yamaguchi prefecture, a visit which renews her recognition that women have once again had to bear the tragedy of the
war and society more heavily than men. Her sister-in-law,
now widowed, changes into a nervous, greedy and calculating
woman, losing all tenderness toward other people. Saddened by
the psychological distortion created in this woman, Hiroko is
struck by the misery which women in the family system have
had to endure. She feels it unfair that the maintenance of the
system depends upon the endurance of women and is at the same
time appalled by the role which women assumed in maintaining
this dehumanizing and sexist system. She calls the strength
produced in the frail woman's body at the time of emergency
and the psychological and mental distortion caused by it "goke
no ganbari," the widow's stubborn strength.

Yet soon this widow's strength/distortion appears in Hiroko-
Yuriko herself, and worst of all, this is pointed out by her husband, with whom she is finally reunited after twelve years of
separation. In Fūchiso (1946), Jyūkichi (Kenji) points out that
her overanxious and protective attitude toward himself and his

family is goke no ganbari and suggests that she return to a more
relaxed attitude. His observation of her widow's hardness and
strength, implying a lack of femininity, is a male chauvinist one,
yet she realizes that her eagerness to protect her husband was
indeed distorted and mistaken, that she was unconsciously adopt-
ing a protective attitude toward him just as a husband might do
toward his wife, and that the love relationship must be based on
mutual equality and independence. The full cycle had come;
twenty years earlier she had suffered from the hypocritical pro-
tectiveness of her older husband, and she was now unconsciously
assuming the same protective role toward her younger husband.

Most importantly, when the question arose of her rejoining the
Communist Party, the executive committee of which Jyūkichi-
Kenji was now a member, she asked him to let her work in a way
that would let her continue to write novels. He replied that she
must work in her own way and must continue to write novels.
With this understanding she joined the party without hesitation,
but later found that he had foreseen a possible conflict that
might have wrecked their love had she not done so. Although
Yuriko's decision to join the party was reached from her own
belief and the decision was hers, ironically it was the same experience which her protagonist in "The Family of Koiwai" had
gone through. Ideological sharing was an important condition
for love. Yuriko here argues that ideal love is the most human
one, a love in which each partner is concerned with his or her
own life without an overinflated confidence in bringing happiness
to others, but a love based firmly on the support of and faith in
each other. Together with such support, complete sharing of
basic attitudes toward life and the same world view are considered necessary; this is the hardest demand made on women, the
demand to participate in political as well as intellectual activities as equals of their men. She calls such a relationship that
of humanistic communism. Women's happiness must be instrumental in the development of their creativity, while there will
be no happiness where creativity is stifled.

Yuriko believed in human growth as the most significant purpose of life. She committed herself to communism only when,

impressed especially by the condition of women in the Soviet
Union, she accepted it as an ideology which facilitates both human growth and social justice. For her, human growth was not
a matter of inner awareness, but could be achieved meaningfully
only in relation to others; it could be achieved only by living
within the real world, within history, in vital association with
other people. For this reason, personal concerns (ideal love
relationships especially) and social and political ones become
interfused in her creative activity. In her understanding, practice takes a central role; the pursuit of art for life's sake and
of intellectual activity for its practical consequences provided
the means for her to unite life and ideas, life and writing. Yuriko's firm belief in human growth, her unending interest in and
love of women, and her commitment to positive male-female
relationships resemble those of such writers as Simone de
Beauvoir. Like Beauvoir, she lived passionately, creating her
own life-style as a woman, and tried to create a unique autobiographical novel in which the protagonist emerges as a modern
as well as an historical hero.

Of the three conflicts, however, the one which gradually came
to concern Yuriko most in her later years was that between politics and literature. As I have noted, she started her creative
career as a bourgeois intellectual, deeply influenced by the humanistic writings of Tolstoy and Arishima Takeo at a time when
the moralistic, introspective "I-novels" had established the
tradition of the modern novel in Japan. The historical perspective of Yuriko's autobiographical novels distinguishes them from
from the traditional I-novels, in which the perspective of the
author-protagonist is exclusively internal and psychological.
This historical perspective grew stronger in the course of her
writings. Although the conflict between consciousness and practice, the realization of which was to become central in Japanese
writers' struggle against the I-novel, was clearly the starting
point of Yuriko's writing and the basis for the development of
her thought, when she was writing Nobuko she understood this
conflict only as a problem of her personal growth, not as directly related to history or society. When she came to realize

that sexism is a political phenomenon, the conflict developed another layer of meaning, that is, the conflict between literature and politics. Writing about one's personal growth, about achieving one's personal freedom, began to appear to her as merely the sterile self-satisfaction of an elite intellectual. Thus the conflict was transformed from a metaphysical-philosophic concern with realization (consciousness) and practice to a socially concrete question of politics and literature.

The early Showa period produced a flood of theoretical arguments with regard to proletarian literature and the writers' role in revolution, yet it did not produce many significant fictional works. Miyamoto Yuriko, with Kobayashi Takiji, undertook the task of creating a communist literature. Yuriko's problems were more complex than those of Takiji, who was committed to presenting situations or dramas in which the oppressed masses attain a revolutionary understanding and commitment to action, or than those of Tokunaga Sunao, another important proletarian writer who, himself coming from a lumpenproletariat background, wrote naturally about laborers — their struggle for change, their limitations, their happiness and their distortions. Yuriko, on the other hand, was an intellectual who was keenly aware of her basic alienation from the masses and of the limitations of her understanding. She had not forgotten the bitter lessons she had learned from the tragic failure of the humanist writer Arishima Takeo, who embraced proletarian literature and gave up his inherited property to become a socialist but later had to admit that the class nature of a writer cannot be transcended. After declaring that he could not pretend to be a socialist and could write only as a member of his bourgeois class, he died in a suicide pact with a woman.[15]

During the first years of Yuriko's life as a communist, her writing suffered from didacticism and dogmatic analysis. Her best contribution during this period was clearly in the field of essay writing, in which she analyzed the conditions of women. Although her belief that literature should contribute to people's progress and should be meaningful to the emerging new class and generation was not shaken, she grew uneasy about the possibility of artistic stagnation in her political life. Although Kenji was more than eager in urging her to pursue her novel-writing in her own way, for him there was no doubt that she should not write as anything but a communist.

In Fūchiso (1947), the protagonist Hiroko hesitates to join the party because she still does not see clearly the relationship between her art and political activities; she is worried about how joining the party might affect her writing.

"Hiroko, will you leave your curriculum vitae since you are here [at party headquarters]."
"My vitae?"
She hesitated, feeling that it was too sudden. To present her vitae must mean going through a formal procedure to join the party.
"Of course, but..."
Hiroko was not prepared to do so here, at this moment. She felt that two kinds of work were pushing her from opposite sides of her body: literary work and political work concerning women, which was the natural consequence of her being a woman. At present she was occupied more with the latter. As a result, what she wrote became entirely educational.

"How would it affect my work? ... If only I knew." Whenever Hiroko wrote short educational pieces, Jyūkichi himself advised her to organize her political work, telling her that otherwise she would not be able to write novels. It was also felt keenly [by the communists] that they must produce specialists in every field of the humanities.... But when Jyūkichi asked her when she planned to write novels, how was it related to his suggestion to present her vitae?

"There is no reason for me to refuse if I know what my writing will be."
"Hiroko, you can only prove objectively through your own writing what is the best."
"I am very glad if I can work in that way."

"But that you can write in a way most appropriate for your present concern does not mean that a writer does not have to assume historical responsibility in her own daily life.... People in the humanities are too preoccupied with it [the relation between politics and literature] in general.... It must be because their life and work are too personal. But in the case of husband and wife, the gap can become too big to bridge."

(Fūchiso, p. 256; author's translation)

Yuriko's only solution was to maintain her determination to

write novels in history and to find out what kind of novel is a
good novel by writing with all her energy. Yet this was an indi-
rect way of saying that she was going to set aside the problems
of politics and literature and would be immersed in writing novels, not political novels, but just novels. Indeed, most of her
communist ideas were expressed in her essays, and her novels
trace mainly her personal growth. She was also totally committed to participating in political activities, organizing, lectures,
and so forth, as if she were trying to bridge the gap between
politics and literature in this way.

When Yuriko started writing as a feminist, however, with her
own life as the central theme of her novels — and that started
with her postwar novels — the gap between politics and literature and that between history and individual life were eliminated. She had discovered new modern heroes, the oppressed
class of women struggling for liberation, a class emerging to
play an important role in the history of human liberation. By
writing autobiographical novels from a revolutionary feminist
perspective, she achieved a unique combination of literature
and politics, of history and individual life. The result was the
overflow of her creativity. The Banshū Plain, Fūchiso, The
Two Gardens, and Road Sign were written within the short years
of bubbling creativity between the end of the war and her death
in 1951. They were all autobiographical works and extensions
of Nobuko, tracing her personal growth as a woman writer and
woman communist, but these later works were distinguished
from Nobuko by their communist-feminist perspective. She had
plans for writing two more such novels, plans left unmaterial-
ized by her sudden death.

The form of Yuriko's novels is closest possibly to the Bildungsroman, a form of novel which traces the moral as well as
social development of an individual. Her works, most simply,
are a communist and feminist variant of the Bildungsroman.
The recent autobiography of Simone de Beauvoir also resembles
her works in its basic attempt to trace the inner as well as the
social growth of the author-protagonist, and to place her in his-

tory. By placing inner growth within a concrete historical and
social framework, history and individual life are uniquely interfused, creating both a personal drama and social intellectual
history; Yuriko's hero is an honest reflection of herself, yet she
emerges as a universal modern hero. Although Yuriko's hero
is by no means portrayed as an ideal, superhuman woman, she
is a positive hero whose faith in female and human liberation
through communist revolution is unshakable.

Yuriko's works present the drama of a woman developing
from a member of the bourgeois elite, dependent on men, into
an independent, mature woman writer and communist, even as
they mirror realistically an important page in the social, moral
and intellectual history of modern Japan. Thus Yuriko created
a new form of autobiography, one in which the protagonist
emerges as an historic figure of the age, experiencing fully its
limitations and possibilities. Her writings interlace uniquely
the tradition of the I-novel with the historical social commitment derived from her political activities.

During the 1920s and 1930s, writers and artists in Japan actively debated the proper relationship between politics and literature, between social values and artistic values. The dispute
over socialist realism appeared as the culmination of this debate. For the Japan Communist Party (JCP) and those writers
committed to socialist revolution, these issues and the question
of socialist realism were naturally of central concern. The
question of the relation of art and literature to society or of
world view to literary creation, however, was of great concern
to nonproletarian writers as well, particularly to those humanist and modernist writers who, discontent with the dissociation
of art from society in the decadent literature and autobiographical I-novels then dominant, were trying to make art once again
vitally relevant to social reality and the modern human condition.[1]

The question of literary realism had been a major subject of
debate from the time of Tsubouchi Shōyō's essay "The Essence
of the Novel" in 1885,[2] and with the development of the I-novel
as a distinct genre in the twentieth century, the debate often
took the form of critiques of the I-novel. An outgrowth of naturalism, the I-novel had become the predominant novelistic
genre in the "modernization" of Japanese literature from the
turn of the century. Narrowing their concerns to the exploration and unveiling of their own internal worlds, the writers of
the I-novels had lost vital touch with the reality outside of
themselves. In this context, the question of how to deal with

life in art and literature, which the socialist-realism debate
fostered, concerned many nonproletarian writers as well as
those committed to revolution.

It was, moreover, not only the radical writers who were subject to the ruthless repression carried out by the national police
in the 1930s; in fact, most of the writers of the period were disturbed and threatened by it, and all were subject to censorship.[3]
Because the period of the proletarian literary movement was the
period of Japan's steadily widening imperialistic involvement
in China and Southeast Asia, the question of politics and literature was one of practical concern to nearly all writers, whose
choices were limited, essentially, to tenkō (forced conversion
of ideology), collaboration with the government in its war effort,
or escape into silence. Under these circumstances, the dispute
over politics and literature (and that over socialist realism) became central to writers lacking political involvement as well as
to proletarian and revolutionary writers. The dispute over socialist realism, therefore, must be understood as part of Japanese writers' larger concern over the relationship between literature and politics, between art and life.

Although the number of works written strictly according to the
theory of socialist realism was limited, the active dispute which
took place with regard to its applicability to Japanese proletarian writing has a significant place in the history of modern Japanese literature, particularly in the context of the larger dispute
over politics and literature. The dispute took place when the
proletarian literary movement was dissolving, and this contributed to the complex reaction of the writers on the left. For although the dispute centered in form around the question of the
applicability of socialist realism to the Japanese situation, it
reflected more basically the desire of many writers to justify
their tenkō by finding new theoretical grounds for writing proletarian literature without political guidance. In this sense, the
dispute must be evaluated as a part of the question of tenkō,
which left a deep scar, moral as well as psychological, on the
history of modern Japanese literature.

The rise of the proletariat as a social force during the middle

to late Taisho period (1912-1926) was reflected in literature
in the formation (in 1921) of the group whose journal was
called Tanemakuhito (The Sowers)[4] and in the growing demand for "mass art," "labor literature" and "art of the
fourth class." Following the publication in Bungei Sensen
(Literature and Art Battlefront) in September 1921 of an article by Aono Suekichi entitled "Spontaneous Growth and Pur-
poseful Consciousness,"[5] an active dispute arose on the
proletarian literary front. Interrupted by the great Kanto
earthquake of 1923 and the brief period of political reaction
which followed, the debate reached its peak during 1927 and
1928. After the period of reaction, the Japanese Communist
Party sought to renew itself and its commitment to the
masses, not only creating a supportive political environment
for discussing the theoretical issues of proletarian literature, but even making the issues themselves matters of political concern. Reflecting the development of proletarian
literary activities, the Federation of Japanese Proletarian
Artists (NAPF) was formed in 1928, creating a brief yet active united front of revolutionary artists and writers.

The united front was soon strained by the mass arrest and
unprecedented persecution of the communist revolutionaries,
climaxed by the brutal murder of Kobayashi Takiji by the
national police in the eighth year of Showa (1933), and the
next year the Federation of Japanese Proletarian Artists was
dissolved. The NAPF period, from 1928 to 1934, is usually
referred to as the period of Marxian or communist literature. The major theoretical activity of this period was represented by Kurahara Korehito's "proletarian realism," which
received the support of Nakano and Miyamoto. Distinguishing
proletarian realism from both the naturalistic recording of
life and anarchistic or subjective protest literature, Kurahara placed realism at the core of the new Marxian proletarian literature, thus making a major contribution to its
theoretical orientation. Appearing when Japanese literature
was dominated by the naturalistic I-novel, whose possibilities
for further development were sharply limited, Kurahara's

writings opened a new way to deal with reality and brought
proletarian realism into the mainstream of the literary concern with realism.

Kurahara's first major essay, "A Path to Proletarian Realism" (1928),[6] appeared in response to the writings of Aono
Suekichi. In a series of essays including "Investigated Art"
(1925) and in particular in "Spontaneous Growth and Pur-
poseful Consciousness" (1926), Aono had argued that although
"spontaneous proletarian literature" can be born without a
specific literary movement, such literature cannot give readers a socialist consciousness of purpose. The frustration,
anger and hatred of the proletariat cannot be organized or
put in proper perspective unless the writer approaches his
or her task with the proper political consciousness. Aono
saw the proletarian literary movement as an injection of
consciousness of purpose in the field of literature.[7] Although
Aono's articles played a key role in the proletarian literary
movement, they represented a rather mechanical application
of the political doctrine of Lenin's What Is to Be Done? to
the literary field, and his crude efforts to impose political
objectives on literary works left many questions unanswered.
Although Aono demonstrated the necessity for and significance of political ideology in proletarian literature, he failed
to discuss the relation between literary values and political
values, and this lack led to considerable confusion in the
discussion and debate among the proletarian writers.

In this context, Kurahara's theoretical writings assumed
major importance. His series of articles on proletarian realism were written to develop Aono's idea of literature depicting society with the proper political perspectives, yet he
criticized as dangerous the introduction of abstract political
ideas into literature. Placing realism — a literary perspective — at the center of proletarian literature, Kurahara discussed with great sophistication the relation between politics
and literature from the standpoint of literary method. According to Kurahara, the three basic conditions for proletarian realism are that proletarian writers must (1) start

from reality and their understanding of reality, (2) depict reality always from the social standpoint, and (3) grasp people in their complexity and their totality. In this way, he combined realism with class perspective, thus establishing the basis for the theory of proletarian realism.[8]

In his articles on proletarian realism, Kurahara focused the discussion on the relation between world view and literature, the evaluation and criticism of the existing literature of realism, and the creative method appropriate for describing reality and people. All of these themes were at the forefront of the subsequent debate over socialist realism. With regard to the relation between literature and world view, he argued that the artistic method cannot be separated from the artist's world view, thus rejecting any dualistic notion of politics and art. Arguing moreover that dialectical materialism is, like realism, a method of looking at reality, Kurahara identified proletarian realism with the realism pursued by dialectical materialism. In his article "Some Thoughts on Realistic Method" (1931),[9] however, he identified world view with the author's understanding of reality and argued that class analysis in literary works need not be merely theoretical escapes from the mechanical application of dialectical materialism as a creative method.

In evaluating the past literature of realism, Kurahara criticized naturalism as external depiction which pays attention only to trivia.[10] Although he depicted idealism as an alternative to realism, he maintained that realism not only portrays reality as it is, but also grasps the social and historical truth of reality. Real proletarian literature exists in the mutual relationship of these two elements, yet to grasp the reality in its totality, it is most important to recognize the superiority of the latter element as well as the interaction. His treatment of historical truth led the way to the discussion of the rising historical force with which revolutionary romanticism has been so concerned and thus to the discussion of the relation between romanticism and realism, a discussion which assumed major importance in the socialist-realism dispute.

With regard to the method of creation, his argument centered around the question of types; although artists should depict living people as they are, they should create artistic types according to class, occupation, age, sex, environment and consciousness. This can be achieved through the writer's severe, realistic attitude, that is, through the writer's class consciousness as a member of the proletariat. He argued that it is not enough to describe any types at random, but the author should select the most meaningful types in terms of the development of the age; that means new, emerging types. Kurahara's argument on types parallels Gorky's advocacy of describing the most conspicuous class characteristics of people, and although not fully developed it represents the first attempt in Japan to clarify the importance of types in proletarian literature.

Kurahara's arguments on proletarian realism left many issues unresolved, yet by arguing or insisting that the fundamental function of literature is the understanding of reality, he partly closed the gap between politics and literature in proletarian literature. Miyamoto Kenji basically supported Kurahara by arguing that the artistic value of literary works is determined by whether or not they supply sensory realization of inevitable social and historical development, whether literary works tell us the truth in concrete creation, and that is what is meant by the social value of literary works. By placing realism at the center of proletarian literature, Kurahara relieved it of the excessive weight accorded politics in literature without denying the importance of world view, and his writings led to further discussion of artistic value, of form and content, and of politics and art, as well as to a reassessment of art history among both proletarian and nonproletarian writers.

The dispute over socialist realism, which started around 1933, followed the dispute discussed above over artistic value and the relationship between politics and literature, and took the form of a dispute over how to adapt Soviet socialist realism to the Japanese proletarian literary movement. The dispute, however, took place at the time when the proletarian literary movement was dissolving, most of its writers having been forced to

convert their political ideology under the pressure of severe in-
terrogation and persecution by the police. From the standpoint
of literary history, therefore, the significance of the debate lay
in the writers' search for a method to continue to write proletarian literature after their conversion and for a method of re-
establishing proletarian literature after its official tie to the
Japanese Communist Party had to be severed. This situation
especially differentiated the history of socialist realism in Japan
from that in other countries. The debate over socialist realism
is closely related to the question of tenkō, then, and must be
treated in relation to it.

Literary censorship has been an integral part of Japanese literary history in the modern period. Although numerous in-
stances of censorship took place in the early part of the Meiji
period before the constitution was established in 1889, only after
the declaration of the new constitution, in which the protection of
human rights was at least proclaimed in principle, did large-
scale censorship and the suppression of freedom of thought and
expression become, ironically, a serious and systematic con-
straint on literary activities. This systematic censorship, con-
tinuing until the end of the Second World War, was carried out
as a part of political repression directed against those groups
opposed to the government and its nationalist policies. These
groups were mainly anarchist and communist, and since their
major literary movement was the proletarian literary movement, it was largely against this that literary censorship was
directed. Thus literary censorship in Japan is deeply intertwined with the pursuit of national goals and with the nationalism and imperialism of the modern state.

Prior to Japan's stepped-up involvement in China in the 1920s
and 1930s and the growth of the revolutionary proletarian movement domestically to a point where it could not be ignored, literary censorship was merely one aspect of a tightly directed
society pursuing national goals. During the twenties and thirties,
however, literary censorship clearly went beyond the control of
expression within a directed society and became more openly
political, as it aimed explicitly at the suppression of expression

and suppression of those movements which questioned the locus and use of power in society.

Those writers who refused to go through tenkō remained imprisoned or were silenced completely. Such writers as Miyamoto Yuriko, Nakano Shigeharu and Tosaka Jun, who were not permitted to publish creative works, continued to write essays which were not related to war issues or political issues, but others such as Kaneko Mitsuharu fell into complete silence.

It was in June 1933 that two of the top leaders of the Japanese Communist Party, Sano Manabu and Nabeyama Sadachika, made a statement advocating conversion to their fellow prisoners.[11] Responding to this appeal, more than 30 percent of the imprisoned communists had converted by the end of July, and by 1935 about 90 percent of the communists had converted.[12] Except for Miyamoto Kenji, Kurahara Korehito and a few others, most of the proletarian writers gave up their ideology. Actually, the conversion of proletarian writers had already started a year prior to the appeal by Sano and Nabeyama and had been reflected in the debate over politics and literature in which writers tried to justify their dissociation from the party by dissociating literature from politics. After the dissolution of the Federation of Japanese Proletarian Artists, a new organization of proletarian writers and artists called the Japan Proletarian Cultural Federation (Nihon Proletaria Bunka Renmei) was formed, but about four hundred of its most important members, including Nakano Shigeharu, Tsuboi Shigeji, Kurahara Korehito and Miyamoto Yuriko, were soon arrested. Only Kobayashi Takiji and Miyamoto Kenji escaped arrest, and they guided the underground proletarian movement.[13] By 1935, it was apparent that the proletarian movement had lost all of its organizational support.

Because the legal activities of the proletarian writers were so limited, those who went underground tended to be further radicalized. This created added difficulties for their followers, who were caught between the radicalism of the leadership and the pressure of the police. Thus the proletarian literary and cultural movement reached its most critical moment, with Kobayashi and Miyamoto fighting against the police and the authority of the state to maintain proletarian literature as a revolutionary movement, while such writers as Hayashi Fusao tried to maintain a space in which writers could write by freeing literature from the direct control of politics.[14] Hayashi's argument was instrumental in the dissolution of the Proletarian Writers' Federation, an autonomous group within the Cultural Federation. The dissolution of the Writers' Federation and the conversion of writers left those who had given up the movement but remained committed to proletarian writing without a clear theoretical and methodological direction.

By 1937, when the Sino-Japanese War resumed in earnest, the division between the proletarian literary movement and bourgeois literary movements, a division which had characterized the early Showa scene, had changed into a division between writers who supported the war (or went along with the government's policy on the war) and writers who resisted the increasingly militarist-nationalist thrust of public policy. This change was foreshadowed in 1933 by the formation of the Art and Literature Freedom Federation (Gakugei Jiyu Domei), organized mainly by Miki Kiyoshi and Toyoshima Yoshio, which included among its members Yokomitsu Riichi and such Communist Party members as Tokuda Kyūichi and Miyamoto Kenji. The formation of a writers' group of this kind, which included both radical and liberal writers, reflects a fundamental change in the direction of the proletarian literary movement, since NAPF admitted only Marxist-Leninists and considered all other literary views to be bourgeois. The attempt, therefore, of such committed communists as Miyamoto Kenji to form a federation of all antiwar writers, whatever their ideology, reflects the change in direction of the proletarian movement and the recognition that unified resistance was necessary.

The debate over socialist realism started as part of the larger debate over politics and literature, and focusing on the question of the relation between world view and creative method, continued until 1938, the year after the outbreak of the Sino-Japanese War. In other words, the debate took place at the most critical time of the proletarian literary movement in Japan, at the moment when the movement was crushed and writers were looking for some way of writing. Unlike the situation in Soviet Russia, where socialist realism was advocated at least in part in order to unite proletarian writers who had been divided into separate factions and to present a new relation between world view and method that might replace dialectical material-ism, some of the advocates of socialist realism in Japan tried to use socialist realism to justify nonideological proletarian writing. Thus while socialist realism was being used to bridge the gap between politics and literature in Soviet Russia (and in the communist areas of China), it was being used in precisely the opposite way by some of its advocates in Japan.

Bungaku Hyōron (Literary Review), which was formed at the time of the dissolution of the Writers' Federation, strongly ar-gued that regardless of the author's world view, if the method is that of realism, revolutionary literature will emerge as a re-sult.[15] In the same period, in his influential essay "New Change in Creative Practice,"[16] Tokunaga Sunao used socialist realism as a theory to separate creative practice from political prac-tice. Attacking such leaders of the Writers' Federation as Ku-rahara Korehito, Tokunaga was responsible, with Hayashi Fu-sao, for its dissolution.

The participants in the debate, which centered around the ap-plicability of socialist realism in Japan, can be divided into three groups. Such writers as Kawaguchi Hiroshi and Kubo Sa-kae argued that in adapting socialist realism to Japanese set-tings, it should be made to take the form of negative realism or revolutionary anticapitalist realism, while such writers as Itō Teisuke and Koyama Shigeo advocated people's revolutionary realism. Miyamoto Yuriko, Nagano Shigeharu and Tsubokawa Tsurujiro represent the third position. Aware of the political nature of the debate, they sought to demonstrate the relation be-tween world view and method without trying to simplify the re-lation for the purpose of adapting it to the Japanese context.

Socialist realism as literary theory never became deeply rooted in the Japanese literary world, mainly because the whole proletarian literary movement was crushed by the time the war

was over. With the almost complete destruction of the Japanese
Communist Party, the wide range of people who resisted had lost
their guiding organization, leaving the activities of proletarian
and communist literature isolated and lacking in social or organizational support. Such resistance literary movements as the
one led by Aragon in France never existed in Japan. Despite the
numerous articles written on proletarian realism and socialist
realism and the active debate carried out among proletarian
writers, relatively few works of socialist realism were produced.
Among those that did appear, Miyamoto Yuriko's short stories
and Kubo Sakae's play Volcanic Ash Zone (1937-38) stand among
the best examples of socialist realism.[17] After the Second World
War, debate over the relation between politics and literature
was renewed among members of the Japanese Communist Party
when the party was reestablished, but the major literary issues
of the postwar period have revolved around the question of the
writers' war responsibility and the question of tenkō.

Tokunaga Sunao, the author of the representative proletarian
novel Taiyo no nai machi (Sunless City, 1928), attacked the use
of dialectical materialism advocated by party leaders as a
method of creation.[18] Although he supported the position that
creative method cannot be separated from world view, Tokunaga
said that writers grow ideologically through creative practice.
He argued that such great writers of realism as Shakespeare,
Balzac, de Maupassant, Chikamatsu and Saikaku have used their
realistic method to produce class figures who are all vivid
characters. Although he was quite cautious about uncritically
introducing revolutionary romanticism to Japan, he advocated
writing about proletarians without using dialectical materialism directly.

Kawaguchi Hiroshi was also opposed to giving ideology excessive weight in literary creation, but his approach to the question
of socialist realism was quite different from that of Tokunaga.
Socialist realism, Kawaguchi asserted in an article entitled
"Negative Realism: A Direction for Proletarian Literature"
(1934),[19] seeks to depict the truth of socialism, that is, the
richness of life and versatility of truth at historical moments

when socialism is developing victoriously. Writers can write
about socialist truth only under such circumstances, only when
the situation is truly socialist. Socialist realism, therefore, is
a positive and active realism that depicts the rise of socialism.
In Japan, however, the situation was totally different; socialism
had not become a rising historical force. Most of the proletarian writers were intellectuals, and there was a great gap between workers and farmers. If writers were to depict reality
truthfully, then the reality presented could only be negative.
Japanese proletarian literature had simply not reached the point
where revolutionary romanticism could be presented. Under the
reality of capitalist rule, Kawaguchi claimed, depicting reality
negatively from the perspective of socialism is not at all reactionary, contrary to arguments presented in the Soviet Union.
In new proletarian literature (by this he meant after literature
had gained a certain independence from politics), negative realism would become the most significant perspective in depicting
reality.

Moriyama Kei, in his article "Criticism of Negative Realism"
(1934),[20] was sharply critical of Kawaguchi's position. Moriyama distinguished between bourgeois, reactionary realism,
which he saw as presenting a cynical understanding of reality
under the pretension of depicting reality objectively, and socialist realism, whose essence he saw in the positive image of
a new world projected by revolutionary romanticism. Negative
realism, according to Moriyama, dissociates the proletarian
world view from literary creation and implies a cynicism that
is bourgeois rather than socialist. The truth of socialism can
be grasped, he believed, only by the author's participation in the
struggle to achieve socialist society. The condition for writing
socialist realism, therefore, is the author's commitment to
revolutionary practice rather than the existence of socialism
or its imminent success.

According to Moriyama, it was incorrect to talk of the Japanese situation as negative. It was only the intelligentsia, dis-
sociated from the "socialistic reality" of Japan, who talked in
this way. Socialist realism depicts the reality which can be

grasped by the proletariat actively engaged in the construction
of socialist society; there are no negative and positive socialist
realisms. Revealing the ugliness of reality is legitimate only
in the writer's attempt to bring about socialist society; doing so
without ideological perspective is exactly what petty bourgeois
intellectuals do in their so-called bourgeois realism.

Itō Teisuke was also critical of the concept of "negative realism." He argued that socialist realism is not the summation of
reality but a selective representation of reality, of what is typical. Above all, it is a representation of the positive effort and
consciousness of millions of workers and farmers who are pouring their energy into the creation of their own future.[21] Socialist realism, according to Itō, is a method of understanding this
positive historical force. Without the world view of dialectical
materialism and without placing this positive proletarian force
in the perspective of dialectical materialism we can never grasp
the socialist reality.

Still another approach to socialist realism was taken by Nakano Shigeharu, who pointed out in his article "Problems of Socialist Realism" (1935)[22] the distortions in understanding socialist realism which had occurred because writers were eager
to use it to justify their own literary theories. He pointed out
first of all that socialist realism had never been presented as
the antithesis of dialectical materialism. Socialist realism in
the Soviet Union was concerned primarily with three questions:
first, the reflection of Marxism-Leninism in the practice of
philosophy, politics, economics and art; second, the evaluation
of the past history of art and literature; and third, the reflection
of the relations of socialist society. Soviet theorists were concerned with the theory of literature on a global level, not merely
with their own social-political situation. To say that socialist
realism is applicable to Soviet reality but not to Japanese reality, Nakano claimed, is irrelevant to the concerns of socialist
realism. If socialist realism has a slogan, it is "anticapitalist
realism."

Both Nakano and Moriyama were the targets of Kubo Sakae.
In his article "Socialist Realism and Revolutionary (Anticapital-

ist) Realism: The Distortions of Nakano and Moiyama" (1935),[23]
he accused them of distorting the theoretical structure of socialist realism. According to Kubo, socialist realism is the antithesis of dialectical materialism and is the highest stage of artistic creation, that is, the socialist stage of art and literature.
Quoting Gorky, he argued that the proletarian nation needs cultural technicians, technicians of the mind. Socialist realism
gives great weight to the technique of literature and the technique of creation. It is a theory that strengthens and broadens
the cultural front, and it should be distinguished from anticapitalist art movements. Socialist realism's emphasis on technique
should not be understood as contradictory to having a world
view, as Nakano argues. Without the creation of new forms, the
ideological fulfillment of the work cannot be achieved.

Miyamoto Yuriko, avoiding the more overtly political positions
in the debate, argued that socialist realism is the strengthening
of the possibilities for proletarian activities in different cultural
spheres for the sake of the creation of socialist society.[24] In
essence, Yuriko argued that socialist realism is the practice of
writers writing about the creation of socialist society in their
own way, according to their own observation of reality. She said
that it is an effective literary method at the time when the proletarian movement has reached a certain height and the prole-
tarianization of intellectuals, farmers, workers and citizens has
become a major historical force. Socialist realism, therefore,
does not deny politics a role in literature; nor does it deny
dialectical materialism as a method of creation. Above all, it
supports neither professionalism in literature nor nonrevolu-
tionary depiction of the masses. It is, to the contrary, a method
of giving literature its proper role on the battlefront of the entire proletarian movement.

The dispute over socialist realism in Japan, therefore, dealt
with the relation between world view (particularly dialectical
materialism) and literary creation on the one hand, and with its
validity and usefulness in dealing with the Japanese situation on
the other. The arguments focused on two points: (1) the relation of ideology to the method of realism in literature — whether

socialist realism is the antithesis of dialectical materialism — and (2) the question of revolutionary romanticism — that is, of the projection of the future, positive society — in realistic literature, particularly in depicting the situation of the Japanese proletariat. Japanese writers rarely discussed the works of such prominent theoreticians of socialist realism as Georg Lukacs, and they had very little understanding of Soviet discussions concerning socialist realism, although various theoreticians quoted Soviet writers to support their ideas. This is partly because their concern was not the examination and evaluation of the theory itself, but its usefulness for their own writing. Since literary creation was considered among proletarian writers to be a revolutionary activity, any theory of literature had to be primarily a theory of creation, one which could help guide their writing. Although Aono's "purposefulness" in literature — the injection of political purpose into literature — presents one definite approach to writing, its assertion that writers must shape their works according to their political purpose provides only an abstract theory of writing. Subjecting literature to the obvious control of politics, moreover, made many professional writers uneasy.

Although Kurahara's proletarian realism, on the other hand, interprets reality from the standpoint of dialectical materialism, it emphasizes realism as a literary method and in doing so provides concrete guidance to writers. Since Kurahara's theory identifies realism with dialectical materialism, moreover, it extends Aono's concept of "purposefulness," making it at once more specific and more rigid. On the basis of his theory, which was soon adopted as the party line, Kurahara advocated working with amateur writers who were true proletarians and exerting strong control over the choice of subjects.

Some professional writers naturally felt that Kurahara's realism was a political theory rather than a literary one and that it did not allow them to write freely and imaginatively. These writers saw in socialist realism a theory separating realism from dialectical materialism and literature from politics, thereby giving literature greater autonomy and priority. For

the writers who were forced to give up their political beliefs and
political ties to the revolutionary movement, and for those who
found the party too radical to follow, socialist realism presented
theoretical support enabling them to continue their proletarian
literary activities without political control. In this context, the
question of tenkō intruded itself inevitably into the debate over
socialist realism and in fact became the central element.

After the forced conversion, most writers turned to nonpolitical writings, mainly writings of internal search dealing with the
disillusionment and sense of sinfulness and futility they experienced after they themselves negated their raison d'être as revolutionary writers. Some writers, however, continued to convince themselves and others that severing the official ties with
the party and superficial abandonment of political ideology would
not change fundamentally the nature of their works. The purity
and legitimacy of their writings, therefore, had to be proven by
presenting a new theoretical basis for writing proletarian literature without obvious political purpose. Tokunaga Sunao, Hayashi Fusao and Hirano Ken were among the writers engaged in
this search, but all of them had been discontent with the radical
abstractness of the party's literary guidance even before the issue of tenkō had arisen. For them, the search for a new theory
to free proletarian literature from direct and obvious political
control was not merely an act of self-justification. For many
writers, tenkō did not mean a conversion to bourgeois writing
but a new start as proletarian writers. It was natural that they
found in socialist realism a theoretical basis for freeing literature from the strict approach to reality dictated by dialectical
materialism.

The question of revolutionary romanticism, the other central
issue of the debate, touches more directly upon socialist realism's applicability to the Japanese situation. Kawaguchi and
Kubo Sakae took the position that since a realistic portrayal of
Japan's social and human condition could not be optimistic or
"romantic," realism must be negative or at best critical. Thus
Kawaguchi used the term "revolutionary anticapitalist realism"
rather than "revolutionary romanticism" in his effort to avoid

confronting the fundamental contradiction between realism and
romanticism in socialist realism.

The criticism Kawaguchi and Kubo received from Moriyama
and Itō Teisuke was based on the question of the writer's outlook
or world view. According to Moriyama and Itō, "negative realism" implies the same cynical approach to reality that one finds
in bourgeois realism. At the same time, they saw the revolutionary romanticism in the writer's positive treatment of the
proletariat and their revolutionary effort as an essential element in socialist realism. What Moriyama called "people's revolutionary realism," therefore, grasps revolutionary romanticism in terms of the writer's commitment to or belief in revolution and the presentation of proletarians as positive heroes.

Itō's argument that socialist realism selects those elements
in reality which are characteristic or typical and is a method of
understanding the positive historical force (that shapes the typical reality) clarifies the relation between the author's world
view and realism, fortifying Moriyama's point that reality can
be grasped only from the perspective of those who are actively
engaged in changing it into a socialist reality. The authors' belief in proletarian revolution as an inevitable and positive historical force, and their commitment to it, are what distinguish
socialist realism from bourgeois, "objective" realism. In this
context, proletarians emerge as positive class heroes. Thus,
although Moriyama and Itō regarded dialectical materialism as
the correct ideology, they integrated most of the arguments
presented by the proponents of socialist realism into their own
theory.

The arguments supporting revolutionary romanticism were
more straightforward and less complex than those marshalled
in the debate over dialectical materialism and literary realism,
yet under the overt police repression and military rule, revolutionary romanticism never gained many adherents, for the
possibility of revolution was remote, and "romanticism" was
indeed unrealistic. Several authors, however, including Miyamoto Yuriko, Nakano Shigeharu and Kubo Sakae, centered their
works around the birth of the revolutionary and the awakening

of the common worker to revolutionary consciousness, as well
as the portrayal of an exploitative and quite desperate reality.
By emphasizing human growth and the attainment of revolutionary consciousness rather than victorious class struggle, these
writers integrated the presentation of positive heroes and their
belief in the historical validity of proletarian revolution with the
portrayal of exploitative reality, creating works of inner growth
and revitalizing realism in Japanese literature.

The dispute over socialist realism climaxed the proletarian
writers' search for an appropriate methodology. While Moriyama was the strongest proponent of socialist realism, Kawaguchi, Kubo and Itō, although advocates of socialist realism, argued that it must be changed to negative realism, revolutionary
(anticapitalist) realism or people's revolutionary realism re-
spectively in using it as a methodology for writing about the
Japanese situation. The choice of any of these alternative forms
raised important questions with regard to the future direction
of proletarian literature. The dispute, therefore, had deeper
philosophic and political implications than the question of methodology itself suggested.

As the war progressed, Japanese writers' alienation from social and political reality deepened. Such writers as Tanizaki
Junichiro and Kawabata Yasunari, escaping into the world of
classical literature and aesthetics, remained aloof from contemporary affairs as well as from the debate over realism. The
writers of the Japanese Romantic Group (Nihon Romanha), nationalistic advocates of defending and restoring Japan's spiritual
and aesthetic tradition, also revealed their fundamental alienation from the reality of contemporary Japan in their search for
the archetypal origins of Japanese culture in classical and
primitive literature. In the postwar period, Mishima Yukio
emerged as a successor to this group. Although the proletarian
literary movement was crushed almost completely by the time
Japan invaded China, the new tradition of realism which it
helped establish provided the basis for the postwar literary efforts to deal with the complex social and cultural changes of the
period, and with the philosophic and political questions that accompanied them.

Kamen no kokuhaku (Confessions of a Mask), Mishima Yukio's second full-length novel, appeared in 1949, the fourth year of Japan's postwar literary activities, and established the literary reputation of the twenty-four-year-old Mishima instantly and unshakably. Although the novel shocked some critics and puzzled others, all of them recognized Mishima's undeniable and "unusual" talent, and agreed that he was a "unique," "new" writer whose writings were a marked departure from Japan's literary tradition.[1] The novel was considered shocking and puzzling not only because its protagonist's confession of his homosexuality was unprecedented as a literary subject, but also because the protagonist's attitude toward the war and his experiences in it was diametrically opposed to the humanistic criticism of the war which characterized the postwar literary mainstream. The publication of the novel, therefore, was a significant event not only for Mishima, whose literary efforts had hitherto met a varied response, but also for postwar literary history. Soon after the novel appeared, Hanada Kiyoteru wrote that after a delay of half a century, Japan's twentieth century had started with the appearance of this novel.[2]

Mishima himself considered the work to be "the logical conclusion" to his temperament, a temperament which infused the world of his early works.[3] Yet Confessions of a Mask is a new starting point for his novels as well as the conclusion to his early works, for the "logical conclusion" meant not only the

metaphysical or aesthetic clarification of his perception and
temperament, but also the rationalization of his methodology, a
way to fictionalize his temperament and thereby to create the
world of his metaphysics and aesthetics.

Mishima, who considered himself a poet by nature, depended
heavily upon his "temperament" in his early fiction.[4]   If Confessions of a Mask marks a new start in his literature, it is because the work is a "novel" while his early works are "poems,"
open expressions of his temperament; yet this "novel," like all
of his others, is poetry in disguise.

Mishima stated that he had come to understand that the true
substance of poetry is realization, and that he had decided to
part from his "sensuous talent" and from his "sensuous perception" itself. He tried to do so by writing Confessions of a Mask,
"forcibly, through the form of the novel."[5]   As Hanada said, the
novel is filled with "logical lyricism" and is basically a poem in
the form of a novel. Mishima created his own type of "novel" in
his attempt to provide the "logical conclusion" to his temperament. Therefore, when Mishima stated that he had "somehow
conquered his inner monster" by writing Confessions of a Mask,
it did not mean merely that he had finally confronted his homosexual temperament, but also that he had found the way to deal
with his desire to express his temperament in literature, the
way to fictionalize his temperament.

Besides being a confessional novel, Confessions of a Mask is
a novel about Mishima's method for the novel; indeed, it is as
significant to Mishima's novel as The Counterfeiters is to Gide's.
If the temperament and "sensuous perception" underlying his
metaphysical and aesthetic world are poetry, this novel is the
logical architecture of that world and the means to give it logical form (by fictionalizing it). For Mishima, the novel meant
the method, and the question of the novel and the question of
methodology were inseparable. Indeed, for Mishima, who pre-
ferred masks to real faces, structure to lyricism, and artificial
effects to real facts, "fiction" was the key term.

When it first appeared, however, Confessions of a Mask was
considered solely as an openly autobiographical work, an I-novel

in which a bold confession of the author's homosexuality takes place. In fact, the protagonist of the novel is meticulously presented as identical to the author insofar as his biographical data are concerned. If the novel is a confessional I-novel, then the identification of the protagonist with the author is not in doubt, and the confession of the protagonist is the confession of the author. The novel must be understood accordingly as the removal of the protagonist-author's social mask, an exposé of the real face hitherto hidden behind the mask.

It is true that the protagonist constantly wears a mask and that he "gestures" in order to carry on his everyday life; he engages in "the masked theater to show it to myself,"[6] and the plot of the novel is the protagonist's realization of his "abnormality" and his analysis of his "life of gestures." There is no doubt that Mishima meant the protagonist to be taken as the author himself, as his meticulous effort to make the protagonist identical to him indicates, and it is also evident that Mishima intended to make his homosexuality public by writing this novel. Indeed, confession exists at the core of modern fiction, and the modern novel is a means for "confession." As can be seen in Flaubert's statement that Emma is himself, the fictional confession provides the basic metaphysics of the modern novel. If characters are masks through which the authors "confess," then the homosexual protagonist of Mishima's novel is the author's mask which enabled him to confess. Confessions of a Mask, then, must be understood as Mishima's self-revelation "in terms of" the protagonist. As Hanada pointed out, Mishima wore a mask in order to confess. The mask was Mishima's means of fictionalizing his inner drama.

What did Mishima intend to do by letting his protagonist confess, and what did he want to reveal by wearing the mask of the homosexual protagonist? Mishima was not like Shimazaki Tōson and Tayama Katai, writers who were urged on in their art by a desire for self-revelation for ethical or artistic reasons; nor was he like Shiga Naoya, a writer for whom the search for self provided the structure and the materials for his novels. Yet in creating his prototypal, ideal heroes, Mishima was al-

most exclusively involved in creating heroes who reflected various aspects of his own personality. Whether Mishima was an
egomaniac seeking to express himself in terms of his heroes or
merely tried fastidiously to identify himself with the heroes he
created, there is no doubt that the protagonists' worlds were
what inspired Mishima's dream and passion as his own inner
world.

Mishima's well-known dislike of Dazai Osamu certainly reflects on the surface his criticism of those I-novelists who use
openly their own weakness and desperation as subjects of literary pursuit. Yet one cannot but feel that Mishima's dislike of
Dazai is due to his disgust at seeing in Dazai his own egotistical
inclination exposed so defenselessly.[7] Mishima's attack on confessional I-novels and their authors — brooding, self-destructive
intellectuals who could be interested only in their own inner agonies — and his criticism of the tendency among Japanese
writers to identify life and art, can best be understood as
paradoxical rhetoric used to hide his egotistical involvement
in himself.

Mishima was consistent, however, in insisting on his creative
theory — that is, that art belongs to a logically constructed fictional world dimensionally different from that of life. Mishima
stated that he started his writing by searching for a method to
hide rather than to reveal himself.[8] With Japanese writers who
confused art and life in mind, Mishima declared, quite deliberately that for him art and life belong to different dimensions, just as intellect and flesh belong to different dimensions.
At the same time, Mishima always revealed the central themes
and essential qualities of his protagonists at the start of his
novels. Whether they are criminals, perverts or madmen is
made clear to the reader from the beginning, and Mishima's art
is a kind of magic — his analysis of the mechanism of the human
spirit — which draws the reader into the depths of the protagonist's world. Mishima's "logical" analytical eyes were always
open, particularly when he described the protagonists who were
masks for himself, and he was never "drunk" in writing the
drama of his alter ego. Although there is no doubt that Confes-

sions of a Mask is about himself, what is revealed by the confession is not the real face of Mishima;[9] the novel is another
"masked play," enabling him to survive not as a man who lives
in daily social life, but to survive as a writer.

Prior to writing Confessions of a Mask, Mishima wrote several nihilistic aesthetic works which appeared anachronistic in
the postwar literary atmosphere.[10] He had already discovered
his central theme, the life whose beauty and brilliance are supported by its impending annihilation. His "sense of ending" had
already found the metaphors of summer and sea, metaphors
which were to occupy an increasingly important place in his
later works.[11] Mishima started as a writer with his "aesthetics of annihilation (ending)" serving as the raison d'être for both
his life and his art. Just as Mizoguchi in Kinkakuji (The Temple of the Golden Pavilion, 1956) felt threatened when he learned
that the temple had escaped, now that the war was over and destruction no longer seemed inevitable, Mishima felt threatened
by having to face the postwar era of peace in which a long life
seemed assured to him, thus depriving his art of its basic metaphysics.[12] The tragic stance which Mishima and his protagonists could assume when confronted by predicaments in which
their death seemed asssured would no longer be possible for
them, and Mishima had to create new predicaments which would
enable them to be tragic heroes, heroes in the world of his "aesthetics of the ending."

In this sense, Confessions of a Mask is his successful attempt
to create a new "fate" for his hero, a fate that would condemn
him to inevitable "destruction." In the novel, his destruction or
death is only a social one, taking the form of absolute alienation
in a spiritual sense from peaceful, "everyday life." The novel is
a deliberate declaration of the identity of the author and his hero
as masochistic homosexuals. The declaration is a challenge to
society, but not a challenge to accept the protagonist-author as
a homosexual. Rather, establishing his "abnormality" was an
attempt to separate himself absolutely from the world of daily
life and to force society, therefore, to condemn him.

The novel is, therefore, a rational articulation of his relation

to the world and to the age. It is a novel in which Mishima made
a statement about his "being in the world," to use Sartre's
phrase, attempting thereby to retain the possibility of being identified as a tragic hero and thus to maintain his aesthetics of
death. If Mishima "confessed" in the novel, he confessed his
deep-seated fear of living in the peaceful postwar world where
his raison d'être as a man and as a writer no longer existed.
The tragic sentiment in the novel is that created by accepting
the protagonist-author's fated destruction as the condition for
his life's fulfillment. Mishima's hero is one who maintains a
heroic stance in exchange for his own death. When there was
no war to demand the sacrifice of young lives for the sake of the
emperor, what fate could a man accept to die gloriously?

Mishima's homosexuality was a "fate" which he deliberately
chose, a fate which separated him (and his protagonist) from ordinary life. For the protagonist, to whom the tragic is the only
salvation of life, leading a daily life in which tragic fate is absent is "gesturing." Life is, after all, a masked play. Mishima's aspiration for the tragic was obviously conceived in
terms of Nietzsche's Dionysus, whose aspiration for the tragic
is an aspiration to transcend himself.[13] The truly tragic hero,
for Mishima, had to possess a beautiful body whose principle
was being and action. The writer, engaged in words, could create a tragedy but could not participate in it. Likewise, the homosexual protagonist suffers from his initial awareness of the
"nonexistence of the self," and yearns for a beautiful body — for
a tragic hero. His homosexuality, therefore, is not only what
separates him from daily life, but also what enables him to participate in tragedy by aspiring to be one with, that is, to love, a
tragic hero. Fulfilling his aspiration for the beautiful flesh he
lacks and for the heroic tragic death which he is not qualified to
obtain requires a sacrifice of blood and death. The protagonist's love for St. Sebastian and Omi reveals this clearly.

In order to make his homosexuality "fate," it was necessary
for both society and Mishima himself to condemn his trait or
temperament. Mishima indicated that he regarded this temperament, a temperament without which his very identity would

have been destroyed, as his enemy. Although his homosexuality or temperament was the fate he chose by his own will, it had to remain a negative element against which he had to fight. To desire not to be oneself was essential. By choosing the identity of a homosexual, he was able to stand alone against a hostile world, one composed of the totality of hostile others. Yet in order to maintain his temperament as negative, he had to remain immersed in the image of himself reflected in heterosexuals and thus exist in the consciousness of others constantly. The protagonist's masochism is a method of existing solely in the consciousness of others and thus gaining a sense of himself and of life.

In Confessions of a Mask, Mishima's protagonist finds that although he is unable to desire women, he can still love them. He feels that although he wears the mask of an ordinary man in his association with Sonoko, his love, when he is not in fact an ordinary man, love can exist between them. The world of love he shares with Sonoko is a world of spiritual eros, a world of harmony in which an aggressive life of the flesh is lacking. The earnestness with which he questions whether he can love a woman without desire makes it appear almost as though he is undertaking a religious quest to overcome the impossible, human limitation, and his agony appears to be that of the religious chosen. The mask almost becomes a metaphor for the human condition, and the novel impresses the reader as a tragic poem in disguise; yet life makes itself felt with a surge that threatens to overwhelm his body.

Life-force — it was the sheer extravagant abundance of life-force that overpowered the boys. They were overwhelmed by the feeling he gave of having too much life, by the feeling of purposeless violence that can be explained only as life existing for its own sake, by his type of ill-humored, unconcerned exuberance. Without his being aware of it, some force had stolen into Omi's flesh and was scheming to take possession of him, to crash through him, to spill out of him, to outshine him. In this respect, the power resembled a malady.... As for me, I felt the same as the other boys — with important differences. In my case — it was enough to make me blush with shame — I had had an erection, from the first moment in which I had glimpsed that abundance of his.[14]

It is when the protagonist meets an aggressive challenge of

life that he is provoked to the eros of the flesh. The first man who sexually provoked him was a night-soil gatherer. His very fear of the crazed mobs at festivals or of revolutionaries driven into an ecstatic state by the aggressive force of life creates his ambivalent attachment to them.

Through it all there was only one vividly clear thing, a thing that both horrified and lacerated me, filling my heart with unaccountable agony. This was the expression on the faces of the young men carrying the shrine — an expression of the most obscene and undisguised drunkenness in the world....[15]

In his fantasies, he is constantly a victim attacked by animalistic mobs in action, pure flesh which is the embodiment of the aggressiveness of life itself. His fear, hostility and attachment to the pure flesh and his desire to identify himself with the aggressor he fears create his masochistic world of eros. Thus his relation to the world becomes his relation to himself. The protagonist's masochistic desire to identify himself with the aggressive force of life and Mishima's later fetishism of the well-built body both stem from Mishima's initial recognition of his lack of flesh and fear of flesh.[16]

Defining oneself as an outsider, a "pagan" who cannot occupy a place in a normal, humane life, is one of the singular means artists have used for self-definition in modern industrial society, a utilitarian society hostile to art. Tonio Kröger's dichotomy definitely underlies Mishima's isolation from the "normalcy" of life.[17]

In modern Japanese literature, such I-novelists as Katai and Toson converted their failure in everyday life into privileges of the novelist which would enable them to concern themselves exclusively with their isolation and to write about it. Dazai Osamu also deliberately acted out the role which others forcibly imposed on him. In Mishima's case, homosexuality presented a stronger rationale for the protagonist's isolation and uniqueness, for the isolation is physically real rather than just mental. As for Mishima himself, in like fashion precisely, his "abnormality" was the license for his art, his license for writing.

Mishima's hero, having lost the "blessing" of a tragic fate with which the war provided him, had to choose his own fate by his own will, a fate that would assure his destruction. In most of Mishima's works, the sense of life, the experience of eros, is inseparably connected with death, the death the protagonist envisions for himself. Yet in Confessions of a Mask, although blood and death provoke the protagonist to a sense of life and eros, he does not envision his own glorious death. Through his masochism, he attains a kind of heroism, but unlike the protagonist in "Yūkoku" (Patriotism), he does not actively seek his own death. This is because he is attracted by the erotic sweetness which the idea of death provokes rather than by death itself.[18] Moreover, as in the case of Mizoguchi in The Temple of the Golden Pavilion, his fulfillment in homosexuality is his attempt to live. Mishima wrote that when he finished the novel, he felt clearly that he wanted to survive.

After writing a novel like Confessions of a Mask, through which I conquered my inner monster in any event, two opposing aspirations appeared clearly in the mind of the then twenty-four-year-old me. One was the feeling that I must live under any circumstance. The other was a leaning toward classicism that is precise, intellectual and clear.[19]

Confessions of a Mask is the story of the birth of an artist, that of Mishima himself. The homosexual protagonist who at once fears and aspires for pure flesh is a metaphor for the writer who, belonging to the world of intellect, writes because he aspires for the tragic intensity of life. In this sense the novel is about himself, about the search for the author. The self-search of the protagonist is identified with the self-search of the author, his ontological quest for what he is; it is the self-search of "a creature, non-human and somehow strangely pathetic." [20] In this sense the novel can be called truly confessional.

The novel is, however, a fictional work and not a real account of Mishima's life. In his notes for Confessions of a Mask, Mishima wrote that true confession is impossible (" the true essence of confession is its impossibility"), for only a mask with flesh can confess, and that he intended to write a perfect fic-

tional work of confession. In order to pursue the ontological
quest of the mask, a mask must deliberately be worn. If Mishima's mask were forcibly taken away, we might discover
that there is neither a face nor any naked facts at all behind it;
there would be nothing, or at best abstract passion, which was
for him the substance of life.

The novels of Tomioka Taeko (1935-   ) contain many autobiographical elements. In Meido no kazoku (A Family of Hades,
1974), Shokubutsusai (The Festival of Vegetables, 1974), and Kochūan ibun (The Strange Story of Kochūan, 1974), many of the
sections are based on the author's real life or personal experiences.[1] It is clear, however, that her novels are not I-novels of
self-search; each of her works has a well-contrived story with
its own fictional devices. Her widely acclaimed use of "Bunraku
narration" is instrumental in bringing into her novels those to
whom her protagonists relate in daily life, however ambiguous
these relations may be. Thus her novels are fundamentally different from I-novels, which are composed of inner monologues
and self-search supported only by the author's self-consciousness. How then should we understand the personal life of the author which exists in the center of her works? What does it mean
that a certain period of her life — a period about which the author obviously feels she must write — is constantly used as the
basis of her novels? For those who know her personally or
those who have read her autobiography and numerous other essays dealing with her experiences, the stories which are told in
A Family of Hades are already quite familiar ones; yet the meaning
of her novels seems to exist in the very fact that, despite the importance of autobiographical elements, they are not I-novels.
A Family of Hades is composed of four independent stories,

---

*A Japanese version of this chapter appeared in Gendaishi Techo, May 1976.

yet the progression of time which encompasses the protagonist's growth — childhood, life with her lover, separation and marriage — supplies the basic structure for the novel, linking the four stories to create an integrated whole. As time passes in her personal life, the lives of the common people around her change too. Through the changes that take place in these people's lives, social and cultural changes — and therefore historical time — are introduced in the novel.

The novel, however, is not a Bildungsroman either, for the growth of the protagonist is not a theme of the novel and it therefore lacks the typical motif of a Bildungsroman, the establishment of the relation between the self and the world by tracing the growth of the self as an historical as well as a personal existence. The protagonist describes the relations between herself and her father, mother, brothers and sister, sisters-in-law, lover, his parents and his wife, but her first-person-singular narration does not indicate an intention of self-search. Rather, skimming lightly over her subjects and treating them in a relaxed manner, she shows great interest in them as individual existences. The protagonist does not exist firmly at the center of the novel like a Jamesean center of consciousness. Although the "I" in the novel, who is a victim of the people surrounding her, must in fact be the most involved character, the "I" narrates her own relation to them as if she were an outsider or, sometimes, as if she were defending them. Moreover, when the story is complete, the reader does not know in what way the protagonist has changed or grown.

A Family of Hades is about two subcultures in Japan, both of which can be called indigenous, and the novel traces the way these indigenous subcultures undergo change in the new circumstances of the postwar period. On the one hand, there is the world of the protagonist's mother and that of her father (although her mother's world has a different logic than that of her father, it belongs to the same subculture), and on the other hand, there is the world of her lover, Sho-chan. The former is a world which demands a strict moral code in human relations, a code according to which one's actions and behavior must be justified. The latter is a world in which one lives according to the circumstances, an easy-going (actually extremely self-centered) world in which one feels everything will turn out all right, absolving one of the need to justify one's behavior to others. If the former is the Edo gamblers' world of duty and loyalty, the latter is the world of the "immigrants" who move from one place to another, seeking a convenient place to accommodate their way of life.

Standing between these two subcultures, the protagonist is surprised, at a loss, impressed and disgusted, and she continues to talk of her relation to them as if she has forgotten that she is a victim of the two. The attractiveness of the narration is not that of the uninvolved narrator whose personality shines out during her story of others despite herself, but is that of the involved narrator who, while telling her own story, is sidetracked into discussing the lives of the peripheral characters, shifting the weight of her story to the stories of others. The same technique of narration is used in The Festival of Vegetables and The Strange Story of Kochūan rests entirely on it.

The protagonist in The Festival of Vegetables, Tsushima-san, herself becomes one of the peripheral characters in the latter part of the novel, changing her role from the central actor of the story to an observer-narrator watching and telling the story of the people around her. Even in this situation, the "I" of Tsushima-san makes her existence felt strongly. In all of Tomioka's novels, in fact, the "I" floods the world, and even when the "I" narrates only the stories of the others, the reader feels that this is a sidetrack necessary to tell the story of the self. The reader feels certain that the stories of the peripheral characters are side plots only, regardless of how central a part they seem to occupy; no matter how well-conceived the fictional structure of the novel, there exists the vivid, almost violent, self-expression of the author. Tomioka's novels differ markedly, therefore, from both I-novels, which aim at self-expression, and well-structured stories, which hide the author's self in the world of the story.

Although they represent opposing cultures, the protagonist's

father and lover live essentially in the same way in that they
live only according to their own way of life; they refuse to
bother intellectually and emotionally with anything which will
not fit in with their way of life. In this sense, her mother, who
identifies herself as the victim of her husband, belongs to the
same type, for she also lived faithfully to her own inner logic
only. Even the protagonist's younger brother Akira, a child of
the new generation, contains a "darkroom" inside of himself
(he is involved in photography), and he too creates his own life-
style according to the logic of the darkroom.

Interest in the secrets of others, others who are lords of their
own castles, is the central theme of The Strange Story of Kochūan. While in A Family of Hades the others are common people, those whose business it is to carry on everyday life, the
characters in The Strange Story of Kochūan are artists — those
who express — and their business is to create. Yet in Kochūan,
Tomioka questions the distance between the existence which
lives and the existence which expresses, refusing to treat the
protagonist, Yokokawa Sōta, who is an obsessed "expresser,"
as a different species. The dichotomy between life and art here
again is the central concern.

In The Strange Story of Kochūan, the narrative methods em-
ployed in A Family of Hades appear in more systematized form.
The novel is about Yokokawa Sōta, a man who is obsessively involved in making tiny books under his artist's name of Kochūan.
The story is told by a narrator who appears to be interested in
understanding Kochūan's "darkroom" — his inner secret. The
narrator's impulse to draw open the curtain of Kochūan's darkroom creates the justification for her storytelling. To listen to
the story of Kochūan, therefore, is to have a glimpse of the nar-
nator's inner world as well.

The novel thus uses the technique of point of view skillfully,
employing a narrative convention which Edgar Allan Poe so ably
systematized. There is a protagonist (who is the hero of the
story) who acts, and there is a narrator who watches the hero
and tells the hero's drama. The moment when the originally detached narrator becomes involved in the hero's drama and iden-

tifies herself with him internally is the moment when the story
reaches its climax. The hero, however, remains outside the
everyday world (most likely he is a madman), while the narrator, although he or she becomes identified temporarily with the
hero, remains an existence of this world, of the world of daily
life. The Strange Story of Kochūan, therefore, can be read at
once as a story about Kochūan and as a story about the inner
search of the narrator. If it is read in this way, the climax of
the novel occurs at the moment when the narrator, after delving
into the depths of the inner world of Kochūan, transcends him.
The novel, however, goes beyond a simplistic relation between
the actor-hero and observer-narrator, with the narrator asking
herself why she investigates the inner world of the "expresser"
and why she narrates his story. In this way, the author questions herself about the relation between the author and her work,
the relation between everyday life and the world of the novel, and
the relation between living and expressing.

The novel is a story about an "expresser" who creates a
"strange thing" — a work of art — in order to conceal a very
private part of himself, but at the same time in order to "possess" it surely. The novel presents a brilliant analysis of decadent art and literature, Kochūan's romance of sexual fantasy
is very close to the fantasies created by Kawabata, Tanizaki or
Nagai Kafu, and in fact, Kochūan is the prototype of the decadent
romantic artist. The perversion in which one fears in extremity
the revelation of one's dark, private secret, yet finds passion
only in expressing and thus possessing it constantly, has been
one of the central themes of dark romanticism.

The "I," the narrator of the novel, attains the key to the darkroom of Kochūan, and although she comes to the verge of opening the room, she states that she is not interested in bringing
out the secret it contains. Yokokawa Sōta has entered a small
pot (Kochūan means "inside the pot-hut") and there cultivates,
as if cultivating pearls, only what he has permitted to enter.
The narrator says that she is not interested in revealing the
secret of the inside of the pot because she is not sure which is
more true, the bottom of the pot or the "pearl" which was nur-

tured there. For the "expresser," who created "toys" of
miniature books in order to conceal himself, rather than
to liberate himself, the creation of tiny books is indeed a kind
of "vengeful masturbation." The narrator, however, sees the
same infantile perversion, the same obsession, in artists, col-
lectors, lechers, and in essence in all of those dreamers who
are basically lacking in the ability to live in everyday life.[2]

Underlying the novel is the narrator's (author's) concept of
art. The narrator says that "between life and the work of creation, neither is weightier than the other," and that she does not
think that the artist's works are lies and "the room which exists
beyond the works is his real world." What she discovered by
investigating Kochūan is that the reality which existed beyond
his books was not that of a madman. Kochūan, the "expresser"
who contains "the disease called caries" inside his body, is a
prototype of the artist, but she finds him in those who live daily
life as well. The gap between the artist and those who just live
life thus vanishes.

The narrator does not consider the self-satisfying works he
produces great works of art, nor does she consider this egotistical expresser — who even involved others in his endeavor —
a great artist. The "elegant" and "erotic" world of five-colored
shells which was nurtured in the dark inside of the pot is dismissed by the narrator as a matter of no concern to her. She
does not even touch the tiny books which are exhibited on the
shelf, for it is meaningless for her to do so. She says above
all that she lacks the slightest interest in peeping into the
gloomy, weak world inside the pot or in taking that world into
the open. The narrator appears to be both sharply critical of
the art of perversion, egotistically self-insistent in its alienation from the reality of everyday life, and embarrasses, as if
her own private world had been stripped bare.

The fact that the narrator is not in a position simply to reject Kochūan and his world, however, is evident just from the
fact that she does take pains to investigate him — to a point
suggesting obsession — and to tell his story. The narrator explains that she became unwillingly entangled in Kochūan's ego-

tism of self-concealment because her lover, for the sake of
survival (obtaining bread), had taken a position as an illustrator
of his tiny books. In order to avenge herself for it, there was
something which she had to understand herself, and for that purpose she began to investigate Kochūan's inner world after his
death. The period in which she was entangled in Kochūan's obsession is the period when she lived with her lover, Mitsuo, and
to confirm her understanding of Kochūan's dark place was to
confirm her own unhappiness in her life with Mitsuo, thereby
unearthing the darkest part of her life in "the pit." Yet the narrator does not tell us about this part, but conceals it.

The same type of self-concealment can be found in A Family
of Hades. Seeing her mother bound to — if supported by — the
logic of her world of duty and loyalty, a logic that demands
clear-cut moral justification for any conduct bearing on human
relations, the narrator pities her mother and is disgusted by
her. At the same time, the narrator is victimized both by her
lover, to whom her mother's logic never makes any sense, and
her father, to whose masculine pursuit of his own way of life she
is deeply attached. Thus the protagonist becomes sick, is loved
and forsaken by one man, fights with her mother, and marries
a young man, all as if it were the affair of some other woman.

Even after the account of her own drama is over, the protagonist does not forget to tell the tragicomic story of her mother
who, having reached old age, lives with her desire to "sit in a
clean and tidied room of her own," surrounded by her children
to whom her logic makes no sense. Her old house was newly
rebuilt by her children, but she still clings tightly to her grudge
against her husband, pursuing it in her dreams now that he is
gone. Watching her headed toward senility, carried by the tide
of history, Naoko, the protagonist, is sarcastic and tender-
hearted at the same time. She is tied to her by the force of
fate, but at the same time is an individual existence completely
separate from her.

Naoko investigates the life of those who embody the indigenous culture and watches the entire process by which it is absorbed by a new culture and thus destroyed, but there is, on

her part, no emotional empathy with or aggressive defense of
the old culture of common citizens. The indigenous culture of
her parents, Osaka's merchant culture, certainly presents a
value in itself and the mark of one way of life, but it belongs to
the past and does not offer any guidance for her own life. Tomioka, who sometimes becomes anachronistically involved in
traditional culture, declaring after the fashion of Tanizaki that
she aspires to be an "artisan" of the old type rather than a modern artist, is supported by her confidence that she will not confuse the elements of the old, indigenous culture with the elements of avant-garde art, that is, by her confidence in her ability to place the old culture correctly in history.

A Family of Hades, although it is autobiographical, is a novel
in which the revelation of the "darkroom" never takes place.
The novel is filled with the self-assertion of the author, but the
"I" of the author always escapes from the reader's grasp. This
is due to Tomioka's understanding that there are no longer any
heroes with a firm internal world to be dramatized or presented
as the theme of the novel. Above all, it is because of the ambiguous relation between the "I" who is the "expresser" and the "I"
who lives life, an ambiguity which is the very theme of her novel.

The "I" in The Strange Story of Kōchūan dismisses the works
of the "expresser," who is obsessed with his dark place, as
something which makes her sad or something which does not
concern her at all. Her criticism of the art of alienation is a
means of strong self-assertion, for by criticizing it she also
denies the alienation caused by her life with her egocentric
artist-lover. The protagonist, however, is also presented as a
comical antihero. In a bride's waiting room in a church, Naoko
orders sushi to feed her relatives who have arrived from Osaka
to attend her wedding. She prepares herself to be a proper bride
by applying makeup herself, puts on a "Western" wedding veil,
and runs around the church in a sweater to prepare for the ceremony, which will be conducted in accordance with a religion
that has nothing to do with her. Naoko is depicted in a spirit of
intellectually masochistic self-parody.

The morality of the common people in the old, urban-merchant culture is replaced by the morality of the middle class in the urban-capitalist culture. Wanderer-immigrants like her artist-lover can climb from the bottom of one culture to the height of the avant-garde easily because they exist outside the framework of any culture. Naoko watches both dramas and herself gets married, anticlimactically, to a young man. She appears to be an antihero, but in what other way can she relate herself naturally to history? Therefore, Naoko is, after all, a hero.

The coexistence of self-insistence and self-parody characterizes the way Tomioka deals with the self who is an artist. Underlying this coexistence is Tomioka's ambiguity regarding her relation to everyday reality; the expresser (artist) "I" considers herself as incapable in everyday life, while the everyday "I" feels self-conscious about being an egotistical artist who involves others in her pursuit of her obsession, whether it is an obsession with self-revelation or with self-concealment. Her ontological view that both life and art-works, reality and fiction, existing between truth and fabrication, are neither true nor false underlies her complex yet brilliant treatment of the "I" in her novels. She knows quite surely that Kochūan was considered mad by common people, who have a firm grip on everyday life; thus she knows how comical and meaningless her endeavors as an artist might appear to them. At the same time, she knows that all human beings, including those who are not artists, have a "disease" of some kind and are in a sense madmen with some obsession. The reason why the self of the protagonist reveals itself at the same time that it conceals itself in the novel is due to the author's intention to present simultaneously the artist-self and the self who lives life. It is due to the same intention that the self and the surrounding characters freely exchange their roles of being the protagonist and peripheral characters. The more the protagonist tries to express herself in her conversational narration, the more deeply she becomes hidden in the ontological abstraction of the relation between life and art.

Tomioka's novels are offshoots of the modern confessional novel, extensions of the I-novel in which the artist's inner confession dramatizes the growth of the artist or the birth of a new

one. As the central theme of her novels, Tomioka deals with the
birth of a tough "expresser" who transcends the alienated, decadent artist dwelling on his or her own misery as the source of
imagination. Tomioka, who has explored through the language of
poetry the distance between meaning and nonmeaning, and between things and consciousness, was reborn as a novelist by
ascertaining the contents of the darkroom of the obsessed, egotistical artist, and then ignoring or rejecting them.[3]   Underlying her treatment of "I" is her criticism of elite intellectual
artists who egotistically insisted that their personal failure or
agony was the license for the greatness of art, a criticism which
in turn reflects the fundamental changes in the identity of artists and intellectuals in the age of mass culture.

NOTES

INTRODUCTION

1. Nakamura Mitsuo, Nihon no kindai shōsetsu (Modern Japanese Novel), Tokyo, Iwanami, 1974, Introduction, pp. 1-9.
2. Saeki Shōichi, Nihon no watakushi o motomete (In Search of the Japanese I), Tokyo, Kawade, 1974, pp. 5-25.
3. Kobayashi Hideo, "Watakushi shōsetsu ron" (On the I-Novel), Selected Writings of Kobayashi Hideo, Tokyo, Chikuma, 1970, pp. 213-226.
4. Ibid.; Nakamura Mitsuo, "Tayama Katai," Selected Works of Nakamura Mitsuo, Tokyo, Taikodo, 1968, pp. 134-180; "Fūzoku shōsetsu ron" (On the Novels of Social Manners), Nihon no kindai (Japan's Modern Age), Tokyo, Bungei-shunjyū, 1969, pp. 157-236.
5. Ito Sei, "Shinko geijyutsu ha to shin-shinrishugi bungaku" (The New Emerging Art School and the New Psychological Literature), Kindai Bungaku, August 1950.
6. Ibid.

1. IRONIC PERSPECTIVE AND SELF-DRAMATIZATION IN THE CONFESSIONAL I-NOVEL OF JAPAN

1. Hirano Ken distinguishes the shinkyo shōsetsu from the watakushi shōsetsu (I-novel), using the latter term for the destructive confessional novel only, in Geijyutsu to jissei katsu (Art and Real Life), Tokyo, Shinchō Bunko, 1974, pp. 15-45, 274-288. It is my contention, however, that the shinkyo shōsetsu is a type of watakushi shōsetsu and that it will be more appropriate to treat the shinkyo shōsetsu and the confessional novel as the two basic types of the I-novel. Kume Masao's 1925 essay, "Watakashi shōsetsu and shinkyo shōsetsu" (Bungeikōza, January and February 1926), is one of the earliest attempts to distinguish between the two types of I-novel. Ito Sei divides the I-novel into the destructive type and the harmonious type in Shōsetsu no hōhō (Methods of the Novel), Tokyo, Kawade Shobo, 1956, a distinction that is basically consistent with my own treatment.
2. Dazai Osamu uses the (dramatic) confession of the protagonist rather than his own confession as the structural basis of his novel, but for the genre of the confessional novel, whether the confession is that of the author or that of the protagonist is not important. Dramatic confession, the confession of a mask, has always been a device for the author's self-dramatization, and in the novels

201

of inner expose', the protagonists are always alter-egos of the author. Dazai's use of the confession, like Mishima Yukio's, only clarifies the basic overlapping of author and protagonist, of life and art, in the I-novel.

3. Iwano Hōmei, "Gendai shōrai no shōsetsu hasso o isshin subeki boku no byōsha ron" (My Theory of Description Which Will in the Future Transform Imagination in the Novel, 1911); "Ichigen byōsha ron to wa?" (What Is the Theory of One Dimensional Description?, 1920); Selected Writings of Iwano Hōmei, Tokyo, Kōdansha, 1966, pp. 375-381, 381-383.

4. There are works of naturalism which are not I-novels (particularly among the works of early naturalism), and the essentially autobiographical I-novels of later naturalism such as Tokuda Shūsei's Kasōjinbutsu (Characters in a Masked Ball, 1935) and Shukuzu (Microcosm, 1941) are simply life studies and are neither shinkyo shōsetsu nor confessional novels.

5. Kobayashi Hideo, "Watakushi shōsetsu ron" (On the I-Novel), Selected Writings of Kobayashi Hideo, Tokyo, Chikuma, pp. 213-226. Nakamura Mitsuo, "Tayama Katai," Selected Works of Nakamura Mitsuo, Tokyo, Taikodo, 1968, pp. 134-180; "Fūzoku shōsetsu ron" (On the Novel of Social Manners), Nihon no kindai (Japan's Modern Age), Tokyo, Bungeishunjyū, 1969, pp. 157-236. Hirano Ken, Art and Real Life (see note 1).

6. Kobayashi, On the I-Novel, p. 220.

7. Ibid., p. 220.

8. Tanizaki Junichiro, "Jōzetsu roku" (Records of Garrulity), Complete Works of Tanizaki Junichiro, Tokyo, Chūōkōron, vol. 20, 1966.

9. See the discussion in Chapter 3.

10. A dispute concerning the I-novel, including discussions of the Ich Roman, the "pure novel," and the "orthodox novel," appears in Tanizaki, Complete Works, pp. 93-138.

11. This is particularly true in the case of Japanese literature in which the monogatari, the earliest form of fiction close to the modern novel (represented by The Tale of Genji), emerged out of diaries, extremely private writings of love and personal life, and the exchange of poems and letters.

12. Cf. Northrop Frye, Anatomy of Criticism, New Jersey, Princeton University Press, pp. 306-308. Frye observes that after Rousseau, confessions flowed freely in the novel and produced the fictional autobiography, the Kunstler-roman and works of a similar type (p. 307). See also René Wellek, The Theory of Literature, New York, 1949, Ch. XVI, for a discussion of the origins of the novel.

13. The major works of Iwano Hōmei (1873-1921) are comprised of a series of five confessional novels, including Hatten (Development, 1911) and Dokuyaku o nomu onna (A Woman Who Swallows Poison, 1914). For discussions of Hōmei and dark romanticism see Akase Masako, "The Influence of Diabolism in Iwano Hōmei," and "The Influence of Charles Baudelaire on Iwano Hōmei," Momoyama University Studies in the Humanities, vol. 8, 1972, pp. 51-78, and vol. 9, 1973, pp. 1-24.

14. Hirano Ken, Shimazaki Tōson, Tokyo, Shinchō Bunko, 1974, pp. 61-163.

15. Translated into English by Edward Stone, The Broken Commandment, Tokyo, Tokyo University Press, 1976.

16. Nakamura, "Tayama Katai," Selected Works, pp. 152-154.

17. Translated into English by Marleigh Ryan, Japan's First Modern Novel:

Ukigumo, New York, Columbia University Press, 1965.

18. A phrase of Chikamatsu Monzaemon, cited by Hozumi Ikan in Naniwa Mi-yage; for an English translation of the relevant passages, see Donald Keene, ed., An-thology of Japanese Literature, New York, Grove Press, 1955, pp. 386-390.

19. Nakamura, "Tayama Katai," Selected Works, pp. 152-154.

20. Katai, Kindai no shōsetsu (The Modern Novel), Tokyo, Kindai Bunmeisha, 1923.

21. Selected Works, pp. 391-393.

22. Katai, "Sei ni okeru kokoromi" (What I Attempted in Sei), Waseda Bungaku, September 1908.

23. Nakamura, "On the Novel of Social Manners," Selected Works, pp. 178-184.

24. Hirano, "Tayama Katai," Art and Real Life, pp. 80-112.

25. Ten years later, Katai said that he indeed intended to write about his Anna Mahr and to reveal his innermost secret, one whose exposure might destroy his mind, thus giving support to Nakamura's contention. Yet at the same time, he said that he tried to destroy the sentimental self, that is, Tokio, by writing about him, and by doing so to clear a new path both as an artist and as a man. This statement gives support to Hirano's argument. Tokyo sanjyūnen (Thirty Years in Tokyo, 1917). This statement may reflect Katai's complex reaction to the success of Futon, and the subsequent drastic decline of the fame of the work and of himself as a writer; he tended to admit the sentimentality of the work and tried to justify it as his attempt to transcend the sentimental self. Despite the contradictions displayed in these statements, however, these two desires can in-deed be motivations for writing the novel.

26. Later, the woman who was the model for the character Yoshiko wrote about the "truth" of their relationship, accusing Katai of deliberately distorting her actions and especially those of her lover in his novels. Tanaka Michiyo, "Aru onna no tegami" (A Woman's Letter), Subaru, September 1910. See Hirano, Art and Real Life, pp. 107-108.

27. Futon, in Selected Works of Tayama Katai, Tokyo, Chikuma, 1960, p. 58 (the translation is mine).

28. Yoshida Seiichi, Shizenshugi no kenkyu (A Study of Naturalism), Tokyo, Tokyodo, 1972, vol. 2, pp. 151-165.

29. Tsubouchi Shōyō, in his influential Shōsetsu shinzui (The Essence of the Novel, 1918) argues that the modern novel must depict human feelings realisti-cally. See Ryan, Ukigumo, pp. 37-95.

30. Yoshida Seiichi, A Study of Naturalism, pp. 151-165.

2. FROM TALE TO SHORT STORY: AKUTAGAWA'S
   "TOSHISHUN" AND ITS CHINESE ORIGINS

1. Tanizaki Junichiro, "Jozetsu roku shō" (From a Record of Garrulity), Kaizō, February 1927.

2. In "Rashomon" (1914), Akutagawa writes, soon after the narrator started his story, "the author wrote previously that a servant was waiting for the rain to stop." Thus the author intrudes freely into the story, denying the distinction be-tween himself and the narrator.

3. Akutagawa also kept writing waka (poems written in a classical form) collected in Koshibito, 1926, in which he openly poured out his emotions.

4. Saeki Shoichi, "The Narrator and I in Akutagawa Ryūnosuke," Kokubungaku Kaishaku to Kansho, August 1974, pp. 6-13.

5. Akai Tori, July 1920; "Toshishun," Akutagawa Ryūnosuke, ed. by Yoshida Seiichi, Shinchō, 1977, pp. 50-65.

6. "Tu Tzu-chun" in T'ai-p'ing kuang chi and Hsu hsuan kuai lu.

7. Li Fang et al., eds., T'ai-p'ing kuang chi, vol. 16, p. 111.

8. Unlike Tu Tzu-chun, Toshishun refuses to take money the third time he is offered it, but instead asks the sennin to make him his pupil.

9. Yoshida, ed., Akutagawa Ryūnosuke, p. 53. However, Toshishun does not become aware of his disillusionment until later in the story; at this point he still wishes to pursue his decadent life.

10. "Aru ahō no issho" (A Fool's Life), Collected Works of Akutagawa Ryūnosuke, Tokyo, Chikuma, 1976, vol. 8, p. 52.

11. Ibid.

12. Yoshida, ed., Akutagawa Ryūnosuke, p. 65.

13. Li Fang et al., eds., T'ai-p'ing kuang chi, p. 112.

14. Reprinted by World Bookstore Press, Taipei, pp. 581-645. Oda Motoi attributes both the change of the ending which Akutagawa made and that which took place in the Ming version to the writers' catering to the taste of the readers (audience); my understanding of Akutagawa's change is in evident disagreement with this view. Cf. Oda Motoi, "A Comparison in Literary Expression Between the Chinese and the Japanese," Tamkang Review, vol. II, no. 2, October 1971-April 1972, pp. 141-155.

15. In "The Hell Screen," the questions of realism and of the relation between experience and art are also raised. The painter must see with his own eyes the agonies of hell in order to recreate them in art, and in so doing sacrifices his humanity.

3. THE PLOT CONTROVERSY BETWEEN TANIZAKI AND AKUTAGAWA

1. "Suji no omoshirosa ni tsuite" (On the Merit of the Plot), Shinchō, February 1927.

2. "Jōzetsu roku shō" (From a Record of Garrulity), Kaizō, February 1927; the essays of Tanizaki which were involved in the controversy were written as part of the series of essays collected under the title Jōzetsu roku. Complete Works of Tanizaki Junichiro, Chūōkōron, 1967, vol. 20.

3. In these essays, although both Akutagawa and Tanizaki distinguish plot (suji) from story (hanashi) and materials of the story (zairyō), these terms are not clearly defined theoretically, causing some misunderstanding between them and confusion in their arguments. While Akutagawa's arguments center around the significance of the story as an essential component of the plot, Tanizaki's arguments focus on the significance of the plot as the structure of the novel.

4. "Bungeitekina, amarinimo bungeikekina" (Literary, Too Literary), Kaizō, April 1927. The essays of Akutagawa which were involved in the controversy were written (with the exception of the dialogue in the Review section of Shinchō,

— see note 1) as part of the series of essays collected under this title. <u>Selected Works of Akutagawa Ryūnosuke</u>, ed. by Yoshida Seiichi, Kōdansha, 1970, pp. 339-409.

5. Most of the essays of both authors concerning the controversy were published in <u>Gendai nihon bungaku ronsō shi</u> (A History of Modern Japanese Literary Disputes), ed. by Hirano Ken and others, Miraisha, 1974, vol. 1, pp. 143-160.

6. See Chapter 5 for a more complete discussion of Tanizaki and his literary world.

7. "Aru ahō no isshō" (1927), <u>Selected Works</u>, pp. 241-265.

8. "Mr. Shiga Naoya," "Literary, Too Literary," <u>Selected Works</u>, pp. 346-349.

9. See, for example, Hirano Ken, <u>Geijyutsu to jisseikatsu</u> (Art and Life), Shinchō, 1974.

10. The questions of story and plot presented in the controversy were later developed specifically as a question of the form of literature, on which the dispute usually referred to as <u>keishiki ronso</u> took place between Yokomitsu Riichi, Kobayashi Hideo and such proletarian and realist writers as Hirotsu Kazuo, Kurahara Korehito and Katsumoto Seiichiro, See Hirano Ken and others, eds., <u>A History of Modern Japanese Literary Disputes</u>, pp. 363-404.

11. On Yokomitsu Riichi's pure novel, see Edward Seidensticker, "The 'Pure' and the 'In-Between' in Modern Japanese Theories of the Novel," <u>Harvard Journal of Asiatic Studies</u>, 26 (1966), pp. 174-186.

12. Miyamoto Kenji, "Haiboku no bungaku: Akutagawa Ryūnosuke shi no bungaku ni tsuite" (The Literature of Defeat: On Mr. Akutagawa's Literature), <u>Kaizō</u>, August 1929. <u>Proletaria bungaku</u> (Proletarian Literature), ed. by Itō Sei and others, Kōdansha, 1969, pp. 355-365.

13. Hirano Ken and others, eds., <u>A History of Modern Japanese Literary Disputes</u>, pp. 11-14.

14. Saul Bellow, "Who Got the Story? The Novel Since James Joyce," lecture given in Tokyo, June 1972.

4. WESTERN DARK ROMANTICISM AND
   JAPAN'S AESTHETIC LITERATURE

1. For a concise history of the introduction to Japan of European aesthetic art and literature, see Okada Takahiko, <u>Nihon no seikimatsu</u> (Japan's Fin de Siècle), Tokyo, Ozawa Shoten, 1976.

2. An especially valuable discussion of Poe's introduction to Japan can be found in Kimura Takeshi, <u>Nichibei bungaku kōryūshi no kenkyū</u> (A Study of Japanese-American Literary Intercourse), Chapter 16, Tokyo, 1968.

3. For a discussion of Hōmei and dark romanticism see Akase Masako, "The Influence of Diabolism in Iwano Hōmei," and "The Influence of Charles Baudelaire on Iwano Hōmei," <u>Momoyama University Studies in the Humanities</u>, vol. 8, 1972, pp. 51-78, and vol. 9, 1973, pp. 1-24.

4. For a discussion of Soseki and Poe, see Noriko Mizuta Lippit, "Natsume Soseki on Poe," <u>Comparative Literature Studies</u>, vol. XIV, no. 1 (March 1977), pp. 30-37.

5. For the influence of Western writers on Sakutaro, see Tsukimura Reiko,

"Hagiwara Sakutaro," Modern Japanese Poetry from a Comparative Perspective, Tokyo, Shimizu Kobundo, 1971, pp. 164-190.
  6. "Zangesha no sugata" (The Penitent, 1916).
  7. "Namamekashii hakaba" (A Sensuous Grave, 1928).
  8. See Jyōjyō shōkyoku shū (Lyrical Poems, 1925), and Hyōto (Ice Island, 1934).
  9. See Sakutaro, "Shi to senkenteki kioku" (Poetry and Transcendental Memory, 1919), "Shi no honyaku ni tsuite" (On the Translation of Poetry, 1933), and "Poe no kankei" (On Poe's Scheme, 1935). For a detailed discussion of this poem see Tsukimura Reiko, "Hagiwara Sakutaro."

5. TANIZAKI AND POE: THE GROTESQUE
AND THE QUEST FOR SUPERNAL BEAUTY

  1. Aeba Kōson's rough translation of "The Black Cat" appeared in the Yomiuri Shimbun, November 3 and 9, 1888; his translation of "The Murders in the Rue Morgue" also appeared in the Yomiuri Shimbun, December 10, 23, 27, and 30, 1888.
  2. Kimura Takeshi, Nichibei bungaku kōryūshi no kenkyu (A Study of Japanese-American Literary Interchange), ch. 16, "Poe to Meiji-Taisho bundan" (Poe and the Meiji-Taisho Bundan, Tokyo, 1958); Shinagawa Chikara, "Nihon ni okeru Poe" (Poe in Japan), Nihon Hikakubungakukai Kaiho (Bulletin of the Japan Comparative Literature Society), nos. 4-21, 1959-1960; Ota Saburo, "Poe shokai no ato" (Tracing Poe's Introduction to Japan), "Monthly Report," Vols. 1, 2, and 3, Poe zenshu (The Complete Works of Poe), ed. by Saeki Shoichi (Tokyo, Kawade, 1970).
  3. Lafcadio Hearn, "Notes on American Literature" and "Poe's Verse," Interpretations of Literature, ed. by John Erskine (London, 1916), II, pp. 150-166. Hearn had lectured at the University of Tokyo on the English romantic poets (including the pre-Raphaelites) and on Gothic writers, as well as on the supernatural in literature.
  4. Ueda Bin, "Eibei no kinsei bungaku" (Modern English and American Literature), Myōjyō, March 1902.
  5. Tanizaki Junichiro zenshu (Complete Works of Tanizaki Junichiro, Tokyo, 1967), XIII, p. 360. Herafter cited as Works.
  6. Precisely speaking, Akutagawa does not belong to the aesthetic school, yet he shared several principal concerns with the writers of this school.
  7. Sato Haruo, "Junichiro: Hito oyobi geijutsu" (Junichiro: The Man and His Art), Kaizō, March 1927; Kobayashi Hideo, "Tanizaki Junichiro," Chūōkōron, May 1931; Yoshida Seiichi, "Tanizaki Junichiro," Tanizaki Junichiro, ed. by Yoshida Seiichi (Tokyo, 1959); Hashimoto Yoshiichiro, Tanizaki Junichiro no bungaku (The Literature of Tanizaki Junichiro, Tokyo, 1965); Fukuda Koson, Introduction to Han kindai shiso (Anti-Modern Thoughts), ed. Fukuda Kōson (Tokyo, 1968); Ikushima Ryōichi, "Tanizaki Junichiro ron" (On Tanizaki Junichiro), Tanizaki Junichiro kenkyū (Studies of Tanizaki Junichiro), ed. Ara Masahito (Tokyo, 1973), pp. 546-562.
  8. See, for example, Maedako Hiroichiro, "Tanizaki Junichiro ron" (On Ta-

nizaki Junichiro), Bungei Sensen, May 1928; Oe Kenzaburo, "Tanizaki ni tsuite" (On Tanizaki); and Ohara Gen, "Tanizaki Junichiro. Shoki no sakuhin" (Tanizaki Junichiro: His Early Works), both in Studies of Tanizaki Junichiro, ed. by Ara Masahito. See also Nakamura Mitsuo, Tanizaki Junichiro kenkyū (A Study of Tanizaki Junichiro, Tokyo, 1952).

9. Itō Sei, "Tanizaki Junichiro," ed. by Ara Masahito, pp. 519-545; "Tanizaki Junichiro," Modern Japanese Literary Masters, ed. by Itō Sei (Tokyo, 1968), II, and "Tanizaki Junichiro no geijutsu to shiso" (The Art and Thought of Tanizaki Junichiro), Tanizaki Junichiro, ed. by Nihon Bungaku Kenkyu Shiryo Kankōkai (Publication Committee, Japanese Literature Research Materials, Tokyo, 1972), pp. 80-85, hereafter cited as NBKSK; Tanizaki Junichiro no bungaku (The Literature of Tanizaki Junichiro, Tokyo, 1970). See also Shinoda Hajime, "Tanizaki Junichiro ni tsuite" (On Tanizaki Junichiro), NBKSK ed., pp. 119-132; Hashimoto Yoshiichiro, Tanizaki Junichiro no bungaku (The Literature of Tanizaki Junichiro).

10. Nakamura argues that "A Fool's Love" (Chijin no ai, 1924) marks a departure from Tanizaki's early themes (A Study of Tanizaki Junichiro, Tokyo, 1952). In fact, however, this novel deals most explicitly with the major themes of the early works, themes which I discuss below.

11. Such critics as Kawakami Tetsutaro point out the naturalistic qualities in Tanizaki's early works. See "Tanizaki Junichiro," NBKSK ed., pp. 25-30. See also Hashizume Ken, "Tanizaki Junichiro," Shin Shōsetsu, January 1926; Yoshida Seiichi, "Itansha no kanashimi" (On "The Sorrow of the Pagan Outcast"), ed. by Ara Masahito, pp. 107-118. On Thomas Hardy and Tanizaki, see Ōta Saburo, "Thomas Hardy to Tanizaki Junichiro: 'Shunkinsho' ni matsuwaru shomondai" (Thomas Hardy and Tanizaki Junichiro: Problems concerning "A Portrait of Shunkin"), NBKSK ed., pp. 143-157.

12. Sato Haruo, "Junichiro: Hito oyobi geijutsu" (Junichiro: The Man and His Art); Yoshida Seiichi, "Tanizaki Junichiro"; Muramatsu Sadataka, "Tanizaki Junichiro to Izumi Kyōka" (Tanizaki Junichiro and Izumi Kyōka), ed. by Ara Masahito, pp. 461-70; Honma Hisao, "Tanizaki Junichiro ron" (On Tanizaki Junichiro), NBKSK ed., pp. 1-3, 212-214.

13. See, for example, "Becoming a Father" (Chichi to narite, 1915), Works XXII.

14. Edward G. Seidensticker points out that the sense of alienation is the most essential ingredient in Tanizaki's literary world. "Tanizaki Junichiro," NBKSK ed., pp. 90-99. On the theme of alienation in Tanizaki, see also, Nakada Koji, "Tanizaki Junichiro ni tsuite" (On Tanizaki Junichiro), in Ara Masahito, ed., pp. 603-625.

15. Death, as I explain briefly below, occupies an important part in Poe's myth: it is a passage for return to the Original Unity from which man has fallen.

16. For a discussion of Tanizaki's detective and mystery stories, see Nakajima Kawataro, "Tanizaki to mystery" (Tanizaki and Mystery), in Ara Masahito, ed., pp. 419-433.

17. For a discussion of Tanizaki's theme of the double and doppelgänger, see Hara Shiro, "Shoki no sakuhin o dokkai suru" (Interpretation of Early Works), ibid., pp. 119-141.

18. "The Black Cat," Poe's Complete Works, ed. by James Harrison (New York, 1902), V. p. 146.

19. This story, with "The Golden Death" (Konjiki no shi, 1914), which I discuss below, is one of the few works in which the death of the hero actually takes place.

20. "The Assignation," Poe's Complete Works, II, p. 123.

21. "Random Thoughts in Early Spring" (Sōshun zakkan, 1920), Works, XXII. For critical analysis of Tanizaki's romanticism, see Takada Mizuho, "Shō shō Shigemoto no haha" (The Mother of Captain Shigemoto), in Ara Masahito, ed., pp. 267-285, and "Tanizaki bungaku no honshitsu" (The Essence of the Literature of Tanizaki), NBKSK ed., pp. 111-118; see also Hino Keizo, "Haha naru mono: 'Yume no ukihashi' ron" (Maternity: On "The Bridge of Dreams"), in Ara Masahito, ed., pp. 304-318.

22. The criticism he received from proletarian writers may be partly responsible for his "escape" into the world of romance. The major reason, however, is literary and not political or moralistic, as I try to demonstrate here.

23. For a comprehensive analysis of the history and aesthetics of the grotesque, see Wolfgang Kayser, The Grotesque in Literature and Art, trans. by Ulrich Weisstein (New York, 1966); see also Arthur Clayborough, The Grotesque in English Literature (Oxford: Oxford University Press, 1965).

24. For an analysis of the transition from the white flesh to the white woman, and of whiteness as a symbol of eternal maternity, see Takada and Hino.

25. For a psychological analysis of Tanizaki's creation of eternal maternity, see Minami Hiroshi, "Bosei karano tōsō: aruiwa kenshin ni yoru seifuku" (Escape from Maternity: or Domination through Devotion), in Ara Masahito, ed., pp. 585-602. Seidensticker discusses this topic briefly in his article cited above.

26. There is ample evidence that Tanizaki consciously started to link his works with the Japanese cultural and literary heritage near the beginning of the Showa period. The shift in orientation is simply expressed by his moving to the Kansai area. Tanizaki started translating The Tale of Genji into modern Japanese during the 8th year of Showa (1933) and devoted himself almost exclusively to this work for five years. In "In Praise of Shadows" (Inei raisan, 1933), Tanizaki develops his concept of Japanese culture. There he discusses the difference between Western and Japanese culture and asserts his positive identification with the latter. In "Textbook on Style" (Bunshō tokuhon, 1934), he is critical of the influence of foreign styles on his early writings and says that he should have learned instead from the language and styles of classical Japanese literature.

27. In "Ave Maria" (1948), Tanizaki not only relates his eternal woman to the Virgin Mary, but also defines the essence of Maria, the transcendental woman, as whiteness, revealing clearly the influence of Platonic ideas. Later, in "The Bridge of Dreams" (Yume no ukihashi, 1959), Tanizaki describes the essence of maternity as the mother's bosom, a "warm, dimly white world of dream." The whiteness of her breasts, existing beyond time and space, reveals the primordial essence of existence itself. See also Takada and Hino.

28. Tanizaki might have found in The Tale of Genji the archetype of his theme of the pursuit of eternal maternity, as Edward Seidensticker argues. The return, even then, was not so much to the world of classical literature as to the areas of archetypal human experience.

29. <u>Some Prefer Nettles</u>, trans. by Edward G. Seidensticker (New York, 1965), p. 139.

30. Edward Seidensticker acknowledges the similarity of Tanizaki's themes to those of Poe, although he dismisses Poe's influence on Tanizaki as anything but significant. See NBKSK ed., p. 95. Ōhashi Kenzaburo points out Tanizaki's "deep empathy with the tradition of Western romanticism." He says, however, that Tanizaki's world is "different from both Poe's Gothic romance and Baudelaire's symbolism and Western fin-de-siècle decadence," and argues rather that Tanizaki's works are similar to Hawthorne's because of their ethical qualities. See "Tanizaki to Poe" (Tanizaki and Poe), in Ara Masahito, ed., pp. 434-435.

6. DISEASE AND MADNESS IN JAPAN'S MODERNIST
   LITERATURE: YOKOMITSU RIICHI'S "MACHINE"
   AND THE SHORT STORIES OF KAJII MOTOJIRO

1. The first manifesto of Japanese Futurism (written by Hirato Yasukichi, Kambara Yasushi, and others) appeared in October 1920.

2. <u>Aka to Kuro</u>, vol. 1, no. 1, February 1923 (the translation is mine).

3. "The First Manifesto of the Red and Black Movement," <u>Aka to Kuro</u>, vol. 1, no. 4, May 1923.

4. The journal is basically a continuation of <u>The Sowers</u>, differing mainly in that, in its effort to reactivate the proletarian literary movement, it adopted a slogan less rigid than that of <u>The Sowers</u> with regard to individual thought and action in the liberation movement. Aono Suekichi's most influential essay, "Spontaneous Growth and Consciousness of Purpose" (1926), was published in the September issue.

5. It was established in October 1924. Kataoka Ippei, Kon Tōkō, and Itō Takamaro were among the other founding members.

6. "Atarashii seikatsu to atarashii bungei" (New Life and New Art and Literature), <u>Bungei Jidai</u>, October 1924.

7. <u>DAMDAM</u> was published in October 1924 by such poets of anarchism, expressionism and Dadaism as Hagiwara Kyōjiro, Okamoto Jun and Ono Tosaburo, among others, but only one issue appeared. <u>MAVO</u> was published in July 1924 by Yanase Masayume, Ogata Kamenosuke, and others.

8. "Shinshin sakka no shinkeikō kaisetsu," <u>Bungei Jidai</u>, January 1925.

9. "Kankaku katsudo — kankakukatsudo to kankaku sakubutsu ni taisuru hihan e no gyakusetsu" (Perceptional Activities — A Reappraisal of the Criticism of Perceptional Activities and Perceptional Creation), <u>Bungei Jidai</u>, February 1925. For a discussion of the relation of New Perceptionism to the Modernist movement, see, Takami Jun, <u>Showa bungaku seisui shi</u> (The Rise and Fall of Showa Literature), Bungeishunjyū, Tokyo, 1958; Senuma Shigeki, "Zenei geijyutsu to shinkankakuha" (Avant-garde Art and the New Perceptionist School), <u>Kindai nihon no bungaku</u> (Modern Japanese Literature), Gendai Kyōyō Bunko, 1959; "Shinkankakuha" (New Perceptionism), <u>Showa bungaku kenkyū</u> (Studies in Showa Literature), June 1952; Hirano Ken, "Nihon no avant-garde" (The Japanese Avant-Garde) <u>Hon no techo</u>, May 1963; Odagiri Susumu, <u>Showa bungaku no seiritsu</u>

(The Establishment of Showa Literature), Tokyo, Igusa, 1969.

10. Yokomitsu wrote a series of articles including "Shinkankakuha to communism" (New Perceptionism and Communism) and "Yuibutsuron teki bungaku ni tsuite" (On the Literature of Materialism), articles later collected in Kakikata zōshi, Tokyo, Hakusuisha, 1931.

11. Kajii belonged to his own group, Aozora (Blue Sky). Although he was not close to the proletarian literary movement, his last, uncompleted work, "Nonki na kanjya" (The Carefree Patient, 1932) shows his interest in social reality and the conditions of the oppressed.

12. Bungei Toshi, July 1929.

13. First published in September 1928 by such poets as Kitagawa Fuyuhiko, Iijima Tadashi, Anzai Fuyue, Haruyama Yukio and Miyoshi Tatsuji, among others.

14. In addition to the members of Poetry and Poetics, writers from Blue Sky, including Kajii and Yodono Ryūzo, formed the core of the group.

15. Itō Sei, Shin shinrishugi bungaku, Tokyo, Koseikaku, 1932.

16. "Shi to shōsetsu," Shin Bungaku Kenkyu (Studies of New Literature), April 1931. The same issue contains Itō Sei's "On Literature," one of the essays collected in New Psychological Literature.

17. Kajii contracted tuberculosis when he was nineteen years old and died in 1932 at the age of thirty-one.

18. "Sakura no ki no shita niwa" (1928), "Kigaku teki genkaku" (1928), "Kōbi" (1931), all collected in The Lemon.

19. Published in Kaizō, September 1930, translated into English by Edward Seidensticker, Modern Japanese Stories, ed. by Ivan Morris, Rutland, Vermont, Charles E. Tuttle, 1972, pp. 223-244.

20. Ibid., p. 224.

21. Ibid., p. 244.

22. Ibid., p. 229.

23. "The Lemon," The Lemon, Tokyo, Kōdansha, 1976, p. 6.

24. Akutagawa Ryūnosuke, "Aru kyūyū e okuru shuki" (A Note to an Old Friend, 1927), Collected Works of Akutagawa Ryūnosuke, Tokyo, Chikuma, 1976, vol. 8, pp. 114-117.

25. The Lemon, p. 81.

26. Ibid., p. 177.

27. Ibid., p. 74.

28. Ibid., p. 166.

7. KAWABATA'S DILETTANTE HEROES

1. Kawabata, calling himself an idle artist, said that he avoided writing about things with which he was seriously concerned. He said also that his works were composed of the coarse, casual impressions of a traveler and that he had bypassed both life and art. "An Interview with Kawabata," Bungei Special Issue on Kawabata, January 1962.

2. Yasunari Kawabata, Snow Country, trans. by Edward G. Seidensticker, New York, Alfred A. Knopf, 1969, pp. 111-112.

3. Kawabata did create such a hero in The Master of Go (trans. by Edward
G. Seidensticker, New York, Knopf, 1972), in which the tragic hero commits
himself to an art, the game of go, sacrificing the sensuous reality of his life.

4. Kawabata, Snow Country, pp. 71-72.

5. Ibid., pp. 44-45.

6. Kawabata lost his parents early in his childhood, and his early works are
concerned mainly with his definition of himself as an orphan. See for example,
"A Funeral Ceremony Expert" (1923), "The Diary of a Sixteen-year-old" (1925),
"Sentiments of an Orphan" (1925), and "The Izu Dancer" (1926). As a young
man, he suffered from rejection by his first love. Her image, fused with that
of his mother, became a prototype of the unattainable dream-woman who appears
in many of his works.

7. Snow Country, p. 3.

8. Ibid., pp. 9-10.

9. Ibid., p. 57.

10. Reflecting on his early youth, Kawabata said that he was unnaturally mature, having always had the consciousness of an old man. He said this was because he was an orphan and had confronted the death of everyone in his family.
See, for example, "A Funeral Ceremony Expert." In "The Eye of the Apoca-
lypse," he defined his point of view in art and life as that of one who is dying at
the end of the world.

11. Snow Country, pp. 131-132.

12. Ibid., pp. 165, 168.

13. Kawabata acknowledged his involvement in and empathy with the world
of Genji. Although his interest in classical Japanese literature went back to his
school days, when he majored in it, his discovery of the essential link between
his literature and classical Japanese literature came during the war, when he
read The Tale of Genji intensively. See for example, "Pathos" (1947).

14. Chikako may appear to the reader as no more than a practical woman of
the world, but it is this very quality of worldliness that is poisonous for Kawabata's heroes. Kawabata's women can be divided roughly into two groups: clean
dream-women, who are the ultimate mother-figures and who are usually undomesticated, socially insecure women; and ugly women, lacking in sensuousness,
practical and sometimes demoniac, through whom the heroes are tied to the reality of life.

15. Yasunari Kawabata, Thousand Cranes, trans. by Edward G. Seidensticker,
New York, Knopf, 1969, p. 54.

16. Ibid., p. 141.

17. Ibid, p. 53.

18. Ibid., p. 104.

19. Yasunari Kawabata, The Sound of the Mountain, trans. by Edward G. Seidensticker, New York, Knopf, 1970, p. 7.

20. Ibid., pp. 8, 9.

21. The novel takes place in the postwar period when the feudal family system was in the process of dissolution. The marriage experience of the three
couples in the novel reflects this. Yet at the same time, the dissolution of the
families is a means of expressing the spiritual homelessness of Kawabata's
characters.

22. Kawabata, writing in the introduction to his translation into modern Japanese of Taketori monogatari (The Tale of a Bamboo Cutter), the oldest Japanese tale, says that the shining princess's return to the moon is the sad return of one who, although disappointed in this life, cannot completely abandon life. The princess rejected everyone around her because of her high ideals and purity, but she had to bear the sorrow of one who rejected reality. Introduction to The Tale of A Bamboo Cutter in Modern Language, Tokyo, Hibunkaku, 1937.

23. For a discussion of the ambivalent attitude toward life and art of the medieval artist-monks, see Karaki Junzō, Chūse no bungaku (Medieval Literature), Tokyo, Chikuma, 1965.

24. In the medieval period, it was widely believed that the Buddha Amida had gone and the Buddha Miroku would arrive in the future as a savior, leaving the present as a dark interval between the two Buddhas. Chomei refers to this dark interval in his Hosshinshu (vol. 5). In The Sound of the Mountain, Shingo, when he encounters his granddaughter's obsessive desire for a beautiful dress, is suddenly reminded of a passage from a Noh play (Kanami Kiyotsugu, Sotoba Komachi): "The former Buddha has gone, the later Buddha has not yet come: I was born in a dream-interval, what shall I regard as real? I have chanced to receive this human flesh, which is difficult to receive...." (Tokyo, Kadokawa, p. 176. The translation is mine.)

25. The same theme is also developed extensively in Mizuumi (The Lake, 1960), another of Kawabata's major works.

26. Yasunari Kawabata, The House of the Sleeping Beauties, trans. by Edward G. Seidensticker, New York, Ballantine, 1969, p. 101.

8. LITERATURE AND IDEOLOGY: THE FEMINIST
AUTOBIOGRAPHY OF MIYAMOTO YURIKO

1. The Japanese anarchists and communists considered women's demands as petit bourgeois and thus not revolutionary. They refused to establish women's bureaus in their organizations for fear that they would lead the movements in a petit bourgeois direction and mar cooperation with the male branch. See, for example, Takamure Itsue, Jyosei no rekishi (A History of Women), Tokyo, Kōdansha, 1958.

2. The complete works of Miyamoto Yuriko were published by Kawade, Tokyo, 15 vols., 1951. There are also selected works published by Aki Shoten (11 vols., 1949) and Shinnippon Shuppansha (12 vols., 1968).

3. Yuriko kept diaries during the years of her love for and marriage to Araki Shigeru (Nobuko jidai no nikki, 1920-23), Tokyo, Yuriko Kenkyūkai, 1976. Such autobiographical stories written during the same period as "Chiisai ie no seikatsu" (Life in a Small House, 1922), "Hitotsu no dekigoto" (One Incident, 1920), "Yoi" (Evening, 1922), "Kokoro no kawa" (The River of Heart, 1925), in addition to the unrevised first versions of Nobuko, supply reliable information about her life during these years. See also Tomoko Nakamura, Miyamoto Yuriko, Chikuma, 1974.

4. Nobuko was serialized in Kaizō in ten installments between 1924 and 1926. This original version was shortened and radically revised when the novel ap-

peared in book form in 1928. The following quotation in the text is from Selected
Works of Miyamoto Yuriko and Kobayashi Takiji, Tokyo, Chikuma, 1969.

5. Nobuko, p. 133; author's translation. The protagonists in Yuriko's novels are
readily identifiable as real-life persons, and for grasping her world, it is as appropriate to use the names of their real-life prototypes as of the characters themselves.

6. In her early works (such as "Yoi") Yuriko had already been writing about
the problems of women artists, especially about the difficulty of fulfilling the
dual role of homemaker and creative woman, a theme which was developed as
central in Nobuko. However, her interest in women in general and her linking
of her personal questions to the larger problems of women took place when she
visited Soviet Russia. Her commitment to women's liberation became apparent
and unshakable only after her return from Russia, where her ideological understanding and perspective took definite form.

7. Jyūninen no tegami (Letters of Twelve Years), 2 vols., Tokyo, Chikuma, 1965.

8. The relationship between Nobuko and Motoko was more than one of friendship between two women, both psychologically and in some respects physically.
It is clear that Motoko was attached to Nobuko as a lesbian while Nobuko was not
attached to Motoko in this way. However, Nobuko's need for close human relations did find an outlet, soon after her divorce, in her friendship with Motoko,
and her new life with Motoko did supply her with a vision of a new start as significant as marriage.

9. Yuriko had never advocated the maternal feminism which characterized
such feminists of the Bluestocking group as Hiratsuka Raicho. Yuriko's own
decision not to have children was based on her concern that women who spend
their psychic energy on child-rearing and the emotional dependency on children
it entails would have little remaining of the energy and emotional commitment
necessary for a creative life. (See Diary); yet her love for Miyamoto Kenji
changed her attitude, and she wished to have a child with him, a desire which
was not fulfilled because of his prolonged imprisonment.

10. As in many cases of women artists and intellectuals, Yuriko's complex
relation to her mother was a crucial factor in her intellectual and emotional
growth and the formation of her character. Yuriko was a keen and even cruel
observer of her mother; yet her admiration and sympathy for her mother as a
woman grew over the years, enabling her to love her mother dearly. Yuriko has
written as much about her mother as about herself in her works.

11. Yuriko saw clearly the class nature of the aspiration for romantic love,
viewing it as the product of the feudal-bourgeois concept of women, a concept
which idealizes virginity, chastity and motherhood. See such essays as "New
Monogamy," "Discussion of Love for a New Generation," "Passion for Homemaking" (Yuriko Zenshū, Tokyo, Kawade, vol. 9), and "On Chastity," "The Wife's
Morality," and "The Morality of Marriage" (vol. 12).

12. Selected Works of Miyamoto Yuriko and Nogami Yaeko, Tokyo, Kōdansha,
1967.

13. Yuriko must have read the essay in Soviet Russia, since she kept receiving
Kaizō, one of whose issues carried Miyamoto's article. She tells of her impression of the essay in her novel Dōhyō (Road Sign). Kobayashi Hideo's essay, "Sa-
mazama naru ishō" (Various Designs), received the second prize.

14. The most outspoken critic was Hirabayashi Taiko, a woman writer and
once an anarchist.

4 Reality and Fiction in Japanese Literature

15. See "Sengen hitotsu" (One Declaration), <u>Gendai nihon bungaku ronsō shi</u> (A History of Modern Japanese Literary Disputes), Tokyo, Miraisha, vol. 1, pp. 11-14.

9. POLITICS AND LITERATURE:
    THE DEBATE OVER SOCIALIST REALISM

1. In 1929 an active dispute over political values and artistic values in liter-ary works took place, mainly in <u>Shinchō</u>, among such writers and critics as Hi-rabayashi Hatsunosuke, Tanikawa Tetsu, Aono Suekichi, Ōya Sōichi, Nakano Shi-geharu, Miyamoto Kenji and Katsumoto Seiichiro. Between 1932 and 1934, such writers as Hayashi Fusao, Kobayashi Hideo, Miyamoto Kenji, Kamei Katsu-ichiro and Nakano Shigeharu argued over politics and literature.
2. For an English discussion of the essay and its significance in Japanese literary history, see Marleigh Ryan, <u>Japan's First Modern Novel: Ukigumo</u>, New York, Columbia University Press, 1965, ch. 2.
3. Under the Peace Preservation Law of 1889, the Communist Party (founded in 1922) and other leftist movements were destroyed. The massive arrests of activists and proletarian writers by the newly formed Peace Preservation (Anti-subversive) Bureau in 1928-29 and again in 1931-32 literally crushed the "sec-ond" Communist Party (founded in 1926) and leftist-oriented literary and cul-tural movements.
4. The journal was established in 1921 by Komaki Ōmi, who had returned from his studies in Paris in 1919, Kaneko Hirobumi and others. Later, Hiraba-yashi Hatsunosuke, Aono Suekichi, Maedako Hiroichiro and others joined, and the journal quickly became the center of the proletarian literary movement.
5. "Shizen seichō to mokuteki ishiki," <u>Bungei Sensen</u>, September 1926. Fol-lowing the publication, an active dispute took place among Kaji Wataru, Hayashi Fusao, Nakano Shigeharu, Aono and others. Four months later, Aono wrote "Shizen seichō to mokuteki ishiki sairon" on the same theme to clear up some misunderstandings the essay had caused.
6. "Proletaria realism e no michi," <u>Senki</u>, May 1928.
7. See note 5. "Shirabeta geijutsu," <u>Bungei Sensen</u>, July 1925; "Bungei hi-hyō no ichi hattengata" (One Pattern of Development of Literary Criticism), <u>Bungei Sensen</u>, October 1925; "Bunka tōsō no kichō (The Basic Line of Cultural Struggle) <u>Bungei Sensen</u>, March 1926.
8. Georg Lukacs emphasizes the importance of perspective in socialist re-alism, the existence of which distinguishes it from objective realism. See <u>Re-alism in Our Time: Literature and Class Struggle</u>, trans. by John and Necke Mander, New York, Harper and Row, 1964.
9. "Geijutsuteki hōhō ni tsuite no kansō," <u>Zenei</u>, October 1931.
10. His criticism of naturalism reflected that of Lukacs. See <u>Realism in Our Time</u>.
11. Their statement, entitled "Kyōdo hikoku dōshi ni tsugu" (To Fellow Pris-oner Comrades), was published in June 1933, while they were in prison.
12. See <u>Gendai nihon bungaku ronsō shi</u> (A History of Modern Japanese Liter-ary Disputes), ed. by Hirano Ken and others, Miraisha, 1974, vol. 2, p. 342.
13. Kobayashi went underground in 1932 but was arrested in February 1933.

He was murdered while being tortured. He was thirty years old. Miyamoto also went underground in 1932. He was arrested in December 1933, after which he remained imprisoned for twelve years — until 1945.

14. Hayashi Fusao was an original committee member of the Japan Proletarian Art and Literature Association (formed in 1925) and was active in the proletarian literary movement until his arrest in 1930. After his release in 1932, he declared the independence of literature from politics ("For Writers," Asahi Shimbun, May 1932), and from around 1936, his nationalistic inclinations became evident. By the end of World War II he was supporting the emperor system and the war. Since the war he has been a strong advocate of Japan's rearmament and has written essays defending Japan's war effort as well as nonpolitical "youth" novels.

15. See Hirano Ken, and others, ed., A History of Modern Japanese Literary Disputes, p. 348.

16. "Sōsaku hōhōjyō no shintenkan" (Chūōkōron, September 1933); collected in ibid., pp. 179-186.

17. Among Yuriko's stories, "Koiwai no ikka" (The Family of Koiwai) is probably the best example of a work of socialist realism. See the translation of the work by Noriko Lippit in Bulletin of Concerned Asian Scholars (March 1978).

18. Tokunaga; see note 16.

19. "Hiteiteki realism ni tsuite" (Bungaku Hyōron, April 1934), in Hirano Ken and others, ed., A History of Modern Japanese Literary Disputes, pp. 189-195.

20. "Hiteiteki realism hihan" (Bungaku Hyōron, May 1934), ibid., pp. 203-210.

21. "Shakaishugiteki realism ka hiyorimishugiteki realism ka" (Socialist Realism or Opportunistic Realism?; Bunka Shūdan, April 1934), ibid., pp. 196-203. His argument for the selective presentation of reality, the reality grasped by those who participate in the effort for socialist revolution, reflects Lukacs's argument.

22. "Shakaishugi realism no mondai" (Bungaku Hyōron, March 1935), ibid., pp. 211-216.

23. "Shakaishugi realism to kakumeiteki (han shihonshugiteki) realism" (Bungaku Hyōron, May 1935), ibid., pp. 216-228.

24. "Shakaishugi realism no mondai ni tsuite" (Bunka Shūdan, November 1933), ibid., pp. 187-189.

10. CONFESSION OF A MASK: THE ART OF
    SELF-EXPOSURE IN MISHIMA YUKIO

1. See Honda Akigo, Monogatari sengo bungakushi (An Historical Narrative of Postwar Japanese Literature), Shinchō, 1966; Tasaka Ko, Mishima Yukio ron, Tokyo, Fūtosha, 1970, p. 14; Noguchi Takehiko, Mishima Yukio no sekai (The World of Mishima Yukio), Kōdansha, 1971, p. 95.

2. Hanada Kiyoteru, "St. Sebastian no kao" (The Face of St. Sebastian), Bungei, January 1950.

3. The original is "ronri teki kecchaku." Mishima, Watakushi no henreki jidai (The Days of My Pilgrimage), Tokyo, Kōdansha, 1971, p. 135. The short

quotations in this essay are from this book unless otherwise specified.

4. Before the publication of Confessions of a Mask, Mishima had written "Tobacco," "An Excerpt from the Philosophic Diary of a Criminal in the Medieval Period," "Tōzoku" (Thieves), and "Hanazakari no mori" (A Forest in Full Bloom).

5. Mishima wrote: "I felt I had finally grasped the true nature of poetry. I came to see that poetry, which had excited me so much in my boyhood days and tortured me so much later, was in truth a phony, that it was nothing but the bad drunkenness of lyricism (sentiment). Thus I came to believe that the true nature of poetry was realization" (Watakushi no henreki jidai, p. 137).

6. Confessions of a Mask, trans. by Meredith Weatherby, London, Sphere Books, p. 117.

7. Mishima said that he found Dazai repellant because Dazai wrote what Mishima wanted to hide. Mishima also disliked Dazai's pathetic attitude of bearing on his shoulders the agony of the age, and argued that novelists must look cheerful no matter how tragic their literary themes might be. Watakushi no henreki jidai, pp. 117-125.

8. Taiyō to tetsu (Sun and Steel), Tokyo, Kōdansha, 1971, p. 64.

9. Mishima, in addition to his two autobiographical accounts, The Days of My Pilgrimage and Sun and Steel, which he said fell between confession and criticism, wrote freely about himself on numerous occasions.

10. Mishima expressed his feeling of estrangement from the immediate postwar literary circle and its activities as follows: "...I found myself to have become already old-fashioned at the age of twenty. I was at a loss. Radiguet, Wilde, Yeats and the Japanese classics, which I had loved, had become opposed to the taste of the age" (Watakushi no henreki jidai, p. 111).

11. While the sun and summer are, for Mishima, the powerful, tragic forces of life, the sea is a metaphor for his aspiration for something which does not exist for him. Therefore the sea itself challenges his aspiration.

12. In Confessions of a Mask, the protagonist states upon receiving the news that the war was over, "It was not the reality of defeat. Instead, for me — for me alone — it meant that fearful days were beginning. It meant that, whether I would or no, and despite everything that had deceived me into believing such a day would never come, the very next day I must begin that 'everyday life' as a member of human society. How the mere words made me tremble" (p. 165).

13. Mishima read with excitement Nietzsche's The Birth of Tragedy during the war, and one of the short stories he wrote during the war ("An Excerpt from the Philosophic Diary of a Criminal in the Medieval Period") was written under the influence of Zarathustra. Not only was Nietzsche a major source of influence in his early days, but his philosophy affected Mishima's later political ideas as well. Both the "nihilism" of Nietzsche's philosophy and the "terror and ecstasy" of Dionysus were especially attractive to Mishima.

14. Confessions of a Mask, p. 61.

15. Ibid., p. 28. The same experiences appear in "The Thirst for Love," "On Ecstasy," and Sun and Steel.

16. See Sun and Steel.

17. According to The Days of My Pilgrimage, the literature of Thomas Mann was Mishima's ideal around 1950, and Mann was certainly one of the significant

sources of influence on Mishima. The Temple of the Golden Pavilion was, according to Mishima's "The Attempt to Reform Himself," Ogai plus Thomas Mann. Mishima discusses Mann in various essays, and in "Is Eros Necessary for Art?" and "Apollo's Cup" discusses extensively the separation of body and spirit in Tonio Kröger; he also said in a talk with the critic Miyoshi Yukio that he was influenced by the dualism of body and spirit of Thomas Mann. There are many indications (such as his references to St. Sebastian) that Mann's Death in Venice was in his mind when he wrote Confessions of a Mask.

18. Watakushi no henreki jidai, p. 159.
19. Ibid., p. 137.
20. Confessions of a Mask, p. 117.

11. "I" IN THE NOVEL: SELF-REVELATION AND SELF-CONCEALMENT IN THE NOVELS OF TOMIOKA TAEKO

1. Meido no kazoku, Kōdansha, 1974; Shokubutsusai, Shinchō, 1974; and Kochūan ibun, Tokyo, Bungeishunjyū, 1974.
2. One of the main characters of the novel is a "collector of women," whose aim is to sleep with a thousand women.
3. Her principal poetry collections are Henrei (The Return of a Favor), Tokyo, Yamakawa Shuppan, 1956; Karisuma no kashinoki (The Oak Tree of Charisma), Tokyo, Iizuka, 1959; Monogatari no akuruhi (The Day After the Story), Tokyo, MXT, 1960; Onna tomodachi (Girl Friends), Tokyo, Shichōsha, 1964; Engeijyutsu hogozōshi (A Book of Anti-Art Scribbles), Shichōsha, 1970; Selected Works of Tomioka Taeko, Tokyo, Shichōsha, 1967; The Collected Works of Tomioka Taeko, Tokyo, Shichōsha, 1967. A selection of her poems has been translated by Hiroaki Sato under the title See You Soon (Chicago Review Press, 1979) and additional translations are included in Kijima Hajime, ed., The Poetry of Postwar Japan (Iowa University Press, 1975).

ABOUT THE AUTHOR

A graduate of Tokyo Joshi Daizaku, Noriko Mizuta Lippit did graduate work at Tokyo Metropolitan University and received an M.A. and Ph.D. from Yale University. She has taught at various universities and colleges in Japan and the United States and is currently an Associate Professor of Comparative Literature and East Asian Languages and Cultures at the University of Southern California.

Dr. Lippit has delivered and published numerous papers on comparative literature, modern Japanese literature and feminist issues, and she is the author of At the End of Spring (1976), A Disturbance in Mirrors: The Poetry of Sylvia Plath (1979), and Crime and Dream: A Study of Edgar Allan Poe (forthcoming).